THE HUMBOLDT

Highroad of the West

THE HUMBOLDT

Highroad of the West

by

DALE L. MORGAN

Illustrated by ARNOLD BLANCH

University of Nebraska Press
Lincoln and London

First Bison Book printing: 1985
Most recent printing indicated by the first digit below:
1   2   3   4   5   6   7   8   9   10

Library of Congress Cataloging in Publication Data
Morgan, Dale Lowell, 1914–1971.
  The Humboldt : highroad of the West.
    Reprint. Originally published: New York: Farrar &
Rinehart, c1943. (The Rivers of America).
  Bibliography: p.
  Includes index.
  1. Humboldt River (Nev.) 2. Humboldt River Valley
(Nev.)—History. I. Title.
F847.H85M6 1985   979.3'54   85-8108
ISBN 0-8032-8128-5 (pbk.)

Reprinted by arrangement with James S. Morgan,
representing the Estate of Dale L. Morgan

TO MADELINE

Contents

viii   C O N T E N T S

The Humboldt

Highroad of the West

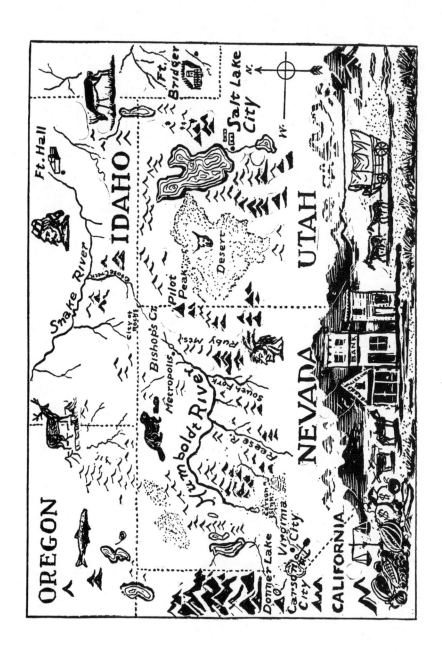

I

River of the West

THE name was armed with adventure. Boston clerks packing their bags, brawny-armed Ohio farmers selling their green acres and lifting their eyes to the western horizon— these could laugh with exultance. Mary's River—the Humboldt, yes, river far across America. They knew the blue waters out of the wilderness intent upon the sea. They knew rivers and the land: America.

In clouds of dust the caravans formed on the plains. Bawling an ever more eloquent invective at their oxen and their mules, digging their heels into the bellies of their horses, the forty-niners rode up the sky toward South Pass. The earth journeyed into grayness as they went, a savage, desolate land, the wind bitter with the aroma of sagebrush. More grimly they descended the western slope of South Pass, excited by a trickle of Pacific water. . . . The gaiety had gone out of them by the time they reached the Humboldt, that turgid, green, barren-banked, and sullen river. Over it hung the choking columns of dust beaten out of the earth by the Golden Army; along its banks at intervals lay alkali like a malice of poisonous white. The Indians skulked in the brush, venting their anger and dismay with venomed arrow and with gunshot. Mountains resisted the sunfire, barren, beautiful and damned. It was not a river such as they had known.

The very necessity for the river gave savor to the hate of it. Mary's River: the Humboldt. Wrote an Iowan in 1850, to "Mary's River":

> Meanest and muddiest, filthiest stream,
>   most cordially I hate you;
> Meaner and muddier still you seem
>   since the first day I met you.
> Your namesake better was no doubt,
>   a truth, the scriptures tell,
> Her seven devils were cast out,
>   but yours are in you still.
> What mean these graves so fresh and new
>   along your banks on either side?
> They've all been dug and filled by you,
>   thou guilty wretch, thou homicide.
>
> Now fare thee well, we here shake hands
>   and part (I hope) to meet no more,
> I'd rather die in happier lands than
>   longer live upon your shore.

The river lay gray under El Dorado. Emigrants came to the harsh test of the Humboldt grimmer and more trail-worn, behind them the long trek up the Platte, the lost elation of surmounting South Pass and that momentary optimism that the journey was nearly done. The oxen, mules, and horses that had been sleek on the plains pulled now at the wagons with red-eyed, lowered heads, their hard skeletal bones thrusting hungrily against their hides. The Humboldt and its Forty Mile Desert were the final judgment of emigrant fitness to climb the Sierras into California. Cholera graves gaped for the men; an open desert space where bones might fiercely whiten awaited the livestock. Over the barren highroad to empire the constant bitterness of alkali dust mingled with the corrupted smell of death and the dank breath of the indispensable river. . . .

This is the paradox of the Humboldt, that it was almost the most necessary river of America, and the most hated. Americans came this way to stand on the mountain passes and look far upon the Pacific; Americans came back. Emigrant and immigrant came this way, Mormon and miner and soldier, Pony Express and Overland Stage, Overland Telegraph and Pacific Railroad, cattleman and sheepman, highway and air line. Indians fought for life in the river bottoms while the West went mad as the Comstock poured out its bonanzas on the heights. . . . The Humboldt was a way, a means: few settled here until they had to, until greener lands were occupied.

It was the last-discovered of the American rivers. The Declaration of Independence was fifty-three years old before a white man pulled up his horse to look upon its green, strangely directioned water and name it Unknown River. It was the Unknown River indeed, close at the heart of the Northern Mystery, that great emptiness mapmakers filled with fanciful streams and lakes because the blankness of that space was too cruel to human complacence. From its discoverer, south out of Oregon's hills in quest of beaver, the river took the name it should still have: Ogden's River. From a wife trapper lore would bestow upon the stocky, energetic brigade leader of the Hudson's Bay Company, the river took an alias: Mary's River. Nor was the fancy sufficient; the river must be canonized: St. Mary's River. None of these names would do

for Frémont, who rode into the Great Basin in 1843 and 1845.
By the weight of his authority the strangest American river
took the name of Baron Alexander von Humboldt, who never
saw the stream. "It does him little credit here," reflected
Thomas Ambrose Cramer in August, 1859, California-bound
along the river. "He was filled with wisdom and goodness;
it only with mineral and vegetable poisons."

Hold in your hands a map of Nevada. The thin blue line
of the Humboldt, bridging the far east-and-west boundaries
of the state, sinks through the map into the reality of the
land itself, a land unimaginable with mountains—range upon
range, lonely and immense, rolling out under the sun stubbornly barren and toughly vegetated, dry and gray-green and
blue, lonely with an inviolate, memorable loneliness and
beauty.

From those mountains the Humboldt gathers itself to
follow in the path of the sun. Out of the north Bishop and
Tabor creeks, Mary's River, and the North Fork of the Humboldt disentangle themselves from the headwaters of the
Snake-bound Owyhee and Bruneau to seek the interior valley.
From the south, creeks tumble off the slopes of the blue Ruby
Mountains into the South Fork of the Humboldt. Yet typi-
cally the Humboldt finds its usually named source in none of
these clear mountain brooks: Out of the shallow valley at the
northeast face of the Rubies rise the Humboldt Wells, swampy
green springs which Mormon Orson Hyde, in 1855 en route
to adventures among the godless, thought excellent approxi-
mations to the bottomless pit. Here the Humboldt has its
beginnings.

Below Wells the river gathers direction. The green waters
fill with strength out of the hills and flood westward as
though in certainty of a sea; they sweep past valley ranches
and plunge down Palisade Canyon, absorbing scant Reese
River and sweeping around Battle Mountain to junction with
a namesake, the Little Humboldt. Now the river gives itself

more sluggishly to barrenness and floods southwest to yield up its waters to the sun. Thousands of years ago the waters of Lake Lahontan spread over the land here, sister to Utah's Lake Bonneville. The years dissolved the lake into barren clay bottoms across which the river finds its way into lower Lovelock Valley. Here, where once wild grasses grew for emigrants, the river knows an unfamiliar usefulness, its waters held for irrigation. But the exhausted river flows beyond into its sink—white and sour with frustration. Westward rises the mighty barrier of the Snowy Mountains, the Sierra Nevada: however weary the river, there is no path to the sea.

Emigrants marveled at the fate of the Humboldt. Conjecture posed an underground mystery, a "sink" through which the foul waters drained into the bowels of the earth. The dizzyingly hot sun suggested a better answer: evaporation into the thirsting skies. The sun caked the land into forty lethal miles. The Forty Mile Desert was an evil name far along the trail to the east. Those in the path to empire tightened their lips, looked to their animals, and spurred west in haste toward streams flowing fresh out of the snowy Sierras. By contrast the toilsome struggle to the summit of the Sierras was nothing; even such formidable mountains were true in the American heritage. Only the river was outlaw to tradition.

Americans never got used to it. A dozen years after the passage of the Golden Army Mark Twain came west to an experience of the Humboldt's waters. "We tried to use the strong alkaline water of the Sink," wrote he, "but it would not answer. It was like drinking lye, and not weak lye, either. It left a taste in the mouth, bitter and execrable, and a burning in the stomach. . . . We put molasses in it, but that helped very little; we added a pickle, yet the alkali was the prominent taste, and so it was unfit for drinking. The coffee we made of this water was the meanest compound man has yet invented. . . . Mr. Ballou, being the architect and builder of the beverage, felt constrained to endorse and uphold it, and so drank half a cup, by little sips, making shift to praise it faintly the while, but finally threw out the remainder, and said frankly it was 'too technical for *him*.'"

The Humboldt. The goddam Humboldt! This is its story.

II

The Unknown Land

I T IS a part of the dream of America. The Western
Mystery, the Unknown Land, the Northern Mystery. From
the time that Columbus sailed in search of the Spice Islands,
the West has been the name of desire, and the land where
flows the Humboldt was the last mystery left out of three
centuries of adventure into the unknown.

In the Year of Our Lord 1540 Francisco Vasquez de
Coronado set out with three hundred Spaniards and eight
hundred Mexican natives to find the marvels of which he
had heard. Three months of northward marching from
Mexico brought him to the fabled cities, to Zuñi in New

Mexico. Bitterly he looked upon this base materialization of a shining dream. Father Marcos de Nisa, in his tale of the Seven Cities of Cibola, had "sayd the trueth in nothing that he reported, but all was quite contrary, sauing onely the names of the cities, and great houses of stone." This iron-fisted conquistador exchanged reluctantly for desert villages of sun-baked earth his dream of shining cities. Hearing of a great northern river, he dispatched Captain Garcia Lopez de Cardenas to explore in that direction. Twenty burning days across the deserts brought Cardenas to the banks of the river, but riverbanks such as had never been dreamed of before. The world here was broken to pieces, shattered into ruins and reft by inconceivable chasms. The earth fell away under his very feet into canyons surely eight miles deep. A river that must be leagues in width glinted in the canyon like the silver thread of a brook.

To that river the captain tried to descend. Roasting in their armor, his soldiers sought for a passage down the precipices. The bright river mocked all their efforts; their waterbags ran dry. They might die of thirst here within sight of water. Cardenas turned back to Zuñi.

The conquistador listened to his captain's report. There was nothing but death in such a land, death without glory. Coronado took his army east, out upon bewildering plains where the sky was too high, and strange humped cows ran in thunderous herds. At a wigwam village under the hot sun he yielded up his dream of splendor. He returned to Spain and died in 1549.

So the canyons of the Colorado set a bound to the unknown. Whatever the mysteries, they promised too little and demanded too much. Through three centuries the Unknown Land maintained itself against all the exploits of adventurers. The Spaniards eventually came north into California, but the Franciscan padres were concerned only that the gentiles, the coastal Indians, should be won to the Cross and taught to live to the greater glory of God. Soldiers sometimes went inland, but tales of the Sierra Nevada, the Snowy Mountains, were no more than reveries in the dream that was life in Spanish California.

The first penetration of the Unknown Land between the Rockies and the Sierra Nevada came in the year of the American Declaration of Independence. Father Francisco Atanasio Dominguez and Father Sylvestre Velez de Escalante, with eight stout soldiers, set out from Santa Fe, New Mexico, to find a way to Monterey: "The God we adore will open the way before us and will defend us, not only from the Comanches but from all others who might wish to do us harm." Six weeks out, and far to the north, they crossed a large river that would one day be called the Green, but which they named the San Buenaventura. Now they rode after the sun, and late in September emerged from the passes of the Wasatch Mountains into Utah Valley. "Those will come," they told the gentle Indians of this valley, "who will teach you to plant and sow, and raise herds of cattle, so that you will be able to eat and dress like the Spaniards, to obey the law, and to live as God has commanded."

A lake to the north was described for them, a large lake with waters "very harmful and very salty," but they had already come north beyond the latitude of Monterey, and on resuming their journey they turned southward. Three days' travel brought them to the banks of a river. Was this the San Buenaventura? The mapmaker thought so; boldly he sketched its course from where they had crossed it before. The priests, however, thought it must be another river—and it was; one day it would be named the Sevier River of Utah.

Bleakly flanking hills invited no westward course. Lowering gray skies on October 8th unleashed a norther upon them. As the snow whistled about the camp, the priests reconsidered their purpose. Monterey must lie an enormous distance to the west, for the Indians knew nothing about

Spaniards and priests. Snows would close the mountain passes, and their provisions were almost exhausted. If they went on to Monterey, moreover, their return to Santa Fe would be long delayed, and they had promised to the Indians of Utah Valley that they should return to work among them. It might be well to return to Santa Fe, perhaps to find a shorter and better road, perhaps to find still other unknown peoples. They should go south to the Colorado River and thence back to Santa Fe.

Their escort took this decision with such bad grace that the priests resolved to seek the will of God. His companions all agreed, Father Escalante writes, "like Christians, and with fervent devotion recited the third part of the rosary, while we recited the Penitential Psalms with the litanies and the other prayers which follow. Concluding our prayers, we cast lots, and it came out in favor of Cosnina. We all accepted this, thanks be to God, willingly and joyfully."

The little company made its wandering way back to Santa Fe. The boldest penetration of the western mystery was ended, though the heart of the mystery, west of Utah's central valleys, still resisted the seeker. The mission was never sent the Utes; the hope of an overland way to Monterey was given up. Only traders came in following years, and these were content to reach the land of the Utes, and from thence return. The Spaniards had come first and farthest, but it was not to their adventuring that the Unknown Land yielded its mysteries.

The Vérendrye brothers, Louis and François, penetrated sufficiently west into the Dakotas to see far on the western horizon the glimmer of mountains. The Shining Mountains, the Montagnes Rocheuses, the Rocky Mountains: Jonathan Carver, who in 1766 came into the Dakota country, wrote of those shining mountains, and of a great river of the West called the Origan.

It was 1793, however, before the great Alexander Mack-

enzie crossed the "height of land" in Canada and made his
way to the Pacific waters. Twelve years later, and five hundred
miles south, Meriwether Lewis and William Clark on Jefferson's orders crossed the continent and descended the Columbia to the sea.

To John Jacob Astor, that ambitious German immigrant,
the West opened as an empire awaiting looters. Capable
traders were dispatched round the Horn to establish Astoria
at the Columbia's mouth. The Astorians who came by sea
were soon reinforced by an overland party. These Astorians,
crossing the Continental Divide and descending the Snake,
that "cursed mad river," thence crossing the Blue Mountains
to the Columbia and so on to the sea, trekked along the
northern boundary of the Unknown Land. Disasters wrecked
Astoria. The discouraged Americans sold out in 1812 to the
British and journeyed back across the Rockies. Left in ex-
clusive control of the Oregon, the British wastefully trapped
that country, heedless of the mysteries of the south, and
during fifteen years after the Astorians set their faces east,
the terra incognita endured.

Mapmakers worried at that 500,000 square miles between the Rockies and the Pacific, between the Snake and the
Colorado. There were no paradises there, no El Dorados, just
the mighty land. . . . Escalante had named a river the San
Buenaventura. Mapmakers wrought wonderfully with that
heritage. West of the Rocky Mountains they traced its course,
a river sometimes devious in its wanderings, sometimes swift
and straight in search of the sea. From white-crowned peaks
the great river gathered its waters to flow through a mighty
mountain barrier to the Pacific. Most likely this great river
flowed into the Pacific at San Francisco Bay. The Spaniards
had not admitted such a river, but the Spaniards were close-
mouthed. The Americans who crossed the Rockies in 1823-24
rode west in the certainty that a river of the West, rising in

the Unknown Land and journeying through its heart, awaited discovery.

It was, even for its dwellers, an unknown land. The land is one of beauty, of grandeur, but a hard land to come to terms with. There are great valleys, spreading plains; and the eye is never freed from mountains. At its northern verge the Unknown Land dips toward the valley of the Humboldt; in the south it is slashed by the black chasms of the Colorado. Between is the dryness.

Survival was dependent on the most minute knowledge of the sources of water—in what places, at what seasons. Every tiny spring, every pothole that held the rain, every trickle from the mountains—this knowledge was the condition of life. An Indian of the Unknown Land might spend all the years of his life within a radius of fifty miles of where he dropped from his mother's womb into the dust, the farthest migration that to the mountains from which piñon nuts were harvested in the fall of the year.

As it was the direct, so was water the indirect condition of life. There were no bison. Sometimes in the mountains sheep and deer might be found; and sometimes antelope were to be hunted in the desert valleys; but the chase normally was the search, hour by hour, for rabbits, ground squirrels, gophers, snakes, lizards, and insects—whatever ran or crawled or hopped upon the earth. Far in the south, in the valley of the Muddy River, a little irrigation was possible; a little corn could be raised for a more stable and enduring society. In the valley of the Humboldt and in a few other places fish could be had in years when low water did not produce such concentrations of alkali as poisoned them. But the routine of life was the hunting of edible roots and seeds, the everlasting rooting into the earth which gave to the people of the Unknown Land their historic designation, the

Diggers. From each dawn to each dark life was a search for the wherewithal to live.

The eternal preoccupation with the belly almost destroyed any social organization but that of the family. Here a man's food-gathering activities were more effective on the individual than on the communal basis. There were no war chiefs—and, indeed, in general no chiefs at all—because war was rare, and then mostly defense against incursions from without. In the Unknown Land war was a luxury—there was insufficient loot, expressed in terms of the belly, to underwrite the expenditure of time.

Except in the extreme west, along the Truckee and Carson rivers where the Washoe lived, the dwellers in the Unknown Land were a Shoshonean people, blood brothers to the Shoshoni, the Ute, and the Comanche. Whites called them later by a hundred names, but ethnologists roughly classify them as (in the west) Northern Paiute, (in the south) Southern Paiute, and (in the east) Shoshoni. To the time that white adventurers entered their country, the desert dwellers of the Unknown Land had no horses, though horses by this time had spread northward to the Snake country. The small bands bordering the Ute country were occasionally subjected to slaving raids, after the Utes got horses; and the Bannocks sometimes rode down from the north into the Humboldt Valley, but the Unknown Land was circumscribed by the belly, and few of its dwellers were far-wanderers.

They were an abject people; whites looked upon them in a revulsion of horror and pity, for the Indians of the Unknown Land dwelt upon a hardly human level. Suffering and squalor was the double face of life . . . and these were the heirs to Cíbola!

They wandered a country marked by the vanished dead. Petroglyphs and pictographs are found in canyons throughout the Unknown Land. The Paiute and Shoshoni, however, had no tradition that these had not been here always; their fathers' fathers' fathers knew nothing of the people who had made them. Archaeologists, excavating Gypsum Cave in southern Nevada, have found the remains of man intermingled with those of the giant sloth. Can man have lived here so long as twenty thousand years ago? Archaeology has only begun the struggle with the mystery. These pre-Basket-Maker people must be accounted for, and their relation to the Basket Makers and Pueblos who followed them, and the disappearance of the Pueblo peoples before the Shoshonean peoples. . . . By digging, by stratigraphy, by careful classification of artifacts and other findings, archaeology may one day establish the structure of the past. But the Unknown Land holds to its mysteries. It defeated the valiant human spirit that took ship across the Atlantic to begin the penetration of the American mystery. It beat into animality the dwellers within its borders. . . . The sun lifts above the hills of the Unknown Land, the purple shadows advancing and retreating along the dry valley floors; wind out of nowhere whips up a mad whirling dust that pursues itself amid the sage and then is a nothingness again. Splendor and death are here in the fire of the sun, reality corrosive in the heart of the dreaming.

III

Desert Wayfarer

THE dark oaks lifted their leaves in the gentle spring winds; the burnt sunny earth was gay with flowers. But Jedediah Smith raised his eyes to the tremendous white barrier that fronted the line of the sunrise, and felt himself half around the world from home.

Twice already he had attempted the passage of those snowy heights. Jedediah turned away, remembering tiredly these five years since that February morning in 1822 when he had laid aside his Bible and Wesleyan hymnbook to read in the *Missouri Gazette* William Ashley's advertisement for *enterprising young men*: "To ascend the Missouri to its source, there to be employed for one, two, or three years." So he had dreamed in reading about Lewis and Clark. He

17

had been only five years old when Meriwether Lewis departed toward the Pacific. Now he was a grown man, and for all the stern zealotry of his Yankee upbringing, another fire in his veins than fear of God had brought him west to this frontier. . . .

The party went up the Missouri to a succession of disasters. It was the Platte that became their highroad into the West.

They crossed South Pass, that new gateway to all the West. In the autumn of 1824 Jedediah turned eagerly to the wilderness beyond. With six men he fell in with Alexander Ross and the Hudson's Bay Company Snake Country Expedition. The suspicious Scot unwillingly took him to Flathead Post.

In December he left the post with Peter Ogden, the new H.B.C. brigade leader. He was glad to part from the ungracious Ogden in May, on Bear River, to ride up that stream in search of the Americans who, the Indians said, had wintered near by. En route to rendezvous he had found them, and listened to the tales of the big salt lake found by the stripling, young Jim Bridger, who had floated down the river in a bullboat of buffalo hide and imagined himself, for an hour, upon the shore of the Pacific. He had listened again to Ashley at the rendezvous on Henry's Fork. Ashley had reached the mountains in April and had embarked down the Spanish River—the Green—in a voyage of discovery. Southward there was a land of lofty mountains heaped together in the greatest disorder, barren beyond imagining. The general had bought horses from the Eutah Indians, circled a mountain range, and come here to rendezvous.

A year later, in August, 1826, Jedediah bade good-bye to Ashley. Rendezvous was over. Ashley shook hands with him, looking beyond Jedediah to the sunlight that glittered on the waters of Great Salt Lake. Ashley had sold out to the young Jedediah and his partners, David E. Jackson and

William Sublette. This stern-eyed, devout young Yankee was such a son as he would have liked to have. . . . He would come, himself, no more to the mountains. With the fortune his furs had brought him, he would enter upon a gentleman's career, politics.

So Jedediah took the seventeen men south, south into a strange country of crumbled red hills, where the vegetation forsook the good northern greenness for tortuous, spined, and lonely forms. A stream scarlet as with a blood of the earth he followed to a great river that flowed south and west. Shrewdly he guessed: the Colorado River of the Spaniards.

Jedediah followed the river four days, the country "remarkably barren, rocky and mountainous," with many rapids in the river. Reaching the fertile valley of the Ammuchabas— the Mojaves—he stayed fifteen days, and then with two Indian guides rode west fifteen days over a country more barren than he had ever thought to see, tumbled plains that held the sun's heat like a province of hell. An inconstant river, appearing and disappearing in the gray waste, gave guidance. At last they climbed snowy ridges odorous with pine, and from a mountain pass looked down upon a land wonderfully green. Far on the horizon was a blueness that met the sky. The sea. He who had been born upon the gray Atlantic shore had come hence to the Pacific.

The road to San Gabriel wound south amid rich fields. Hungrily his men rode past herds of fat cattle. The soldiers who came out to meet them, for all their dark faces and strange language, knew the needs of a man's belly. They killed a yearling and feasted with the Americans while Jedediah rode on to the mission with the commandant.

The good friar, Father José Bernardo Sanchez, received him with gracious hospitality. There was fine wine at the meals, even cigars. While Jedediah waited for an answer to his letter to the governor, he spent pleasant days and hours with Father José. His men were bountifully fed and given cloth

to replace their ragged shirts. Remembering the hard cold of
the north, the wading, half frozen, in mountain streams,
Jedediah exclaimed with wonder at a sun that could be so
beneficent in November, fields that could be so fruitful in
December.

But the life was too gracious, too easy. Jedediah walked
about the mission buildings, his bronzed young face turning
to the tawny hills or to the distant blue sea. Echeandia sent
for him at last. But at San Diego the governor was urbanely
hard to pin down to anything at all. Letters must be written
to Mexico City; opinion must be had on this trespass upon
the soil of the new Republic of Mexico. No, he could not permit the young American captain to leave. Perhaps all was as
it appeared to be; perhaps not. Jedediah found quarters aboard
Captain William Cunningham's *Courier,* trading on the coast
out of Boston. With five other mariners, the captain went to
talk to Echeandia. Mr. Smith no doubt had been compelled
to enter California by lack of provisions and water; he had
no other object than to hunt beaver and other peltry, and
desired to move north through California only because he ran
a grave risk of perishing if he returned as he had come. They
persuaded the governor. Echeandia sent to Jedediah a docu-
ment permitting him to take his departure.

Having got conveniently out of sight of the Mexican
settlements, Jedediah turned north. No matter what any man
might say, or any government, he would find out what lay in
the unknown country north, whether a Buenaventura flowed
to the sea.

That mighty mountain rampart, the Sierra Nevada, rose
along the eastern sky to shut them off from home. By May,
Jedediah and his men, encamped on what came to be called
the Rio de los Americanos, had given up hope that the Buenaventura was easily to be found—if indeed it existed. Only six
weeks away was rendezvous at the Little Lake. They rode east
into the mountains.

They climbed into a snowy world in which the horses floundered and starved. Alternating snow and rains beat upon them. There came a moment when Jedediah lifted his rifle in a signal of negation. "We must go back." He tried again to the south, but again the mountains defeated him.

Now Jedediah looked once more at the mountains, stained by the sunset to an unearthly amethystine beauty. Suddenly he resolved to leave the company here. He would take the blacksmith, Silas Gobel, and toughhearted Robert Evans, and once more he would try the passes. His imagination kindled. Surmounting the summit, they should look a thousand miles across a wilderness unknown to any. Across that uncharted wilderness they should find their way to the rendezvous. After rendezvous . . . he would return.

Eight days of nightmare. Two of the seven horses and one of the provision-laden mules were lost in the crossing of the tremendous range. But the going became easier as they crossed the summit. The snow was packed so hard that the horses sank only a foot in traversing it. The land to the east opened to sight, range upon range. The three men struck out southeasterly, for the Big Salt Lake. Quickly the fresh streams from the Sierra sank into the ground, and they traveled over dry, sandy plains, sometimes two days at a time without water. Indians whom they encountered seemed a travesty upon the human race, naked and miserable, feeding on grass seed and grasshoppers. There was no game. They ate a horse, and then another. The sun passed overhead and their shadows moved around them in a world of mountainous sand, blistered bare rock, thirsty sage and dry greasewood. Choking for water, Jedediah thought with a bitter humor of his dream of the Buenaventura, that proud river to the sea.

On June 22nd, twenty-four days since they embarked upon the passage of the great sandy desert, and thirty-two since saying farewell to the company, Jedediah turned from contemplation of his gaunt-faced men lying exhausted on the ground to write the record of the day:

> North 25 Miles. My course was nearly parallel with a chain of hills in the west, on the tops of which was some snow and from which ran a creek to the northeast. On this creek I encamped. The country in the vicinity so much resembled that on the south side of the Salt Lake that for a while I was induced to believe that I was near that place. During the day I saw a good many antelope, but could not kill any. I however, killed 2 hares which when cooked at night we found much better than horse meat.

Next day another thirty-five miles, across a plain of salt that held the fury of the sun and twisted the world into unreasonable mirage. They camped without water. Jedediah started early in hope of finding a spring. From a ridge he could see nothing but sandy plains and dry, rocky hills, unless that was indeed a snow-topped mountain sixty miles northeast. He returned to Gobel and Evans, but when he would have told them of the desolate prospect ahead, his heart failed him. "I saw something black in the distance. No doubt we'll find water near by."

They struggled north and east through the sand. Even had they been in the best of health, able to eat and drink when they desired, they would have found the soft sand maddening to walk through; now, Jedediah thought, it was more than man could bear. By midafternoon the sun was so bad that the three men dug holes in the sand and lay in them for an hour in hope of cooling their blistering bodies. They traveled on until night and encamped without water.

> Our sleep was not repose, for tormented nature made us dream of things we had not and for the want of which it seemed possible, and even probable, that we might perish in the desert unheard of and unpitied. In those moments how trifling were all those things that hold such an absolute sway over the busy and prosperous

world. My dreams were not of Gold or ambitious honors, but of my distant, quiet home, of murmuring brooks, of Cooling Cascades.

They roused from such misery, and plodded on through the night. The sun rose upon the parched waste, and it seemed that in all the world the flood of light poured on no more unhappy beings. Four hours after sunrise Robert Evans fell on his face. They moved him into the shadow of a juniper and pushed on. Watèr alone could help Evans, and that only if found soon. Three miles brought them to a stream. Gobel jumped in bodily; Jedediah flung himself on the ground and poured the water into his belly regardless of consequences. But then he filled a small kettle and set out on the back trail. Evans was far gone, scarcely able to speak. Jedediah handed him the kettle, with its four or five quarts. Evans drank it without taking his lips from the kettle, and was so much revived that he was able to go on to the stream.

Another two days' travel, seeing Indians now who spoke, encouragingly, the language of the Shoshoni and knew of Lewis's River—the Snake. But they knew nothing of the Salt Lake, and when on the morning of the 27th Jedediah saw from a ridge an expanse of water extending far to the north and east, he was afraid to believe. But there was no mistake. "The Salt Lake, a joyful sight, was spread before us."

They circled the lake and made a raft of cane grass to carry their things across the Utah Outlet (Jordan River). Jedediah swam before the raft, holding between his teeth a cord attached to the frail vessel; the men swam behind. Neither Gobel nor Evans was a good swimmer, and the current swept them a considerable distance; Jedediah reached shore, indeed, with great difficulty, being "verry much strangled." They made a fire of sedge to dry their clothes, and had another meal of horseflesh. During two days they journeyed north, talking but little, "for men suffering from hunger never talk much, but rather bear their sorrows in moody silence, which is much preferable to fruitless complaints." Again north, killing a fine fat deer on which they fed gratefully; once more, then, twenty-five miles along the shore of the lake. From this country they had set out highheartedly some ten months ago; they returned in circumstances different indeed. Up Bear River they journeyed into Cache Valley, where Indians told them the whites were assembled twenty-five miles away at the Little Lake. Jedediah hired a horse and guide and went on to the rendezvous, arriving at three in the afternoon on this third day of July in the year 1827. The arrival created a sensation in the camp; he had been given up for lost.

He had been gone ten months. In that time he had crossed the Unknown Land in the south; he had recrossed it centrally. He had found it everywhere a terrible country, a sandy waste men ventured upon at the peril of their lives. He had thought, as the mapmakers believed, that a great river ran thence, another Columbia. He had found, instead, that even springs were scant, and likely to be bitter with salt. There were no beaver there—no riches. As Jedediah gathered eighteen men to rejoin his company in California, he gave no consideration to retraversing the great sand desert. "I had learned enough of the San Plain in my late journey across it," he reasoned, "to know that it would be impossible for a party with loaded horses and encumbered with baggage to ever cross it. Of the nine animals with which I left the Appelamminy but two got through to the Depo, and they were, like ourselves, mere skeletons." The circuitous route by way of the Colorado presented serious difficulties but was far better than that over the Sand Plain.

The Buenaventura sought by this splendid wayfarer did not exist. He died, perhaps, without the knowledge that there coursed in the stead of the great river another stream, the shallow Humboldt, which alone for adventurers in the beginning joined California to the Rocky Mountains. For lack of a central route to travel, Jedediah went south. The treacherous Mojaves killed ten of his men as the party crossed the Colorado. The valiant Silas Gobel died under their arrows. The remaining eight went on with Jedediah to California, joining their comrades on September 18, 1827. Jedediah turned north to Oregon after the long ordeal of jail and official inquisition that followed his visit to the Spanish settlements in quest of supplies. All of his company save three died on the Umpqua River of Oregon after a hard march up the coast. The officials of the Hudson's Bay Company recovered for him from the Umpqua Indians the furs they had plundered in the massacre . . . yet had he known of a desert river that flowed in the course of the sun, all the company might have returned safe to the mountains.

Jedediah's adventures on the Pacific Coast kept him from rendezvous until the summer of 1829. Next year he left the mountains. His experience in the Unknown Land loomed large when he came at last to define something of the fire in him that drove him to adventuring in strange lands, which was not alone the passion for discovery:

It is that I may be able to help those who stand in need, that I face every danger. It is for this, that I traverse the mountains covered with eternal snow. It is for this, that I pass over the sandy plains, in heat of summer, thirsting for water where I may cool my overheated body. It is for this, that I go for days without eating, and am pretty well satisfied if I can gather a few roots, a few snails, or, better satisfied if we can afford ourself a piece of horse flesh, or a fine roasted dog, and most of all, it is for this, that I deprive myself of the privilege of society and the satisfaction of the converse of my friends!

In 1830 he came from the mountains, and visited briefly with his friends and family. Next year he set out for Santa Fe. Suffering from thirst on the Cimarron plain, he went ahead searching for water. Comanche raiders came upon him as he drank. His horse was frightened with a mirror: Jedediah killed the chief as his horse whirled, but the Comanche lances thrust into his body. Far from the mountains where he had lived so valiantly, the blood of Jedediah Smith ran out upon the sand.

IV

Unknown River

NOVEMBER in the year 1828, forty-eight days out
of Fort Nez Percé. Forty-eight profitless days on Powder
River, Burnt River, Malheur River, blistered by September's
blazing days, crippled by October's hills and stony roads.
The rivers yielded nothing. Peter Skene Ogden led south the
fourth expedition he had brought into the Snake country.

The brigade leader for the Hudson's Bay Company rode
in the midst of his men. Astride his horse he looked small,
but the breadth of body between shoulders and hips drew the
eye twice to this dark-faced young man. The muscles rippled
powerfully with the lithe movements of his body; a formidable fellow. There was, moreover, a quality to his voice—a

27

voice that was remembered, even as the peculiar twist of his lips that passed for laughter.

On November 1st the trappers scared two Indians out of the brush. Nothing could be made of them, nor did they seem to understand a thing. He had given each a looking glass and his liberty. Liberty, at least, they understood. They exploded into the brush like frightened hares. . . . He had not been so far south, Ogden conjectured, since the disaster near the Big Salt Lake in 1825. The Indians were more numerous as they advanced; they fled in all directions from their grass huts. Quite evidently they had never seen whites before. The Americans had not got into this country.

Southward the company followed a winding stream of many lakes, the lodgepoles scarring the earth with their passing. That first stream—not large but certainly long—they abandoned, crossing a plain to another river of similar size. On the forty-eighth day out of Fort Nez Percé, November 9, 1828, they encamped where this river, which one day would be named the Little Humboldt, lost itself in a marshy lake.

The hunters in advance reported no stream beyond, only hills of sand. But lakes always had some kind of outlet. Below the lake the river emerged out of the ground. Ogden followed in its path and rode over a sand ridge into full view of a large, willow-lined river south in the wide plain.

Galloping at the risk of his life through swamps and over hills and rocks, Ogden drew up his horse on a riverbank to the warning, sharp sounds of beaver tails cracked on water. A large, well-stocked beaver lodge obstructed the river not a hundred paces away.

The gloomy faces of his bronzed trappers lifted to that news. By the time the stars were lost in the dawn, the camp was deserted. The Indian women dismantled the lodges and packed the horses; as the sun rimmed the dusky hills with gold, Ogden rode with the women and boys on the heels of his men. The sun marched down the velvet, gray-green flanks of the hills to fill the valley bottom with yellow warmth. Ogden gratefully lifted his broad shoulders to the sun. It was as warm as September. Even the rattlesnakes had not yet denned up. Perhaps the winter would be mild; perhaps they would be able to take beaver throughout the season.

From clumps of sage on the hillsides, scrawny, brown-bodied men peered out upon their passage. Down the valley, now and again, the Indians scurried into the brush ahead of them. They were clothed, if at all, in twisted rabbit skins; they had no horses. They lived on seeds, and what wild fowl they could bring down. Ogden had never encountered a race of animals less entitled to the name of man.

Yet they were an improvement on the thieving Snakes. He could have loved even the Americans, had they shot a few dozen of the insolent rascals. A little wailing in the lodges would work miracles among those gentry.

The wide plain opened ahead. Hai! The women laughed to see the sun-brightness of the water, the dusty green willows through which the river glinted. There should be work for their skinning knives here! Ogden listened to the cheerful hum of the voices. The sun was quiet on the land, the dust-dry land. Ogden remembered all at once the intense lush greenness of Oregon below the Dalles. There was no such greenness here. He wondered where this river went, this unknown river.

Next morning, Ogden rode alone down the river to judge its course. The river ran south and west as far as he could see. Shortly after noon he turned back. He had given his men orders to trap upstream, since they could expect cold soon, the cold that congealed rivers and sealed beaver safe in their lodges; the river would freeze, and there appeared neither wood for fuel nor any quantity of game. Yet, he decided, turning back, he would take the camp downstream a distance.

His trappers were in when he reached camp. The bright flicker of the fires was made cheerful by their voices, gay

after these fruitless days on many streams. They had brought
in fifty beaver—prime, sleek pelts notwithstanding the fact
that they had found the beaver very wild. If only the returns
continued so satisfactory!

The Indians were more numerous as they descended the
stream. The banks of the river, indeed, were lined with
deserted Indian huts, sometimes as many as fifty together.
Bolder than most, a band of miserable wretches came into
camp. Most were naked and few carried arms of any kind.
Yet they were fat and in good condition; evidently they fared
well on seeds and fish. These Indians had thought them, at
first, a war party of Snakes; they chuckled among themselves
at the knowledge that the trappers warred only on the beaver.
The Indians were worse than dogs in the camp, yapping
underfoot every second, insatiably curious to handle things.
Some of those things disappeared, two traps. Moreover, they
followed the trappers too closely and frightened the beaver.
Saturday night Ogden sat in the firelight with his
journal. A wind from the south whistled among the lodges.
Ogden dipped his quill pen in the ink and scratched the
record of the company's fortunes:

Thursday 20th Nov. Again 60 beaver to skin and dress. I wish
the same cause may often detain us. Recovered one trap. 300 Indians around our camp: very peacable. This river takes a southern
course.

The firelight chased shadows over the handwritten page.
. . . These Indians made their footwear of beaver; that accounted for their wildness. The Indians said there were more
beaver toward the sources than below. *Friday:* there had been
nothing of moment.

Saturday 22nd. 52 beaver; the river still fine; dead water and
willows in abundance: gale of wind from the south and appearances
of rain.

There was more than an appearance of rain. Suddenly it came in gusts; the lodges resounded like beaten drums. The rain had an inexpressible freshness. It brought out of the earth a fragrance strange for November. Ogden stood for a moment at the opening of his lodge, lifting his head to the driving rain.

It was still raining in the morning, a steady downpour. The bedraggled camp plodded through the mud down Unknown River. The skies leaked grayness upon the world and shut off the far ranges. They still lacked two hundred of their first thousand beaver, but their three thousand no longer seemed out of reach.

By nightfall the wind had risen again, and the rain was turning to sleet. The dripping trappers straggled in, grateful for the fires in the lodges and the steaming kettles of antelope flesh. An hour after midnight one of the Iroquois came in with Joseph Paul. The man was hardly able to mount his horse, unconscious even of the snow that mantled his head and shoulders. They carried him into his lodge and buried him in blankets.

There was no question of moving camp. After daybreak Ogden came to squat beside the blanket-swathed figure and look into the black, burning eyes.

"How do you feel, Joseph?"

Paul twisted in the blankets, moving his head to a delirious babble. Yet out of the incoherence he was suddenly begging, "M'sieu Ogden, in the name of the Holy Virgin, M'sieu Ogden, have the men throw me in the river!" He wept, sinking his fingers into Ogden's arm, clinging in frenzy to his idea. "Be quiet!" Ogden said harshly. "Lie quiet," he said more gently. "You will be better."

He walked out into the gray world, that lie upon his lips.

Death was irresolute, or cruel. On the third day Ogden dispatched the trappers up the river. He would have to follow with the camp when the man died, or could be moved.

. . . Five days of cold were powdered with snow, a dry snow that flaked out of the sky two feet deep. The hunters found no antelope or deer. There were no buffalo in this country. If only the weather would moderate! If the cold would relent a little, he would make an attempt to move. Nobody in the camp believed Paul could live. . . .

As yet the men had said nothing, which was surprising, for they had no overstock of tender feelings, but the women let their voices rise as he walked among the lodges. There had been nothing said while the provisions lasted; that must be said to their credit. This hard country scarred whites and Indians alike. . . . Ogden recalled suddenly the Snake woman he had encountered in Oregon two years earlier. The winter had been so severe, she said, that her people had had to resort to the bodies of relations and children. She had killed no one, herself, but had fed on two of her children who died.

He took up his journal.

By care and attention we shall not hasten his death, nor prevent recovery; but are in a critical situation, our horses starving, our provisions low. Granting it may hasten the death of our sick man, we have no alternative left. God forbid it should hasten his death. At the same time the interests of the others who are now becoming most anxious from the low ebb of provisions must be attended to.

He would break camp in the morning. He would assign two men to aid Paul. They would keep him well covered with robes and blankets. Beyond that, God would have to answer in this matter.

The emaciated horses carried them five days upstream through heavily drifted snow. The sick man seemed to stand it fairly well. But the fifth night was very bad. Ogden left Paul after sunrise, squinting his eyes against the wintry

splendor of the snow. There was no question of raising camp
this day.

The man would certainly die. Paul was only twenty-
nine, steady and a first-class trapper; he had been in this
country ten years, since he came with Donald Mackenzie in
1819. Of Mackenzie's noble company only two still lived.
Their graves were everywhere in the Snake country; only
one had died a natural death.

Ogden shook his head against gloomy thoughts. There
had been times when his starving men had stolen out of
each other's traps—not for the skins but for the very flesh
of the beaver. He had seen the skeletons of his men come
through their skins until it was a company of death that
rode with him. A man could stand against the Blackfeet or
the Snakes, but this country withered the years from him.

Many of the trappers came in, almost froze naked as the
greater part are, and destitute of shoes, it is surprising not a murmur
of complaint do I hear; such men are worthy of following Franklin.
Two-thirds without a blanket or any shelter, and have been so
for the last six months.

So he had written in his journal of 1826, wondering
later, when he turned it over to John McLoughlin, whether
the bewigged gentlemen in London would trouble to read
this tribute to their wilderness men.

He remembered that his father had wanted him to be a
clergyman, or perhaps a lawyer. But into Montreal from the
west came the gaily blanketed voyageurs with their high-
piled packs of furs, their tales of adventure along the great
rivers. The Hudson's Bay Company and the great North
West Company were warring for possession of that rich and
fragrant land west to the Pacific. In the year 1811, in the
fullness of his seventeen years, Ogden had joined the North
West Company.

There were seven eventful years near Fort Isle à la Crosse. The H.B.C. post a quarter mile away was a temptation. . . . So in 1818, when indictments were being found in the legal warfare between the two great fur companies, he had been transferred inaccessibly to the Columbia. There followed two good years, then in 1821 the firm to which he had given ten years of his life merged with the Hudson's Bay Company.

He went to England. Stony London made him restless, its narrowness, its crookedness, its hived people, its interminable fogs. It was good to return to the Oregon.

The fall of 1824 brought distinguished visitors, Governor George Simpson and white-haired Dr. McLoughlin. Simpson brought promotion coveted indeed: at the age of thirty Ogden was named a chief trader for the Company. Simpson looked him over with approval, this broad-shouldered, confident young man. There had been too much waste, too much incompetence, in the Columbia Department. All that was to be changed. He had come himself to see to it. "Mr. Ogden, I think we will send you to the Snake country."

Wincing under perennial deficits in this country, the Company had considered withdrawing from the Oregon into Canada. The aggressive young governor changed all that. He outlined his ideas to Ogden. The Americans were moving westward. Last fall they had been on the upper Missouri; there had been H.B.C. desertions, tales of the riches of the west. If the British waited passively, they should have the Americans trapping even on the Columbia. Ogden should revitalize the Snake Expedition, strip the Snake country bare of furs. The Americans would recoil from a fur desert.

Ogden reached Flathead Post only a few hours before Alex Ross came in with the Snake Expedition of 1823-24. That dunderhead had picked up seven Americans led by a Bible-quoting young Yankee named Smith, and he had no better sense than to bring them with him to the fort. The southeastern country, said Ross, was swarming with Americans. They had posts on the Big Horn and Yellowstone, and Major Andrew Henry, he who had trapped the upper Snake country fifteen years ago for the Missouri Fur Company, planned next spring to lead an American party into that country. This Mr. Jedediah Smith and his six men were probably here to induce the H.B.C. trappers to desert. So Ross had brought them here! Simpson had properly taken the measure of this man: full of bombast and marvelous nonsense, and interested only in his salary of £120 a year.

Ogden gathered his expedition. There were two gentlemen, as many interpreters, 71 men and boys, 364 beaver traps, and 372 horses, not to speak of women and children and their 25 lodges. Ross was delighted. "Never," he swore, "has so formidable an expedition been gathered for the Snake country!" Yes, Ogden remembered now, darkly, it had been formidable—surly, misbehaved fellows, shiftless and irresponsible . . . formidable, yes!

He left Flathead House on December 20, 1824, taking the Americans with him to get rid of them. Simpson had told him to go straight into the heart of the Snake country, toward the banks of the Spanish River, and then to take a western course into the unknown, find the sources of the Umpqua, and by way of that river and the Willamette make his way to Fort George at the mouth of the Columbia. An ambitious assignment.

The party went first toward the sources of the Missouri. But this country was too hazardous, infested with those inveterate enemies of all trappers, the Blackfeet. In twenty appalling days they forced a passage through the Salmon River Mountains, and in April reached the Snake. The returns were good, but a man was killed by the Blackfeet, and Blackfeet raiders made off with twenty horses. "To what end do we work ourselves down to the bone?" groaned the free trappers. "We are only at the beginning of the season, and already one man is dead and half our horses gone! We get nothing from our furs, hardly enough to keep our bones inside our skin; the cost of goods is too high. We are nothing but slaves for the Company!"

He cajoled and threatened, and they went on with him. At Bear River he parted from the seven Americans, who ascended the stream. The Snake Expedition had now three thousand skins—a pretty tale for an enemy ear! Going on down Bear River, Ogden discovered that this stream poured into a mountain-hemmed lake whose waters were extraordinarily salt. Over the lake he looked to misted blue hills. Somewhere there must lie the sources of the Umpqua.

His trappers scattered on the streams tributary to the big salt lake. Fifteen of his men, two days absent, returned to camp with a score and a half Americans. Those villains encamped a hundred yards away and raised the Stars and Stripes of their country. "You now," their leader bellowed, "are in United States Territory. Whether indebted or engaged, you are all free!"

In the morning the American leader came to see him: "Do you know in whose country you are? The Oregon has been ceded to the United States of America. You have no license to trade or trap here. I tell you to get out!"

That rascality would take in nobody. But the disaffected Iroquois seized upon this moment: "You may as well know, Mr. Ogden, we are joining the Americans. We have long waited for a chance, and if for three years we have not, that was our bad luck in not meeting them!" And the intolerably virtuous American: "You have had these men too long in your service. You have imposed on them shamefully, treating them as *slaves*, selling them goods at high prices and giving them nothing for their furs!"

There followed a scene of confusion. The Iroquois seized their furs; the Americans came running with their rifles.

Mr. Kittson and Mr. McKay laid hand upon their guns, and
Ogden also, but this was not a moment for violence. The
Iroquois, with a galling obscenity, made off to the American encampment with their furs. Ogden kept guard through
the night and at daylight raised camp. Two more of the
freemen deserted. He rode off from the scene of the debacle
with the American's threat sounding in his ears: "You shall
see us shortly in the Columbia. . . . We are determined
that you shall no longer remain in our territory!"

Fortunately, he had kept his temper. Had they been
able to goad him into firing, the Americans would have had
an excuse for making an end of the whole British company. But there could be no question of trying to trap
further here; that might end with the desertion of everyone. And it was equally out of the question to search westward for the Umpqua. He returned to the Snake.

That ill-starred expedition of 1824-25 had far-reaching
effects. McLoughlin ordered in the books for an investigation, and swept the old rate structure into limbo. The freemen had been assessed too much for supplies, and paid too
little for their furs. With the Americans in the country,
offering high prices for furs, any H.B.C. expedition courted
disaster unless changes were made. So he had been given a
basis to go on, and he had stripped the upper Oregon of its
furs, shut out the Americans from the lower Oregon. It had
been a hard and dangerous three years.

But he must dwell in the present. The camp was pinned
here to the close earth under cold skies. The river wound
east and west with its column of willows, gray and frozen.
Death could not hold them here, only the imminence of
death. Ogden turned in the cold and looked back upon the
camp, huddled, weather-scarred lodges, the reluctant smoke
from the fires. They could not abandon Joseph Paul. He
could not be moved. They could not stay here any longer.

This wintry, strange, mountain-girt land held them as though they were staked out upon its snows.

Two men came forward with a solution. They would stay with Paul until he died or could travel.

There was probably no danger from the Indians. And there was no alternative. It was impossible for the whole party to remain here and feed on horseflesh four months. A hundred horses would scarcely suffice, and what would become of them afterward? He gave the men a bag of pease and a three-year-old colt; he clapped them on the back and started up the river.

For a week they traveled east. One horse after another disappeared into the kettles. Frozen Unknown River dwindled in size, and they struck off across the country. Somewhere to the east, Ogden conjectured, lay the Salt Lake. "I am fully aware," he admitted to his journal, "we shall find nothing but salt water not palatable in our starving state." This was a gloomy, barren country. Except for the tracks of wolves, there was nothing to be seen of any animals.

They fell at last upon antelope. The flesh was poor, but incomparably better than the tough flesh of their starved horses. On the day after Christmas, Ogden had a distant view of the Great Salt Lake; heavy fogs shrouded the low waters. The salt lake had looked more kindly in May, three years ago, on the opposite shore.

On December 30th they reached the plain of the Malad River, tributary to the Bear. Two camps of Snakes had a little food they could purchase; moreover, eight men sent in advance had succeeded in killing two buffalo. On New Year's Day a horse stumbling with exhaustion brought into camp one of the trappers who had been left with Paul. The sick man had died on Christmas Day, after suffering severely. Ogden sent two horses back to assist the remaining trapper into camp. One man alone now remained out of Mackenzie's company of 1819.

The severe winter cold continued. One thing alone made it endurable; they found beaver in numbers. On January 15th they commenced the second thousand of beaver, and Ogden permitted himself to hope that they would yet bring three thousand to Fort Nez Percé. A woman was lost and found, treated with a strange chivalry by the Indians. There was some sickness in the camp, but on the whole health was good. To one who came complaining Ogden lectured: "I have given you all the purges I have. It is your duty to recover, for you can expect no more assistance from me!"

It was two months before he turned again to Unknown River. He divided his party, sending one division to Fort Nez Percé in his track of 1826. As the Blackfeet and Snakes were now scattered in search of fish and roots, this seemed reasonably safe, but with only fifteen men he would have to be careful in his intercourse with the Indians of Unknown River. Twelve of the men he sent on in advance, while he followed with the women and children, and the camp equipage.

It was April 8th before he reached the forks of Unknown River. He found some of the trappers waiting with 43 beaver. Indians were fishing salmon trout from the stream. It was strange to see such a wealth of food taken from this river, so implacably frozen last winter. They continued downstream, overtaking their trappers, laden with beaver. On April 13th they encamped only a mile from Paul's grave. Ogden decided to strike north into the hills toward Sandwich Island River. But first he visited the grave. In this lonely immense land, threaded by a greenly murky river that flowed to nowhere, it was good that Paul's bones remained inviolate.

Two weeks on Sandwich Island River were disappointing. Ogden led his little company back to Unknown River.

By the second week of May they lacked only three hundred of the second thousand beaver. The Indians here dressed in beaver skins, a criminal waste. The valley of Unknown River opened ahead, level as far as the eye could see. Where could the river discharge?

Through May the heat grew greater, and the country wearied the horses, who sank half a leg deep in beds of sand. The American, Smith, must have crossed such a country as this, without the grateful reassurance of a river—though now the waters were becoming brackish, as though the stream tired of the unequal struggle with barrenness. The Indians seemed less numerous, but at night their fires burned in the mountains. Ogden saw carefully to the horses. This was no country to be left afoot with furs, women, and lodges. Yet the traps continued to produce abundantly. It was amazing: one day 75 traps produced 37 beaver. In the best country a trapper never looked for more than one skin from every three traps. The engagés were exultant; the privations of the winter faded.

One of the trappers showed him the tracks of pelicans. They were near a lake, then. A salt lake? If so, there should be no more beaver. On May 21st the company remained in camp to dry their beaver. One of the trappers rode back upstream a distance to visit his traps. His horses were stolen; before he could get out of the bushes, the Indian had vanished. Even as Ogden listened to this tale another trapper panted into camp from the opposite direction; four Indians had set upon him and seized his gun. He was lucky to escape with his life; arrows winged into the ground around him as he ran. These were not Indians such as they had met upstream. They were a savage and daring tribe, perhaps from Pitt River in California. Ogden called his sober trappers around him: "Go out only in twos, and be strictly on your guard."

He hesitated. They had been so successful that it might

be foolish to venture farther in the course of this Unknown River. They had followed it west many days, and then southwest again, a strange long river. But he was reluctant to abandon a stream so productive and so challenging.

The river spread in swamps. On May 27th the company encamped within a mile of a lake that spread all along the southwest horizon: "We may now think of retracing our steps. It is too far on in the season to proceed on discovery."

The men went out in the morning with their traps while the women dressed the skins brought in yesterday. Three of the trappers came in late in the morning, angry over stolen traps. One had pursued and beaten the thieves, but had not recovered his traps. As Ogden listened, a man who had gone to explore the lake galloped up, crying alarm. Only the fleetness of his horse had saved him. He had stumbled upon twenty Indians, who uttered war cries and ran toward him. One was almost upon him before he could flee; he had had to fire into the man's face.

"Secure the horses," Ogden snapped. Four of the men he named to stay with the animals; the other ten he ordered to advance on the Indians and see what they were about. "But," he said sharply, "you are not to risk a battle. We are too weak."

The ten men rode down the river south and west. Ogden put the camp in shape for defense. Before he was done, the ten scouts were back. Two hundred Indians were marching on the camp. Indeed, they came over a distant ridge almost on the heels of the trappers.

Ogden picked up his gun and walked out to meet the Indians. It was a war party. That was obvious from their dress and drums, and from the fact that all were young save one. He held up his hand forbiddingly, and the two hundred Indians halted, no more than five hundred yards from the white camp. He gestured for them to sit down. There was a moment of indecision; Ogden was acutely conscious that in all his camp there were only twelve guns including his own. Then the Indians sank down upon the earth.

Sweating a little, not taking his eyes from the arrogant faces that watched his, Ogden summoned his Snake interpreter to talk with several who seemed to be leaders. The lake had no outlet. Eight days' march westward was another river, large but without beaver. Salmon were plentiful there. There was another river also—Ogden wondered if this might be Pitt River of California; but white men one day would call these rivers the Truckee and the Carson.

"They want to enter the camp," said the interpreter.

"Tell them no." Ogden looked at the brown faces, conscious of his advantage and determined not to lose it. The sun glittered on a rifle, on another. Perhaps these Indians had ammunition also; they must have picked up arms somewhere on the Pacific—possibly part of the plunder from Smith's party. Had they not been discovered, they certainly would have fallen upon the white company.

Ogden stood by the interpreter uncompromisingly, sliding his hand up and down the barrel of his rifle. The voices ceased. There was a silence. Then, slowly, the Indians got up from the ground. Gradually they withdrew. Taking a deep breath, Ogden became aware that the day had turned gray. He looked up. Clouds were filling the sky. Far in the western mountains lightning flashed.

It was too dangerous to break camp immediately. The clouds overspread the sky. It began to rain. Darkness closed down early, and the whole camp watched through the stormy night. Indian fires blazed on all sides until the night seemed multiplied in angry fire. But dawn came uneventfully. The horses were packed; the trappers mounted their animals.

Wiping the rain from his face, Ogden turned on his horse to look at the gray lake that one day would be known as the Sink of the Humboldt. Smoke from Indian fires blew acridly to him on the wind. He ought not to infringe upon

McLeod's territory. McLeod's territory was the water discharging into the ocean. Ogden grinned. But his party was too weak to advance, and only fifty traps were left. It was high time to return to Nez Percé.

Seven days later he reached the stream down which he had come in November to find this unknown river. He decided to turn north up this winding stream, go on to the Blue Mountains and thence to Nez Percé. They had no cause to complain of their returns. It had been a good trip, this fifth of his expeditions to the Snake country. But his mind returned to Paul, to the grave that none of them might ever look on again. . . .

We are directing our course to Sylvaille's River, Day's Defile, and Snake River. Unknown River is known as Swampy River or Paul's River, as he must remain here till the great trumpet shall sound.

V

Trail to California

FROM the time the rampart of the Rockies was breached at South Pass, a wary-eyed, hard-handed, dangerous breed of Americans roamed the West, more savagely able than the Indians whose realm they invaded. From the fragrant forests of the Blackfoot country to the hot-walled Mexican towns, from the green farms of the Missouri Valley to the placidly sunny missions of California, the mountain men roamed the land with a fierce, knowing energy and a superb self-sufficiency.

Beaver was the quick wealth of the West, looted ruthlessly from all this empire of the mountain-desert. From the year's hunt the trappers turned in midsummer to rendezvous. The supply trains wound up the plains from St. Louis with ammunition, traps, food to tickle mountain palates, "fofar-raw" to adorn mountain man and squaw alike, trading goods, tobacco, liquor. Above all, liquor. Down his gullet in the week at rendezvous the free trapper might pour the labors of a year. There was much feasting, much gambling, much horse racing, much dancing.

Some came back to rendezvous laden with fur; for others the year might have been one of hard doins—the horses stolen by the Crows, or beset by the Blackfeet, or game and forage vanished. Rendezvous summed up the year's far ranging, and unbridled the imagination. There were tales of the Mun-chies, a strange race of white Indians never quite found by any of the far-travelers. Legend placed them sometimes in the Sierras, sometimes in the south where immense, cavernous ruins remained out of antiquity. Legend placed them even inaccessibly on an island in Great Salt Lake, a race of giants never seen by mortal eye, and known only by gigantic logs, cut by axes of extraordinary size, which floated to shore; they lived on corn and fruits, and rode on elephants. There were stories of the river that ran so fast the rocks in its bed were heated by the friction; stories of the mountain of glass that was a perfect lens and brought to within a few hundred yards an elk twenty-five miles away. There was the tale of Bridger, Old Gabe himself, about a land of "peetrified" trees, with peetrified birds on the branches singing peetrified songs. Petrification here was, indeed, so far advanced that one moun-tain man who carelessly rode over the lip of a chasm was saved only because gravity itself here had been peetrified.

At rendezvous there might be deserters from the Hud-son's Bay Company, and tales of the country where the American mountain men had not penetrated. Tales, perhaps of Ogden's River. (John Work, who succeeded Ogden as H.B.C. brigade leader in the Snake country, visited Ogden's River in the spring of 1831, that year of floods; the flooding waters made profitable trapping impossible.) Ogden himself

was central in the legend of rendezvous. Tradition had it
at last that in the early years Ogden had come to rendezvous
and that one day his horses stampeded to the rival camp,
among them the horse of his Indian wife, her baby hanging
to the saddle; she had followed her horse and child into the
enemy camp, seizing its bridle and also the halter of one of
the fur-laden pack horses, galloping fearlessly back to her
husband's camp despite angry outcries. . . . Legend hallows
legend. If the mountain men at last gave to Ogden's "Unknown River" its other name of Mary's River, to honor such
an Indian heroine, who shall stare the mountain man in the
eye?

From the Pierre's Hole rendezvous of 1832 mountain
men swung west toward the land of the Humboldt. Milton
Sublette took a party to its headwaters and those of the
Owyhee: Joe Meek long remembered that expedition. So
arid and barren were the plains, no game to be found but
beaver whose flesh was poisonous from feeding on the water
hemlock, that Sublette turned north to the Snake. The company ate everything that could be eaten. Joe Meek remembered holding his hands in an anthill until they were covered
with ants, then licking them greedily; he remembered crisping
in the fire, and eating, the soles of his moccasins. Even the
large black crickets infesting this country were welcome game.

The poor wealth of the Humboldt went quickly; after
Ogden the record of the mountain man in this country is
meager. John Work was there in 1831; Sublette approached
the headwaters in 1832; a company from the camp of the
baldheaded little army man, Captain Bonneville, was now
about to blaze a terrible trail through the country. In later
years there would be others, like Kit Carson who in 1838
rode down the river with a company of H.B.C. men from
Fort Hall. But by then the murky green waters of the Humboldt would be trapped out. The mountain men would withdraw to the recesses of the Rockies while in the world of

fashion silk hats replaced beaver, the price of peltry slashed and slashed again. . . . In the sunset of their lives emigration's flood time would return these masters of the West to the Unknown Land. But before that time, before the passing of his own matchless era, the mountain man would have a climax of adventure, and he would do what Jedediah Smith had not: he would establish a trail to California.

Captain Bonneville's first year in the mountains produced a poor catch if furs be the criterion. The packs he sent to the settlements in the summer of 1833 were hardly sufficient to pay the wages of his men. But with the furs went a report on what he had seen during this year, a report Washington might find interesting. He announced his intention of visiting the lower Columbia. He ventured the opinion that if the government intended seizing Oregon, it could never be done better than now. But there were limits to what a man might confide to paper, and he neglected to advise the War Department that he was also organizing a company to march through Mexican territory, without passports, to the California settlements.

Named to take the company to California, Joe Walker had no difficulty finding recruits. On July 24th they set out from rendezvous. Warned by the Indians, they loaded upon their horses sixty pounds of buffalo meat per man before they left the north shores of Great Salt Lake to ride into a desert already legendary among the mountain men.

Before them flattened the desert, glittering under the sun, a white, desolate plain stretching to lonely mountains that held no promise of green. Springs were infrequent, and sometimes so bitter and salt that the horses closed their lips against the water, and sniffed dejectedly at the salt-encrusted grass. Indian trails were beaten from spring to spring, and naked brown men to whom they talked said they should be all right if they followed these trails. South in the desert there was no game of any kind, nothing. It never rained in this great desert, these Indians said, except in the spring of the year. Far to the south and west they should come upon a mountain whose top was always covered with snow. From this mountain flowed rivers in opposite directions. The rivers gathered in small lakes and sank at last into the ground. Far, very far, in the west, they should come to a tremendous mountain across which none of them had ever gone. Near this mountain lived Indians who might be unfriendly.

Walker nodded to that far-knowledge of a brown, naked, grimacing man who stood beside his horse. The last must be the great snowy mountain Smith and his men had crossed six years ago. The river? Smith had not found a river. But the Norwesters, Ogden, had found a desert river somewhere west.

The company journeyed two weeks through a dry, sandy, hilly land where water and game were scarce. They came out at last upon a plain, excited to look on the chill majesty of a mountain that rose blue from that plain. Westward, willows marked the straggling course of creeks. Was it here that Ogden's river had its sources? Were these creeks the gathering streams of which the Digger had told them?

It was a barren country. From the Indian huts that lined the creeks crawled the alarmed, filthy natives, fleeing to the brush to peer out with dejected starved faces. There were old signs of beaver along the stream, but, Walker thought, all had been caught for food by these Diggers. Anything, indeed, was food here: even crickets—those demoniac-looking insects that hopped about in the brush.

The mountain men scattered on the creeks. Some beaver lodges were found. But when the trappers made the rounds of their traps, some were missing. Damned, thieving Diggers! Despite Walker, some were shot down.

The scattered creeks ran together into a river. As they rode west down the stream, depressed by the treelessness, by the seared grass which had sucked all life and color from the rolling earth, by the starved squalor of the Indians, they named it Barren River. A strange river! There were not even sticks to make fire, except now and then driftwood cached by the river in its sullen course; there were not even buffalo chips for fire. The Indians were shy and afraid. Little was to be seen of them, but as the company rode farther west, Indian trails appeared, more and more of them. From the hills climbed thin columns of smoke—signals marking their passage?

Through a palisaded canyon of burnt dark rock they passed to valley bottoms less drearly barren, sometimes grassy. Days later, there spread before them glinting lakes: of such the wizened Indian near the Salt Lake had told them. Ducks wheeled in the sky, and cranes flew overhead with long stiff legs to descend into the reeds that lined the brackish water. . . . At sunset the grass began to burn, and they knew themselves beset by red niggurs.

There was no timber, nothing but the tall reeds and grasses as far as the eye could reach, the turbid waters of the lakes at their back. The mountain men tied their horses together, then picketed them with sharp staves driven into the swampy earth, and tumbled the baggage off the animals in a rough barricade. The lake would protect their rear. Andy Jackson's men had been no better situated when they whupped the British at New Orleans. Walker heaved at the baggage like any pork-eater. They had seen nothing yet except the waving grasses and the smoke. There was no sound of an enemy, only the disgruntled loud croaking of frogs amid the reeds.

Now, however, Indians began to emerge from the grass, scores of them, hundreds—perhaps eight or nine hundred. Singing and dancing, they marched straight on the still-forming breastwork. The mountain men waited for the booshway's signal. These were not such terrible foemen as the Blackfeet, not so cunning nor so savage as Comanche, Arap-

ahoe, or Apache. But on this barren river horses were irre-
placeable.

At 150 yards the Indians sat down upon the ground. Five
chiefs came on alone to the earthwork, gesturing. They wished
to come into the camp and smoke with the whites. Walker
shook his head emphatically. Some of the whites would, he
signed, be willing to smoke with them halfway between the
barricade and where they now sat. It was easy to conceive
the sequel if these Indians, outnumbering them eight to one,
were admitted to the camp. At close quarters a bow and
arrow was a more formidable weapon than a rifle.

The five chiefs returned gloweringly to their tribesmen,
greeted with angry outcries. Some of the brown men leaped
up, signing that they were coming to the white camp. Instantly a dozen of the mountain men mounted the barricade,
signing that the advance of another step would result in their
death. The Diggers halted, loudly crying derision. Five ducks
were swimming at a distance on the lake behind the white
encampment. Upon these, the Indians signed, the whites might
demonstrate their powers.

Five rifles swung toward the lake. At the sound of the
gunfire every Indian fell flat upon his face. It was several
minutes before they had any attention for the ducks. More
respectfully, then, they stretched a beaver skin along a bank
of the river as a target for the whites. Despite the lengthening
twilight, the guns of the mountain men filled it with holes.

The Indians withdrew. They had been given something
to think about. Nevertheless, Walker stationed a strong guard
for the night.

At dawn the cry to arouse: *léve, léve, léve, léve, léve!*
The sky filled with color as the sun pulled itself above the
horizon. The lonely music of wild geese, southward flying,
re-echoed over the lake waters. The company resumed its
wary journey.

The Indians seemed at first to have vanished. After sunrise, however, they began to appear in the high grass, in front, behind, to either side. The mountain men rode nervously ready to fire, but as though the encounters were accidental, the Indians seemed alarmed. These grassy meadows were, however, too dangerous; Walker ordered the company out into the salt-encrusted plain. The Indians came after them, emerging at first in twos and threes, then in larger parties; finally, in formidable companies. The track of the company filled with them. For several hours this strange processional continued—the whites on their horses, the pack horses and pack mules securely led, the unmounted Indians following behind.

Presently the Indians began to send forward small companies, entreating the whites to stop and smoke with them. They were shaken off, but more and more of the Diggers trotted up. Their purpose, Walker decided, was to delay the whites until the whole Indian force could come up, to surround them or get to close quarters with their bows and arrows.

Undismayed by warnings, some four or five of the Diggers, saucy and bold, converged at an angle on their course. A quiet man, quiet-voiced, Walker roared his anger. The red niggurs needed a lesson.

A score and a half of the company had never fought with Indians. Tying their extra horses to clumps of sage and greasewood, they mounted their best horses and rode toward the Indians. At the cry *fire!* the white rifles volleyed death.

The shrieks of the dying mingled with the howling of those who ran for their lives. Swiftly reloading, the exultant mountain men fired again and then with loud whoops leaped off their horses, quickly put their knives into the ribs of the Diggers still living, and lifted their reeking hair. Triumphantly they rode back to the company.

"The severity with which we dealt with these Indians," reflected Zenas Leonard, clerk of the company, "may be revolting to the heart of the philanthropist; but the circumstances of the case altogether atones for the cruelty. It must be borne in mind, that we were far removed from the hope of any succour in case we were surrounded, and that the country we were in was swarming with hostile savages, sufficiently numerous to devour us. Our object was to strike a decisive blow."

The company resumed their journey down the swampy river. They had desired to teach the Indians a lesson. It had been a terrible lesson. There was to be seen now only the mountains on every horizon, shimmering blue, white-peaked; there was to be seen only the swampy course of the river, which flooded into lakes stagnant and green-scummed, from which the wind lifted a foul breath. One of these Battle Lakes opened at last so widely before the company that Walker decided to cross the turbid waters at their head and strike out into the country south and west.

On rafts built of rushes the company crossed the sluggish, defeated waters of the barren river that had brought them so far, and over a desolate salt plain such as they had traversed west of the Great Salt Lake, trotted toward the great range that for days had bulwarked the sky. Before nightfall they reached the shores of another lake without outlet—the Carson Sink—formed by a river that flowed eastward from those white mountains. Zenas Leonard injudiciously tasted the alkaline water, and spat it out. "The water in this lake is similar to lie."

Up the new river they had found—the Carson—Walker's company journeyed a day, then encamped and dispatched hunters to the mountains, to search for game and a pass across the mountains. Provisions were nearly exhausted. The hunters were away all day, returning with word neither of game nor of any mountain pass. They had, however, found a colt, belonging to Indians who had fled at sight of the whites. The colt was killed, and its flesh divided among the party.

The mountains lifted before them, whitened by October snows. On the second day several scouting parties were sent out. None of the parties found game. But one found an Indian trail that might lead over the mountains. Next morning, the hungry company set out in search of the path, and joyously marked the print of horses' hoofs. Horses could have come only from the west. They had feared they should have to abandon their horses and cross the mighty range on foot.

The upward trail, for two days, was steep and rocky; the enfeebled horses fell often and climbed with drooping heads. They climbed into snow. The peaks that lifted their heads into the high clouds seemed composed only of rock and sand, impotent of vegetation. The second night they encamped with nothing to eat except some berries that grew sparsely on south slopes, and an Indian meal composed of dried flies recovered from the stagnant green scum of the lakes below. They had not been unduly cold since leaving rendezvous, but on this night they thought to freeze.

The third day the company got perhaps ten miles farther toward the summit. A dozen men had to break a trail for the horses. Even so, the horses now and then floundered in the drifts, and had to be extricated by force. It was an exhausting day's travel, the snow in the ravines sometimes a hundred feet deep. The weakened horses, forty-eight hours without food, stumbled on stupidly, or huddled stiff against one another. The men began to mutter. By evening some were openly rebellious. The only chance was to turn back to the buffalo country, back a thousand miles to the salt lake.

Walker argued with them, and finally called around him the entire company. Should they go on or turn back?

The majority voted with him: go on. When the rebels refused to listen, Walker lost his temper. "The distance is too great for you to go back without provisions. There are no provisions." He turned to the clerk. "See that they get no ammunition, and that they make away with no horses. They can go on with us or starve here in the snow." He looked in the direction of the horses. Some were skin and bones. "Kill two of them. We must have something to eat."

Food was what they needed. The men feasted on the black, tough horseflesh as though it were the choicest beefsteak, some stuffing themselves so wolfishly that their stomachs revolted, and they must begin again. The camp settled down for the night, and after breakfasting again on the horseflesh, started on in better heart.

They climbed over snowbanks and over rocky ridges cruel to the horses' feet. Late in the afternoon they found a little poor grass which the famished horses cropped eagerly; here they encamped, to recruit the horses. As yet no slightest sign of game had been seen and a week of the most exhausting labor had not brought them to the summit. Through another day they climbed toward the clouds, and in the evening killed three horses, grown worthless from lack of food and severe traveling. In the morning men were sent in all directions, to find a pass over the mountains or some promise of game. They returned at night, having found neither. "We are at a complete stand," wrote Zenas Leonard. "No one is acquainted with the country, and no person knows how wide the summit of this mountain is. The vigour of every man is almost exhausted—nothing to give our poor horses, which are no longer of any assistance to us in traveling, but a burthen, for we have to help the most of them along as we would an old and feeble man." This mountain range, he thought, must be as high as the main chain of the Rockies.

Days later they crossed the summit, without exultation. The descent was one of snowbanks, rocky hills, precipices that fell a thousand feet into nowhere. The horses died daily, the flesh stripped at once from the bones by the starving adventurers. On one day they encountered an Indian who fled, dropping a basket of acorns. Greedily they ate the nuts; and strangely they were comforted, reflecting that they had come safely so far, when an Indian who lived in these mountains could find nothing better to subsist on than acorns; moreover, here was evidence that a better country was at hand, for since leaving Missouri for the mountains they had seen no acorns anywhere.

The trail became a little easier: there was still much snow, but fewer boulders to obstruct the way, and despite the chasms they were able to find trails downward. They came at last to the brink of a precipice from which they could see the dull gold of a far plain. Walker thought that the sea itself could not be much more distant than the range of their telescope.

Zigzagging, they descended the sheer face of the mountain. One man killed a deer, which he carried to camp on his back. The animal was dressed, cooked, and eaten, remarks Zenas Leonard, in less time than a hungry wolf would devour a lamb. This was the first game larger than a rabbit that they had killed since leaving the salt lake two months ago. For fourteen days they had lived on nothing but bad horseflesh. Moreover, when a horse has spent its energy for its master and rolls its eyes to bespeak willingness surpassing its strength, it is hard for even a starving man to shoot the animal through the head and cut from its flesh all the parts that he can hunger for. Twenty-four horses had died in crossing the mountains, and seventeen of these had been eaten.

So came the company into California, descending now through green forests, threading their way through a great, still forest of redwood trees sixteen fathoms and more in circumference, trees that brushed their tops against heaven. They came out upon plains so rich in game that they cried aloud in wonder and would not believe that buffalo was not to be found until they had hunted fruitlessly in all directions. Within a few days they reached the Bay of San Fran-

cisco; thence traveling southerly, they came suddenly in view
of the great Pacific. Proceeding to Monterey with some doubts
as to his reception—Smith had by no means been welcomed
with open arms—Walker was relieved to be granted cordial
permission to remain in the country as long as he wished, and
to hunt and forage as he would.

The weeks in California were gay. There were bullfights
and horse races, soft-fleshed women, wine and tobacco, all the
food they could eat. When, in February, Walker gathered his
company to return, six stayed behind, among them George
Nidever. Skillful mechanics, they saw here an endlessly profitable life; Zenas Leonard thought they would be "of great
advantage to the indolent and stupid Spaniard." It was like
parting with brothers.

The fifty-two who turned east were joined on the second
night by two young Mexicans who rode into camp sitting
their horses with so casual a grace as to stir the instant envy
of all the mountain men. The Mexicans drove ahead of them
twenty-five very fine horses, which Walker bought without
inquiring too closely where they had come from. These Mexicans had deserted from the army a second time, and, if taken,
would be shot. Walker accepted them into the company;
some of his horses were wild and intractable, and the Mexican
talent for the lasso would serve the company well.

Remembering the snowbound heights over which they
had come in the fall, they were patient enough to find an
easier passage over the mountains, even if they must go as
far south as Smith twice had gone. Game was scarce; they
had presently to kill one of the cattle. Indians seemed innumerable, and sometimes they fled in alarm, for some of
them warred upon the mission herds of horses and looted the
outlying ranches; they lived in dread of punitive columns.

Of the Indians they inquired for passes over the great
mountains, and two men were found to guide them. Climbing up into the snow, remembering with misgivings their other

passage over the range, they shouted for joy when the Indians brought them, in four days, across the mountains. They had come by what would later be called Walker's Pass; Walker rewarded the Indian guides with a horse, tobacco, and shining trinkets, and announced to the company that they would march north along the base of the mountain until they intersected the outbound trail; thence they would return by the old trail to the far-distant Green.

West, across the mountains, the earth was glad with the spring sun. Here the soil was thin and sandy, the grass scant and poor. Wildflowers grew amid the sage; there were purple fields of wild iris, and again the vermilion of Indian paintbrush taunted the desert; sometimes sego lilies held in their creamy cups the brilliant sunshine. But the spring was too far subdued; there was no loveliness of green reclothing the world. There were traces of Indians sometimes, but few. There was no game, and the horses and cattle failed on the scanty grass.

The northward journey was maddening. The Pacific itself would have been less a barrier than this desert. Now and then a member of the company would cry his certainty: there ahead rose a peak surely seen the previous autumn: there lay the way clear for them, the trail to Barren River. But the dispirited feet of the horses destroyed the illusion; the men slumped in their saddles as the angle of view changed.

Walker himself, hardened to optimism, at the end of a day's march swore he saw a landmark remembered from the autumn; he ordered the men to march east into the plains. The sun came up pitilessly upon this illusion, but Walker clung to his decision. The desert could not be wide here at this point; they would risk a march direct into the sand plains to intersect the barren river. The company cheered. They had traveled without ever getting nearer their destination; anything was preferable.

The creeks soon sank into the ground. The wind lifted

the sand to scourge them onward, and hurled it in blinding,
cruel clouds. Encampment was made at a deep hole dug in
the sand by Indians; the stagnant water was not enough, by
half, to water the animals. Before dawn whitened the sky,
the company turned their faces into the brightening day;
the animals already were suffering greatly from lack of
water. They rode all day under a broiling sun, and at nightfall camped again, still without water, wood, or grass. Two
of their dogs died of thirst during the day, and many of the
animals were crippled by the sand.

At nightfall Walker ordered a brief halt. To encamp
without water was meaningless. They should press on through
the night in search of water.

The men listened in gloomy silence. None moved to
mount his horse. "Let's turn back while we still have strength
to reach water!" The shout became an angry argument.
Walker, not a man who did things by halves, tried to shout
down the dissidents. "We must be half across the desert.
Better push on than turn back!"

The angry altercation resolved itself into a vote. The
majority voted to turn back.

Yet none mounted his horse. The company had followed Walker in everything, trusting him in everything.
Walker stalked off into the darkness, and the mountain men
looked at each other wretchedly in the starshine. It was
almost midnight when Walker returned. Quietly he ordered
the company to make ready to return upon its trail. Water,
he said, might again have gathered in the deep hole they had
found the first night out.

From some of the dead cattle moccasins were fashioned
to protect the feet of the lame animals, a useful improvisa-
tion against the scouring effect of the sand. More light-
heartedly the company rode through the night.

The cheerfulness vanished at dawn. Somehow, during
the night, they had strayed from the trail. Men were sent

fruitlessly in all directions. Except for the comfortless solace
of the compass, they were utterly lost, and this was the third
day without water. The horses, cattle, and dogs seemed beyond the point of exhaustion, sustained only by an im-
measurable nervous energy. The dogs dragged themselves
piteously to the men's feet, looking up with faces twisted in
an almost human anguish to howl faintly. The animals gave
out all through the day, while the sun turned the broiling
world about and blistered earth and sky. The company at
nightfall was scattered in all directions for a mile, and they
halted briefly to gather together lest in the night's travel they
lose themselves from one another forever.

The food they carried seemed a mockery; none wanted
food; they perished for water, the men with the animals.
The night march was attended by such suffering that when
cattle or horses fell by the wayside, they were bled at once
and the blood gulped down. Toward midnight the horses
became unmanageable. At last given their head, they plunged
through the darkness to stumble down low banks into a
beautiful river of cold fresh water.

Beasts and men stood together in the water, shuddering
in the repletion of the senses.

It was necessary to drive the animals back before they
killed themselves with drinking; through all that remained
of the night the men fought to keep the animals from the
water. After sunrise they rode on, to get the animals farther
from the water and to find feed for them. A few miles distant they encamped amid fair pasturage. The Walker River,
on which they had chanced, had barely saved them. The
desert jornada had cost them 64 horses, 10 cattle, and 15 dogs.

After a day's rest, the company pushed on to the north
as rapidly as the weakened animals could move. There was
more grass now, and water. After several days' marching,
they crossed a divide and saw before them the Carson River,
its sink a metallic glitter to the east. They had come again

to their old trail; they knew where they were, now; they knew how many days distant they were from the Rocky Mountains and their comrades. They rested a day in Carson Valley, and then struck out for Battle Lakes by their trail of last autumn.

Now and then, in the passage to the Humboldt, they saw Indians, but at a distance. As they neared the site of the autumn's massacre, the Indians became visible in more hostile number, twice as many as had alarmed them in the fall. They distributed presents to Diggers they enticed to camp or came on unawares; they signed their friendship, and offered to do battle for them. But the Diggers hid in the brush, and the mountain men seeing again the need of decisive measures, ferociously fell on a band of them, wounding many and killing fourteen. The Indians fled in all directions. It was a cheap victory; only three of the whites were even scratched.

There was no more trouble with Indians. Walker's company rode up winding Barren River until the third week in June, and then, as provisions were dangerously low, struck off northerly in the direction of the Snake, where they could expect to find game in quantity, and beaver. A few weeks later they found Captain Bonneville on Bear River. From the mountains they had found a long and dangerous trail to California. For American adventurers a hard way had been blazed.

As Smith had learned in his time, there was no River of the West rising in the deserts, rending asunder mountain ranges, and pouring its waters into the California seas. There was only a vast, inimical desert, stretching between the Red River of the South—the mighty Colorado—and the great Columbia. Between the Rockies and the Sierra Nevada lay a mighty desert empty of game and verminous with degraded Indians—a desert with a desert river only.

Washington Irving pondered what could come of such a

land, what could come of the West, its great mountains, its parched deserts, its inconceivable immensities that dwarfed seaboard America. "Some new system of things, or rather some new modification, will succeed among the roving people of this vast wilderness; but just as opposite, perhaps, to the inhabitants of civilization. . . . An immense belt of rocky mountains and volcanic plains, several hundred miles in width, must ever remain an irreclaimable wilderness, intervening between the abodes of civilization, and affording a last refuge to the Indian. Here roving tribes of hunters, living in tents or lodges, and following the migrations of the game, may lead a life of savage independence. . . . The amalgamation of various tribes, and of white men of every nation, will in time produce hybrid races like the mountain Tartars of the Caucasus. Possessed as they are of immense droves of horses, should they continue their present predatory and warlike habits, they may in time become a scourge to the civilized frontiers on either side of the mountains, as they are at present a terror to the traveller and trader."

Thus Washington Irving, looking comfortably out upon the gray Atlantic and the shores of Europe. But America surged already in the Mississippi Valley, and the floodcrest of empire was breaking upon the plains.

VI

To the Pacific

THE Frenchman, Robidou, seemed to talk of Paradise. The Missourians who listened in the autumn of 1840 stirred to the picture he painted. A land of boundless fertility, of perennial spring, of wild horses and cattle without number, of friendly Indians, of hospitable people, a land of sunshine . . . California.

Here on the frontier money had been tight since the panic of '37. Goods were sky-high, and there was no market for anything a farm yielded. Besides, a man liked to pioneer new lands. When farmhouses started to go up within a quarter mile of a man's house, he began to itch to get a little farther west, find a new country. There was no farmland so rich that the country over the sky line did not promise something better. A man might brag about the fertility of his farm— on some acres it was actually dangerous to plant crops, for the seeds sprouted so swiftly that a man might be skewered by the green shoots before he could get out of the way—but it was a part of American experience that the beat of the beatinest land could somewhere be found.

It clinched matters when they asked the man, Robidou, about the California climate. "Why," said he, "there are no chills and fever there! A man in the country who had the ague was such a marvel that the people came from fifty miles around to see him shake."

Young John Bidwell was among the spellbound listeners. As a youth of twenty, he had come west from Ohio in the spring of 1839 to locate a homestead in Missouri's newly acquired Platte Purchase. It was beautiful land, but in the summer of 1840 a blackguard had jumped his claim, loudly denying his right, as a minor, to hold land.

Robidou's listeners, John Bidwell taking the initiative, organized the Western Emigration Society. In a month five hundred had pledged themselves to meet next May at Sapling Grove on the Kansas, with wagons and teams reeady for the trek beyond the Rockies. Over in Jackson County a man had a letter from a California doctor named Marsh, which likewise lauded the country.

Eager inquiries came to the Western Emigration Society from as far east as Kentucky and Illinois, and as far south as Arkansas. There was, indeed, more enthusiasm than gumption. California lay west, they knew, but that was about the extent of their knowledge of the route. Maps were baffling; west of the Rockies they showed a lake some three or four hundred miles long, draining into the Pacific through two outlets that dwarfed the Mississippi; the emigrants pondered whether they should take tools to make canoes, and float down one of these rivers to the Pacific. Dr. Marsh, however, said nothing in his letter about any such rivers. He advised following the trail to Oregon as far as Fort Hall on the Snake River, then ascending southwesterly the tributary Portneuf. Thence emigrants should strike out into the desert, where they must locate Mary's River or perish amid the sand hills. Mary's River would take them west to a sink, Mary's Lake. From Mary's Lake they should bear southwesterly to the Snowy Mountains and traverse a pass, beyond which they would find a southward-flowing river. That river emptied into the San Joaquin. Sixty miles beyond the mouth of the San Joaquin in a great bay, emigrants would be welcomed at Marsh's rancho, at the foot of Mount Diablo. Marsh appended the latitude of San Francisco Bay.

In February the newspaper in Liberty printed the letter by the traveler, Farnham, who had gone to California in 1839. Robidou had long since departed and there was none to gainsay Farnham's sour words. To John Bidwell came friends with long faces. They had changed their minds.

Stubborn young Bidwell stuck to his purpose. With the scanty means he could rake up, he bought a wagon, a gun, provisions. When everyone had backed out, even including the fellow who had engaged to furnish the horses to draw the wagon, he crossed the Missouri despite the ice running in the river to cajole men in Jackson County into going with him to California. And at almost the last moment before the time for departure, up rode George Henshaw, a young man from Illinois with ten or fifteen dollars in his wallet and mounted on a spirited black horse.

Persuading Henshaw to trade the horse for a yoke of steers and a bedraggled, one-eyed mule, John Bidwell set out for Sapling Grove. In Weston four or five persons with a wagon joined them, and they were escorted a mile by nearly half the town.

At Sapling Grove only one wagon awaited them, but

after five days the company had swelled to sixty-nine, including men, women, and children. John Bartleson was named captain, because he threatened not to go if he could not be captain. They could ill afford to lose even six or seven from the company.

It was a singularly motley party, this first emigrant train to the Pacific. The teams were composed of mismatched oxen, mules, and horses. There were no cows, and no great quantity of provisions. In all the party there was not, perhaps, a hundred dollars; but they wanted to go to California, and by God they would!

On the fifth day they were ready. But even the captain scratched his head when asked where they were to go. While they wrestled with this difficulty, they heard that a party of Catholic missionaries en route from St. Louis to the Flathead Indians was coming up, guided by the famous mountain man, Thomas Fitzpatrick.

The emigrants debated whether they could afford to wait upon the pleasure of a slow company of missionaries. But those independent spirits who found intolerable the loss of a day looked foolish when asked to point out a way to follow.

The blackrobes who rode quietly up to the emigrant encampment were men of purpose. The white-haired, stern-faced guide, whom the Indians called Broken Hand for his crippled left hand, rode respectfully beside young Father Pierre Jean De Smet, who headed the priests. Only a year ago the young father had journeyed into the mountains to answer a strange missionary call from the Flatheads and Nez Percés, and now he was fulfilling his promise to return.

Uneventfully the company climbed the plains. Now and then they saw old wagon tracks. These were made by the wagons of the fur traders. Sometimes the company straggled out for half a mile or more; usually, however, they were more compactly bunched, for much had to be done to this new road into the West—steep banks dug down, gulches filled, stones dragged out of the way. At night the wagons and carts were drawn into a hollow square, the animals picketed within. To attract no Indians, cooking was done by daylight, and no fires were kindled at night.

Two weeks out, just before they reached the broad and shallow Platte, one of the men who was hunting in the rear of the company, ran up screaming alarm. His mule was gone, and his rifle and pistol and most of his clothes. "Indians! A thousand of them surrounded me!"

Despite Fitzpatrick's peremptory shouts, every man whipped his team into a run. Mules, horses, and oxen alike stretched out against the ground and in bawling confusion made for the river. Fitzpatrick galloped ahead, and as fast as they reached the river, formed the wagons into a hollow square around the animals. Apprehensively, then, the company waited for Indians to appear through the billowing dust.

With majestic unconcern, forty Indians rode up at last to camp a hundred yards away. It was evidently a war party, for there were no women with them except one, a medicine woman. But, Fitzpatrick gently explained to the men who peeked out in alarm upon these neighbors, they meant no harm or they would not have approached the camp in this fashion.

He strode over to talk with them. When he came back, he was leading a mule and carrying a rifle, an ironic enjoyment lighting his eye. The Cheyennes had intended the man, Dawson, no harm, but so apoplectic had he looked that they had disarmed him to keep him from shooting someone. His pistol and clothes were gone—where they knew not. He had thrown them off in his flight. So was named "Cheyenne" Dawson. The camp haw-hawed. But, reflected John Bidwell soberly, it might as well have been any of them.

They ascended the Platte. In a day they saw more buffalo than all the cattle they could expect to see the rest of their lives. The plains were black with them; as far as the eye could reach the earth flowed darkly, and the ground thundered through the nights with their passage. They reached the great landmarks—O'Fallon's Bluffs, Court House Rocks, Chimney Rock, Scott's Bluffs. The Wind River Mountains rose from a glimmer on the horizon to a range singularly crested with white—John Bidwell gaped to see snow in midsummer. They crossed South Pass, that immense, gently-sloping plain so different from what was expected of the spine of a continent, and followed the faint trail of fur traders' wagon wheels to the Green. The rendezvous of the Fur Brigade was no more; it had been held for the last time the previous year.

From Ham's Fork the teams pulled across country to Black's Fork—there was no Fort Bridger here yet, nor would be for another year. Thence they climbed the divide and descended to Bear River. So on August 10th they arrived at Soda Springs, those famous mineral springs at the bend of Bear River.

Just at dark Father De Smet, with the young Flathead, Francis Xavier, set out for Fort Hall on the Snake, fifty miles distant. The camp seemed more empty; the young Jesuit had been well liked. Now, too, that the moment was at hand to break away into the unknown, leave those bound for Oregon and strike off into the deserts for California, their hearts sank. Fitzpatrick urged them to abandon their wild plans and go on to Oregon; he drew them a picture of death in the snows of the Sierra passes.

Next morning, only thirty-four of the California company had courage for their purpose. Thirty-two were men, the other two the wife and daughter of Benjamin Kelsey. Mrs. Kelsey had said in Missouri, "Where my husband goes I can go. I can better stand the hardships of the journey than the anxieties for an absent husband." She was no less resolute now. The Californians pulled their wagons from the trail and hallooed their oxen south and west in the course of Bear River; three men they sent on to Fort Hall for provisions and—if to be had—a pilot.

They had intended stopping in fertile Cache Valley, but still searching for it, they passed through it and down through Bear River Canyon to a rolling plain through which ran a salt creek to mock their thirst. "The sun beamed heavy on our heads as the day advanced," John Bidwell says, "and we could see nothing before us but extensive arid plains, glimmering with heat and salt. . . . The mid-day sun, beaming with uncommon splendor upon these shining plains, made us fancy we could see timber upon the plains, and wherever timber is found there is water always. We marched forward with unremitted pace till we discovered it was an illusion . . . the river was thickly bordered with willows—grass plenty but so salt our animals could scarcely eat it; salt glitters upon its blades like frost." They encamped and sent two men to explore. These returned to report the camp within ten miles of the great salt lake of which they had been told. "This," thought John Bidwell, "is the fruit of having no pilot—we passed through Cache Valley, where we intended to stop, and did not know it."

Two days later the men from Fort Hall arrived. They brought only advice. The company must strike out west from the salt lake. If they got too far south, they would get into a waterless wasteland and perish with their animals. If they got too far north, they would get into a badland where they might wander until they died of exhaustion. There was no road to California. None had gone to California except the men of Bonneville's company, seven years ago. The only trail to California was Mary's River.

It was now August 24th. They had perhaps six weeks to cross the great desert and get through the Sierra Nevada. By late October the snows would begin to fill the passes. They had come this far without event, but the great test was before them. Yoking their oxen to the battered dusty wagons, they turned north and west around Great Salt Lake.

The trackless country had a savage monotony, the sagebrush gray and daunted, junipers darkening the hills like a straggling, irrational, fruitless orchard. The eye wearied for color, something flowering and vivid. The stubborn sagebrush resisted the wheels of the wagons; John Bidwell cried his exasperation at these dry, barren plains "producing nothing but sage, or rather it ought to be called, wormwood, and which I believe will grow without water or soil." A fine white dust blew up from the feet of the oxen and settled on everything, smarting in cracking lips, reddening irritable eyes.

At some springs at the foot of the Hansel Mountains they encamped and sent Captain Bartleson and Charles Hopper west into the deserts to find the head of Mary's River. The days dragged by until grass became scarce. They decided to yoke up and push slowly on. It was definitely colder, now; the water froze in the buckets. . . . It was September 9th before Bartleson and Hopper rode into camp. They had found the head of Mary's River west five days' travel.

The hollow-eyed oxen could not keep up. The wagons resisted like live things, now and then overturning, hooking their wheels stubbornly in the sagebrush. On September 12th Benjamin Kelsey abandoned his wagons, packing his wife and daughter and belongings on horses. Southward the Salt Desert witnessed their passing, a great white plain veiling itself in mirages that plucked deceptively at their hopes. The plain was ridged by mountains; to the west lifted a snowy peak in promise of water: Pilot Peak, rising above the flat salt plain as a symbol of life to these first emigrants to seek the springs at its base.

They were perhaps six or seven hundred miles from the Sierra Nevada. The horses and oxen were failing; the wagons would grow heavier as they lost strength. Moreover, the wagons forced interminable detours, constant, backbreaking

labor, innumerable lost hours. . . . They decided to abandon
the wagons, pack what they could and throw away the rest.

They had seen the mountain men make pack saddles.
But packing, they now found, was an art supreme among the
crafts of men. A day's labor had not sufficed to produce packs
that would stay in place. Within a few minutes of starting,
the packs began to turn. The frightened horses ran in all
directions; the mules kicked desperately; the oxen jumped
about bellowing. Damning California, emigration, and all the
beasts under Creation, the men tried again. They did better
this time, but throughout the dry day's journey the packs
continued to fall off, bursting apart, tripping the animals,
scattering their contents on the desert salt. The company
straggled out under the sun. At nightfall not all the animals
had come up, and John Bidwell went back with Cheyenne
Dawson to find them. The sun rose blazing; and for hours
they could not find the trail of the oxen. "The hell with
them!" Dawson groaned. "There's thousands of horses and
cattle in California!" John Bidwell went on alone. Indian
sign aroused gloomy apprehensions, but at sundown he found
the oxen placidly lying in some tall grass at the side of the
trail. He secured their packs and started them on the back
trail. It was not the packs that were important. He might
end with abandoning those anyway. But they had only thirteen oxen now; they had already begun to kill them for food.
For the company these oxen might make all the difference
between life and death.

Throughout the night John Bidwell moved the oxen
along. Soon after daybreak he arrived at some springs, the
first water he had had in hours. The company had eaten
dinner here yesterday, but had not waited for him. It was
impossible to say which way they had gone. Leaving the oxen
at the springs, he cast about in wider and wider circles for
the trail. To his relief, three men rode at last through a

mirage that veiled their identity almost to the last minute: they had come back for him.

For days they had had to travel south, under the frown of high mountains. Anxiously remembering the counsel given at Fort Hall, they found a high pass over these mountains—the Pequop Mountains—and descended into a valley of many hot springs. Lime incrustations caught and broke up the sunlight into rainbowed color, a loveliness foreign to this hard-handed country. Some of the men came to dangle fish in the hot water—they cooked in ten minutes.

On September 23rd they struck a small stream which they thought might be a branch of Mary's River. Hopefully they followed it to a larger creek; the bright water was a defiance of this earth. Scrubby dark junipers sometimes blotched the tawny dryness of the hills, but the only fresh green was grass and scattering willows and cottonwoods along the stream bottom. Presently this creek ran dry, but they made their way into another valley through which a fine, sparkling stream flowed westward. As the last days of September passed, they followed this creek west-northwest. They had been told that Mary's River ran generally southwest. John Bidwell recited in his journal the information they had got at Fort Hall: "If we got too far South, we would get into the Great Sandy Desert—if too far North, we would wander and starve to death on the waters of the Columbia, there being no possibility of getting through that way." They had now been six days on this stream, their course consistently north of west.

Two days longer the river played with their doubts and hopes—it flowed first almost due north, even a little east of north, and then again northwest. But at last, to everyone's delight, its course changed to the southwest. They passed through a great meadow in which the grass grew shoulder high; Indians swarmed in this valley. Their sable heads, John Bidwell observed, were seen in groups of fifteen or twenty,

just above the tops of the grass, watching the travel-stained
caravan, this vanguard of the American wandering.

Down the long valley of the Humboldt they made their
way, the sun coming up behind their back, passing overhead
and filling their eyes in the western sky before night replaced
the day. More and more of the company walked as animals
gave out. The river spread into swamps and tule marshes.
Observing that the Indians cut the tules to gather honeydew,
they bought balls of the sugarlike stuff, but they found that
the gray balls were made up in large part of the aphids which
had secreted the sweet substance. The only game seen were
antelopes, extremely hard to kill. Moreover, there was little
tobacco left. For an ounce from a plug, tobacco lovers would
surrender their horses for a day.

The monotonous westering wore on their nerves as it
would with all whom the years would bring this way; Mary's
River was a chemistry that worked upon the blood. Captain
Bartleson and the others with horses fretted at the pace of
those who must walk. It was no companionship of the trail
that held them back; there was no food but the oxen. The
eight or nine men with horses and mules pushed on as rapidly
as possible, at whatever cost to the oxen; when the oxen fell
behind, perforce they encamped until the animals were driven
up. One day John Bidwell was left behind, and did not come
up with the company until late next morning. He was thoroughly out of temper, and gave them a piece of his mind.
Bartleson nor any of his eight had a word to say while an ox
was killed, but late in the afternoon he came up with a pro-
posal.

"Boys, our animals are much better than yours, and we
always get out of meat before any of the rest of you. Let us
have the most of the meat this time, and we'll pay you back
the next ox we kill."

When the meat had been handed over and they were
ready to move on, Bartleson was roused to belated indigna-

tion: "By God, we've been found fault with long enough, and we're going to California. If you can keep up with us, all right. If not, you can go to hell!"

With the seven of his eight men who would follow, he disappeared in a cloud of dust.

The twenty-six who remained plodded on down river. Water was bad, and there was no fuel. Indians were numerous, but few approached closely. On October 9th they crossed Mary's River above the point where it spread into the lake of its sink, but Bartleson's trail through the sand hills was exhausting. To the west another lake opened, the bright silver of the Carson Sink. All down the Humboldt and now across the deserts they had found more water than would flow for most who trekked this way hereafter, although in this year California burned with drought.

Leaving the farther lake and proceeding southwesterly through low mountains, they came to a river which seemed more rapid and larger than Mary's River. For the balm of Gilead trees that grew amid its cottonwoods and willows they named it Balm River and thought it a headstream of the San Joaquin (actually they had reached the river which had saved Walker's company seven years ago, and one day it would bear the mountain man's name).

Slowly they climbed the dwindling river, realizing at last that the stream had its origin short of the summit of the Great California Mountain. On October 16th, as they were preparing for the ascent, they were overtaken by Bartleson and his men, trailworn and gaunt with hunger. They had gone much farther south. From some Indians they had obtained fish and pine nuts, but the fish, perhaps because caught from alkaline waters at this season, set them to retching. Bartleson, a man of imposing embonpoint five months ago, seemed now reduced by half. "Boys," he said feelingly, "if ever I get back to Missouri, I'll never leave that country.

I'd gladly eat out of the troughs with my hogs." An ox was killed—the last but three—to feed the men.

Though scouts were not sanguine about getting through the mountains here, it was decided to make the attempt. Provisions were too low to turn back to the lake they had encamped on days before, and attempt to cross the mountains there.

They began the steep climb, up through great forests redolent of the sun-sweet earth, tall pines and firs that towered into the sun two hundred feet, and dappled the earth with green and gold. They climbed all day without reaching the summit. In this thin, cold air the ice did not wholly melt in the bright creeks even at mid day. At nightfall another ox was killed.

Next morning, after the ascent of half a mile, the world outspread appallingly before them—"naked mountains whose summits still retained the snows perhaps of a thousand years: for it had withstood the heat of a long dry summer, and ceased to melt for the season. The winds roared—but in the deep dark Gulfs which yawned on every side, profound solitude seemed to reign." Winding among the peaks, unexpectedly able to avoid most of the mountains, they struck a small chuckling stream that invited them westward: one of the headwaters of the Stanislaus. Now they descended rapidly, sometimes balked by precipices, but always finding a way. The river was growing swiftly, and ever about them were the great trees . . . they had been so long absent from trees. To a person fond of a retired life, John Bidwell thought, this place of roaring winds and hollow-murmuring waters would be a perfect earthly paradise.

On October 20th John Bidwell and Jimmy Johns were dispatched by Benjamin Kelsey, who had been accorded the captaincy, to see whether the gorges of the Stanislaus could be penetrated; others were dispatched in other directions.

Three-quarters of a mile was enough for Bidwell. "Let's go back. We can't get through here."

"Yes, we can," Jimmy Johns argued, and he pulled out his old dragoon pistol and fired the agreed signal that a passable way had been found.

Swearing under his breath, Bidwell turned about, to reach the company before they got under way. Kelsey listened to him but Bartleson and his men did not; while the rest climbed into the mountains northerly, the small Bartleson company got itself entangled in the canyon, so exhausting its horses that they had to be rested a day before the men could climb back out of the impasse and go in search of the others.

The travel on October 21st, John Bidwell says, "was much better than expected, though in any other place than the mountains it would be considered horrible. Capt. B. with his 7 or 8 overtook us, but we heard nothing of J. John's. Distance about 10 miles, could see no prospect of a termination to the mts. mts. mountains!"

Next day the last of the oxen was killed—"let this speak for our situation and future prospects!" Hunters were sent in various directions; Bidwell was lost for a day, and Alexander Kelsey and J. M. Jones did not return to camp at all. They fed, on the night of the 24th, on horseflesh. Indians skulked about. The ragged, half-starved company occasionally caught a glimpse of a rascally old Indian who had engaged to pilot them, but who had abandoned them after they got into the mountains. The suspicion grew that he had designed leading them to their deaths. And on the 27th it began to rain.

They lightened their packs, throwing away old clothes to aid their tired horses. Even if snow did not follow, the rain might make the mountain trails too slippery for travel. Shivering, they saw that the mountains across which they had just come were whitened with new snow. "As we left this

place," John Bidwell says, "one of the men, G. Cook, remained concealed to see if the old Pilot was among the Indians, who always rushed in as soon as we left our encamp-
ments to pick up such things as were left. The old gentleman
was at the head of this band, and as HE HAD UNDOUBTEDLY
LED US INTO THIS PLACE TO PERISH, his crime merited death
—A RIFLE BALL LAID HIM DEAD IN HIS TRACKS."

They struggled downward. Horses and mules less experienced, John Bidwell thought, could never have descended
the difficult steeps; even so, several tumbled head over heels
in bruising falls. This night a mule was killed to supplement
the last of the beef. During the night, moreover, two of the
remaining horses were stolen; next morning, when they approached scattered Indian huts, the natives vanished into the
brush, and they saw, roasting on the fire, the bones of a horse
that probably was theirs. And still no end to the mountains.
Far to the west, a high range discouraged any hope that they
might be nearing the Pacific.

"If California lies beyond those mountains," said Charles
Hopper gloomily, "we shall never reach there." The whole
company was gaunt and worn, but still there were reserves
of strength, and food of a kind. Some wolfed down raw the
flesh of the mule killed this day, while others were content
with meat half-roasted and still dripping blood.

On the morning of October 30th they thrilled to the
sight of a large valley, well timbered and evidently rich,
lying between them and the high mountains they had sighted
yesterday. It was, indeed, the valley of the San Joaquin, and
still doubtful whether they were within five hundred miles
of California, they were almost down to tidewater. They did
not descend wholly to the valley on this day, and next morning John Bidwell was only too happy to breakfast on the wind-
pipe and lights—lungs—of a fat coyote shot by one of the
company. By nightfall, however, he was able to turn to his
journal in almost a delirium of delight: "Bore off in a N.W.

direction to the nearest timber, day was warm, plain dry and dusty, reached timber which was white oak. (very low & shrubby) and finally, the river which we had left in the Mts., joyful sight to us poor famished wretches!!! hundreds of antelope in view! Elk tracks thousands! killed two antelopes and some wild fowls, the valley of the river was very fertile and the young tender grass covered it, like a field of wheat in May. Not a weed was to be seen, and the land was mellow, and free from weeds, as land could be made by plowing it 20 times in the U.S."

The first day of November was spent in hunting; wildfowl without number, and thirteen deer and antelope, were brought in. Next morning all but the obstinate Bartleson and his men set out northerly. Bartleson waved them farewell: "By God, I'm going to kill enough game to last me to California!"

Late in the morning J. M. Jones rode up. He and Alexander Kelsey, missing since the 23rd, had found their way down into this valley and had stumbled upon an Indian naked save for a cloth jacket, riding a horse bareback. "Marsh," the Indian said to them.

It was a name they had sought out from half across a continent. "Marsh," they repeated. "Dr. Marsh!" They followed the Indian to the doctor's ranch house, at the foot of Mount Diablo. Kelsey stayed there, while Jones came back to guide in the company. Arriving November 4th they completed the first overland journey by American emigrants. Up the plains and west through the valley of the Humboldt they had made a trail to California, though their wanderings near the Great Salt Lake and in the Sierras were unfruitful except to warn others who came later.

They had had to abandon their wagons, throw away their clothes, eat their horses and mules, feed upon wildcats and coyotes. They arrived penniless, and their reception by Marsh was ungracious; they would experience some diffi-

culties with the Mexican authorities. But by their own un-
yielding purpose and by something of the grace of God they
had trampled out a trail for westering America. None had
died along the way. Even Jimmy Johns, who had plunged recklessly down the canyon of the Stanislaus, had come through
safely. With his Indian horse which, John Bidwell said,
"could come as near climbing a tree as any horse I ever
knew," undaunted Jimmy Johns had found his way to Sutter's establishment on the Sacramento, arriving two days before his trailmates got to Marsh's. To Alta California had
come the first leaven of a new and vigorous blood; and the
Humboldt River, Mary's River, in the passage of this vanguard had been given the first intimation of its imperial significance in the American westering.

VII

Destiny's Son

H E WAS the illegitimate child of a high-born Virginia girl and a French émigré who had loved her passionately and run away with her. His life, from his birth, had a heady romantic flavor. John Charles Frémont: the name itself is exotic, falling in unfamiliar accents upon the plain Anglo-Saxon ear. It is perhaps an appropriate paradox that a dark, flashing-eyed cavalier, sheerest stuff of romance, should answer to the long tradition of the Unknown Land, strip that land of glamour and fit it unequivocally into the reasoned pattern of the American land.

The American westering had begun again when, in 1841, young John Charles Frémont, by runaway marriage with spirited Jessie Benton, became son-in-law to Missouri's Old Bullion. The Rockies glimmered under the western sky, an intolerably mingled challenge and lure. Through the forested Alleghenies and the valley of the Ohio Americans had come with ax and long rifle and restless eye to the Father of Waters. Jefferson had fixed the nation's western boundary along the crest of the Rockies, but through almost three decades the nation halted in the Mississippi Valley. Explorers and mountain men might trample trails into the West; missionaries might embark into the swelling emptiness; but the men who had come through the trees to the treeless central plains waited thirty years to claim the farther grasslands and the mountains beyond.

Now, however, Texas had fought a war of independence in the south, and men urged annexation, even at the cost of war with Mexico; and year by year it seemed more and more intolerable that Oregon should be shared with Britain, the traditional enemy. Others, who cared nothing for Texas or Oregon, ached lest Europe wrest from the nerveless Mexican grasp a land called by the golden name of California.

Missouri's Linn and Benton were the spearheads of the developing expansionism. As long ago as 1824 Thomas Benton had proposed establishment of an American military post on the Columbia, to encourage Oregon emigration. In 1838 his colleague had proposed to the Senate the immediate occupation of Oregon. But, although the American people surged uneasily along the edge of the plains, they were not yet prepared for the adventure.

Benton and the expansionists threw their influence into sending an expedition to South Pass, to swing wide the gates of the nation's mind. Named to head that expedition was a young lieutenant in the topographical engineers, known vaguely as a subordinate in Nicollet's recent exploration of the upper Mississippi, but more celebrated as Tom Benton's son-in-law.

So was John Charles Frémont launched into the blood stream of American life. For that blood stream he found arteries, and the finding gave his land a plumed hero.

The expedition to South Pass was sheer adventure. Frémont took with him nineteen voyageurs, the hunter Lucien B. Maxwell, and two boys. On the steamboat that puffed up the Missouri from St. Louis Frémont encountered a young man four years older than his own twenty-nine years—a short man with broad shoulders and deep chest, light-haired and flat-featured. For all his quietness and for all the strangeness of his language (a mixture of frontier English, Mexican, Indian, and Canadian French) he filled a man's eye. His name was Kit Carson, and since 1826 he had been a mountain man. When he asked to go along, Frémont was glad to take him.

On June 15, 1842, the expedition set out up the Kansas, following its course for a distance and then crossing to the Platte. This was no exploration; it was an inventory of the country. Three weeks in Frémont's van was the first great Oregon emigration, led by Dr. Elijah White. Eighteen wagons carried some 112 emigrants; like the Bartleson-Bidwell company of last year, none of them knew all the route to Oregon, but one man had been as far as the Green River, beyond South Pass. In White's company traveled Lansford W. Hastings, who would soon again be heard from; but none this year was bound for California. To a young topographical engineer heading an expedition to dramatize the West, an actual wagon road to follow to South Pass established its own moral.

At Fort Laramie the Oregon emigrants sold most of their wagons, their animals too weakened to draw the heavy wagons across the mountains. But guided by the Broken Hand—Thomas Fitzpatrick—they went on despite reports of Sioux raiders.

Rumor multiplied apprehension in Frémont's camp, and that Carson, veteran of Indian battles, should see fit to make his will put the camp into a panic. Frémont, however, left at the fort the two boys and one man who declined to go on, and took the expedition beyond South Pass to the Wind River Mountains: "a view of the utmost magnificence and grandeur . . . a grand bed of snow-capped mountains . . . pile upon pile, glowing in the bright light of the August day." What he judged to be the highest of the peaks he named for himself and climbed. It was a thrilling moment to stand, as he thought, atop the continent. He returned with that warm climax for his official report, and it was exciting to tell, though there had been no real difficulty in the ascent nor had he, actually, climbed the highest peak even of the Wind River chain. On October 29th he was again in Washington. Lewis F. Linn, in a stirring speech to the Senate, described the adventure for the nation, and then presented another Oregon bill, providing for military posts all along the Oregon Trail to the Rockies and for a final post at the mouth of the Columbia, with a promise of 640 acres to every adult American emigrant. This bill was lost, but when Frémont's glowing report issued from the government presses, there were men so eager to have it that they stole it out of the libraries.

So in the year 1843 emigration was already in flood on the frontier. Farmers and frontiersmen, irritable with the constriction of the wilderness about their homes, could read Frémont's report and know that the tales of the Great American Desert were exploded, wagon roads already beaten to the Rockies. The news echoed in many strange places; even the Mormons in Nauvoo, embroiled in the conflicts that would end with the murder of Joseph Smith, wondered whether this boundless West might not offer a haven for the Kingdom of God.

Even before the report was published, Frémont had left Washington on a new mission. The first expedition had been fabulously successful; Benton and Linn had no difficulty in obtaining orders for a reconnaissance of the country west from South Pass to connect with the surveys of Lieutenant Charles Wilkes in Oregon. Arriving on the Missouri frontier in May, 1843, Frémont found himself rubbing elbows with a remarkably heterogeneous company—all bound for the Pacific. Here was J. B. Chiles, back in Missouri after his California trip of 1841; around him were wagons bound for the Sacramento, loaded with goods, furniture, and farm implements, including "an entire set of machinery for a mill." Here was the missionary Marcus Whitman with a great company bound for the Columbia. "Trains of wagons were almost constantly in sight; giving to the road a populous and animated appearance, although the greater portion of the emigrants were collected at the crossing, or already on their march beyond the Kansas river." There were, this year, some nine hundred emigrants westbound along the Oregon Trail—a late day for exploration!

The hallmark of change was on the West. Climbing the plains, the soft-spoken young topographical engineer found that none could be located able to guide him into the mountains in search of another emigrant road to the Pacific; "the race of trappers who formerly lived in their recesses, has almost entirely disappeared."

Abandoning his proposed exploration of a new route through the Rockies, Frémont bore northwardly to regain the emigrant trail on the Sweetwater. The sage was beaten into the dust of a broad, smooth highway by the passage of the innumerable wagons of the emigrants. Content to follow in this beaten track, he rode through South Pass to Green River, and over the sage barrens to the valley of the Bear.

Frémont now could feel himself upon the bounds of the unknown. The Oregon Trail bore northwardly to the Snake, thence across sage-pocked and lava-scarred plains and cloud-mantled mountains to the Columbia. South and west, how-

ever, in the direction of California, was a land wreathed in
legend—perhaps a motherland of great rivers, of rich and
beautiful valleys. (There were still those persistent stories
of the Buenaventura.) Nearer at hand, and certain of reality,
was a lake fabled in trappers' yarning. Only the wandering
mountain men had seen the great salt lake; never, thought the
romantic young man, had its islands been visited, nor had
any ever made the circuit of its shores. Eager for adventure,
Frémont decided at Soda Springs to take a detachment of his
company south for an exploration of the lake, while the remainder went on to Fort Hall. Twelve days later, from an
eminence in Great Salt Lake Valley, Frémont saw "the waters
of the Inland Sea, stretching in still and solitary grandeur far
beyond the limit of our vision . . . to travellers so long shut
up among mountain ranges, a sudden view over the expanse
of silent waters had in it something sublime." A thunderhead
over the lake veiled the islands first in mystery and then in
more impenetrable storm.

In a rubber boat Frémont, Carson, and three others set
out down the Weber River toward the lake. It was not until
the second day that they reached its waters, emerald above
the salt-sand floor. They landed toward sunset on the nearest
island and immediately ascended to its barren, castellated
peaks, naming it Disappointment Island, although it would
finally be known by Frémont's own name. From the summit
of the island Frémont searched with his telescope for indica-
tions of a channel connecting this lake with other waters, or
of the entrance of large rivers, but the vague horizons clung
to their mysteries.

Reluctantly he turned back. Snow whitened the Wasatch
Mountains and provisions were seriously depleted. The company moved north, low-spirited and hungry. The young
leader gave permission for a young colt to be killed, but with
his lieutenant, Charles Preuss, chose to starve a little longer

rather than resort to such fare. Luckily, Fitzpatrick came up, laden with flour, rice, dried meat, and even a little butter.

September now was well advanced. Ice thickened in the streams at night. At Fort Hall Frémont decided that his party was too large, and eleven were speeded on the back trail. With the others he bowed his head to a driving cold rain and rode on toward the Columbia.

A few miles west of Fort Hall he became aware, suddenly, that the wagon road had turned to the southwest, brave in the direction of California.

He remembered the man Chiles whom he had encountered at Elm Grove. No practicable passes were known, and emigrants to California must surmount the *Great California mountain*, but Chiles swore that wagons could be taken to the Sacramento. Here was their trail, cut through the gray sage toward the heart of California. At Fort Hall he had learned further of Chiles. The California emigrants had hired Joe Walker to find them a trail through this desert and south around the mighty mountain barrier—"A long and a hazardous journey," Frémont thought, "for a party in which there were women and children. Sixty days was the shortest period of time in which they could reach the point of the mountains, and their route lay through a country inhabited by wild and badly disposed Indians, and very poor in game; but the leader was a man possessing great and intimate knowledge of the Indians, with an extraordinary firmness and decision of character." Chiles himself, believing a better route could be found to California via the headwaters of the Malheur, had with a few companions gone down the Snake, expecting to traverse California and meet his companions with wagons before they could round "the point of the mountain."

Frémont's own allegiance must be first to the Oregon Trail. He turned back to the Road to Oregon. The trail pursued its way west through a country sullen with cold lava flows. The uniform dark gray of the sage was a somber gloom fallen upon the land; even the sunlight brought the earth no vitality, and the Snake River, paralleling the route, ran a strange, violent, inhospitable course.

The Boise River Valley afforded a grateful interval in the desolation; below the Boise they crossed the Snake for the last time and ascended Burnt River. The descent of Powder River and the crossing of a ridge brought them into that lovely mountain valley, the Grande Ronde. Beyond this mountain basin rose the Blue Mountains—the great barrier to the valley of the Willamette. Leaving the traveled emigrant roads for an Indian trail, on October 24th Frémont reached Marcus Whitman's little mission at Walla Walla, and on November 4th he arrived at the Dalles—the Falls of the Columbia.

So his responsibilities were done. The thirty-year-old army engineer had made "a connected survey" of the emigrant trail across America, joined his scientific observations to those of Wilkes. What was now to be done—retrace the beaten trail to the Missouri outposts of American civilization?

Instead, Frémont lifted his head eagerly to the south. He had heard of a lake, called Mary's Lake, deep in the mountain-desert country. He would go southeast to this lake, thence to the fabled Buenaventura. On this river he would winter, and in the spring return east by way of the Arkansas.

On November 25th Frémont and his twenty-five men rode through flurrying snow into the mountains south of the Columbia. It was a majestic country of snowy white peaks and dark pine forests, peopled, said the Indians, with evil spirits, a beautiful, forbidding land greatly dissimilar to any he had seen.

The River of the Falls afforded a trail south, the sunshine warming the days as the distance from the Columbia increased. On December 10th they reached Lower Klamath Lake. From this point their travels would be exploration. The

Klamath Indians had no advice, and maps misled rather than helped. Southeastward they rode, through a mountain country set now and then with beautiful lakes and sheltered valleys, but as often so convulsed that only twisting Indian trails enabled them to proceed. By December 27th, as they descended these mountains southeasterly, they began to look for Mary's Lake, but by New Year's Day they had found nothing but dry shallow basins, their way "broken by gullies and impeded by sage, and sandy on the hills, where there is not a blade of grass." Gloomy fogs overhung this desert, and they proceeded with desolate feelings. On January 3rd the fog was so dense that the men could not see a hundred yards, and those sent out for the horses were lost for hours. They had reached and overrun the position where, according to the best maps, they should have found Mary's River or Mary's Lake. Evidently they were on the verge of the desert that had been described to them. The appearance of the country was so forbidding that they feared to enter it.

Frémont decided to veer southward in the hope of reaching the Buenaventura. The party set out through the dense fogs, all the men on foot. They encamped without water and with only a few tufts of grass for pasturage. The animals were in an alarming condition.

They were now on the Granite Rock Desert, in the latitude, indeed, of "Mary's Lake"—the Sink of the Humboldt —but too far west. In the desolation they could look in vain for a desert river, for a desert river flowing bright. The fogs lifted a little, and they saw a smokelike column rising into the sky; near these hot springs they found better pasturage, but fifteen horses and mules had been lost since leaving the Dalles, nine in the last few days. Until they reached a country of water and vegetation Frémont decided to proceed with greatest caution, sending scouts fifteen and twenty miles ahead, moving from no encampment unless the next was known.

On January 10th, threading their way through the mountains south, the party came suddenly upon a lake some twenty miles across, its color as darkly green as the ocean. Was this Mary's Lake? Rugged mountains rose from its very shores, and all the tales of Mary's Lake spoke of low, rushy beaches and open country. Frémont observed rising from the waters a rock which was the very image of the great pyramid of Cheops, and so the lake was given a name it still bears, Pyramid Lake. An Indian, naked except for rabbit skin tunic, whose Snake dialect could hardly be understood, told them of a river at the end of the lake, but whether it ran in or out was not clear. There was still a chance that they had come upon Mary's Lake. In the afternoon they reached the river. It ran in; it was neither Mary's River nor the Sacramento, so that they had evidently found a large interior lake without an outlet. This new river yielded to the Indians along its bank enormous salmon trout; Frémont named it the Salmon Trout River—a name it would bear until Truckee was fixed upon it.

These Indians drew upon the ground a map of the river —it issued from another lake (Tahoe) in the mountains three or four days distant, in a direction a little west of south. Beyond this lake was a mountain, and beyond this two rivers (the Carson and the Walker). On one of these rivers, said the Indians, whites had traveled. "Whether they alluded to the settlements on the Sacramento, or to a party from the United States which had crossed the Sierra about three degrees to the southward, a few years since, I am unable to determine," Frémont confessed to his journal.

Hopeful that the Buenaventura might not be far distant, the company moved eighteen miles up the Truckee. With every stream, they expected "to see the great Buenaventura; and Carson hurried eagerly to search, on every one we reached, for beaver cuttings, which he always maintained we should find only on waters that ran to the Pacific; and the absence of such signs was to him a sure indication that the water had no outlet from the great basin." Even Kit Carson could let fancy burden his judgment, for he had seen beaver on the trapped-out Humboldt in 1838, and on the tributaries of Great Salt Lake.

They left the Truckee to follow an Indian trail across country to the river that would become known by Carson's name; hoping it to be a branch of the mysterious Buenaventura, they followed it for a distance, but in the open plain its waters joined with another stream to the eastward, and which way the waters ran it was impossible to say.

Looking out over this level-glinting watery plain, hedged about with blue mountains, Frémont was gazing upon the union of the Humboldt with the Carson in their double sink. Walker had come this way in 1833, and again only last summer; the wagon tracks of the emigrants scarred the earth not far distant.

Discouraged, Frémont returned to camp. The Buenaventura was not to be found. The hoofs of his mules and horses were worn to the quick; and not only were the horseshoes worn, but there was absolutely no iron from which to fashion new ones. It was impossible to cross six hundred miles of such country to the Rocky Mountains. Well, then, he would cross the Sierra Nevada into the Sacramento Valley.

In every direction white signal smokes rose into the skies, rising columns of alarm. The Indians here dreaded the whites. Unknowing of Walker's terrible passage through this country ten years earlier, Frémont thought this a proof of their ignorance: if they knew the whites, they would understand that the only object for whites to come among them would be to trade, and these Indians had nothing to trade.

It was snowing again, the mountains dark under the lowering clouds, and the company turned once more southward from the Carson in search of an easier pass through the Sierra Nevada than the peaks to the west afforded. Their

cross-country course brought them presently to the Walker
River, and up this they traveled to its forks. The east fork of
the Walker seduced them into the hills and canyons of the
Sierra. A tributary of the east fork brought them at last to
a peak from which they saw the west fork bearing northwest,
and they hoped they had found the tributary of a California
river. Through snow and broken country they struggled to
a summit which, however, they learned from Indians was not
the spine of the great California mountain; they had still the
tremendous ridge to surmount. Asked to guide the company,
these Indians "looked at the reward we offered, and conferred
with each other, but pointed at the snow on the mountains,
and drew their hands across their necks, and raised them
above their heads to show the depth; and signified that it
would be impossible to get through. . . . They told us, about
two years ago, a party of twelve men like ourselves had
ascended their river, and crossed to the other waters. They
pointed out to us where they had crossed; but then, they said,
it was summer time; but now it would be impossible."

One Indian was induced to guide them from the Walker
over a broad trail to the east fork of the Carson; here they
were informed that it was "six sleeps to the place where the
whites lived," but that the journey could be made only in
summer.

It was now February 1st. Frémont gathered around him
his worn company. "I reminded them of the beautiful valley
of the Sacramento, with which they were familiar from the
descriptions of Carson . . . and drew a vivid contrast between its summer climate, less than a hundred miles distant,
and the falling snow around us. . . . I assured them that,
from the heights of the mountains before us, we should
doubtless see the valley of the Sacramento river, and with one
effort place ourselves again in the midst of plenty." The men
were willing. The following morning they began climbing

toward the icy pinnacles; all were silent, knowing how hazardous the enterprise and how doubtful the issue.

Through four days they struggled upward through the snow, even after deserted by their Indian guide. On the fifth day Frémont went with Fitzpatrick and Carson to reconnoiter. Climbing on snowshoes to the summit of a pass since known by Carson's name, they looked out upon a great, snowless valley bounded to the west, perhaps a hundred miles away, by a low range of mountains that wrung from Carson a cry of delight. "There is the little mountain!" He pointed to a peak rising above its fellows. "It is fifteen years ago since I saw it; but I am just as sure as if I had seen it yesterday." The distant peak was Mount Diablo. This great valley was that of the Sacramento.

Ten days' terrific labor was required to get the animals over the summit, which they found some two thousand feet loftier than South Pass, at the supposed backbone of the continent. The desert was difficult, but they were spurred by a shining line of water etched toward a broad large mirror set in the dull earth; the Sacramento flowed under their eyes toward the Bay of San Francisco. Another bright line southward raised once more in their minds the question of the Buenaventura, but now they were intent on reaching Sutter's Fort, and this they accomplished on March 6th.

At Sutter's they rested two weeks. What, Frémont wondered, of those emigrants whose wagon tracks he had seen in the sage west of Fort Hall? How had they fared in the desert and in crossing this tremendous mountain range?

He found that Chiles was living on a farm across the Sacramento, while negotiating with the Mexican government for a land grant. With his ten or twelve associates Chiles had successfully ascended the Malheur and by way of the Sacramento had made his way to New Helvetia. The company with wagons, led by Joe Walker, had taken a course far to the south; they had come safely across the mountains, but their wagons, with mill irons, saws, and other useful goods, had been abandoned in the Sierra. Mary's River brought them through the barren deserts to the great California mountain, but that mountain still, by the emigrant, was unconquered; it had stripped to nakedness these emigrants of 1843, even as it had the emigrants of 1841.

Two weeks of rest Frémont permitted himself before turning toward home. The direct course was east, but the Sierra would force them south some five hundred miles, to a pass at the head of the San Joaquin reportedly discovered by Walker.

The country through which they traveled was a land to lay a spell on a man's heart. The valley bottoms were broad and rich, the uplands shaded by vigorous oaks. Flowers of extraordinary beauty blossomed along the banks of the river and perfumed the air. Fields were blue as the heavens with flowering lupine, and again the California poppy turned whole acres to bright orange. Elk and antelope fled from them in this richness. A beautiful land! And flowering under the immaculate range that shouldered all the eastern sky.

On April 13th they traversed Tehachapi Pass, guided by an Indian vaquero. Frémont entered the pass with the half-formed intention of striking out directly east toward the Great Salt Lake, to obtain some idea of the nature of this great interior basin. But the vaquero dissuaded him; the land to the east was "an arid and barren desert, that had repulsed by its sterility all the attempts of the Indians to penetrate it." At the summit of the pass the little cavalcade halted for a moment. Behind them lay the fertile valleys of California, good and rich and green, the sunshine fragrant with the smell of growing things. Before them lay the seared mountains, the rock naked and burnt, the valleys dry browns, parched yellows, verminous grays and whites.

The company began the descent. The pass was a justification, a way from the east into the heart-filling reality of California. With a little labor it might be made practicable for wagons. Americans needed nothing more than a way to follow. And when their white-topped wagons jolted through this pass and down into the valleys of California, Mexican dominion in this land was doomed.

They had come inadvertently to California. Yet, Frémont reflected, consider their discoveries: There was no Buenaventura. The mighty range of the Sierra, more lofty than the Rockies, shut off California from the east. The lines of communication opened north and south: the essential importance of the Columbia to American dreams of empire was made manifest. Here was news for Benton and Linn to thunder in the Senate.

The young vaquero rode on with them a day or two, pointing out a dim trail. It would lead them to the Spanish Trail. Gratefully Frémont followed the faintly traced route, and on April 18th, suddenly, "a general shout announced that we had struck the great object of our search—THE SPANISH TRAIL. . . . A *road* to travel on, and the *right* course to go." Between here and the Colorado River the country was poor in grass and scarce for water, with many waterless jornadas of forty and sixty miles. But these were inconsiderable difficulties.

They had struck the Spanish Trail fifteen miles south of the Mojave River, up which Jedediah Smith had come in 1826 and again in 1827. At the last camp on the Mojave, as they headed northeast, they were joined by two Mexicans, a man and a boy. These had belonged to a party of six, who with a cavalcade of thirty horses had come out in advance of the annual caravan to New Mexico. They had been set upon by Indians, and only these two, on horse guard, had escaped. Frémont promised to help them as he might be able. Kit Carson and Alexander Godey returned triumphantly from a pursuit of the horse thieves, driving the horses before them and with two bloody scalps dangling from Godey's gun.

They had trailed the Indians until night, and then had charged. Two were killed, the rest put to flight. Quickly the mountain men had stripped the scalps from the fallen, killing one of the scalped who came horribly to life, and gathering up the fifteen surviving horses. They had been gone thirty hours, and had ridden a hundred miles.

A night march to avoid the desert heat brought the company to the spring where the Mexican party had been attacked. Two men lay dead upon the ground, but the two women of the party were gone. The Mexican boy, Pablo, ran about frantically, *"Mi padre! Mi madre!"* "When we beheld this pitiable sight," says Frémont, "and pictured to ourselves the fate of the two women, carried off by savages so brutal and so loathsome, all compunction for the scalped-alive Indian ceased."

They continued across the sterile desert to Las Vegas, where they watered the animals in preparation for the jornada between this point and the Rio de los Angeles (known later as the Muddy). On the Rio de los Angeles they encountered Paiutes who evidently "were the same people who had murdered the Mexicans; and towards us their disposition was evidently hostile, nor were we well disposed towards them. . . . In these Indians, I was forcibly struck by an expression of countenance resembling that in a beast of prey; and all their actions are those of wild animals." These were Indians who made the Southern Route to California so unpopular in later times. Frémont watched them roast lizards, and eat with the relish of men always nearly starved.

They lost the trail and were forced to hunt for it, the Indians following them like hungry wolves. A man of the company was shot through the lungs with an arrow; he had been dragged to the riverbank and flung in. Horse, gun, and clothes were gone. But the horses were desperately in need of grass and rest. They had to ride on.

On May 12th they reached the Mountain Meadows of

later tragic notoriety, and soon after were joined by Joseph Walker, now en route back east. He had left California with the annual caravan, but, seeing that a party of whites was ahead, he with eight other Americans had run the gantlet of the desert raiders, killing two in passing, and come in safety to this stronger company.

North of the meadows, along the foothills of the Wasatch Mountains, the country was much greener and more promising, though this fertility did not extend far west. Walker said that all the country along the western horizon was unknown to him, and that even the Digger tribes who frequented Lake Sevier could tell nothing concerning it.

Rafting across the Sevier on May 23rd, Frémont pushed on to Utah Lake, a mirror of bright silver under tall white peaks. Now the company had completed an immense circuit of twelve degrees diameter north and south and ten degrees east and west. This circuit had cost them eight months and 3,500 miles of traveling. The interior of this great basin was still unknown, but its character was clear. No great river rose therein; rivers might rise to debouch into great unknown lakes, with fabulous whirlpools and underground channels, but these waters needed no outlet; legend need not provide one. Evaporation sufficed to establish an equilibrium. This Great Basin was peopled miserably and sparsely by humanity in its lowest form, the peoples scattered in single families, eating seeds, insects, and roots. This was not an American but an Asian desert. Here were interior basins with their own lake and river systems, often sterile and sun-parched, with scattered inhabitants fixed to the animal search for food.

Frémont turned east through the canyon down which Escalante had come sixty-eight years before. By way of the Duchesne, Brown's Hole, the Yampa, the upper Platte, and the Three Parks of the Rockies, the company crossed to the waters of the Arkansas. On July 31st they arrived at the Missouri River, and a few weeks later, in Washington, Frémont was settling down with his wife to write his brilliant report on the West. In the nation's consciousness it would fill a blankness that had hardly been touched by all the exploits of adventurers. But Frémont had traveled only the perimeter of the Great Basin; he had seen the river that flowed through its heart only from the west, beyond the farthest reach of its dying waters. What that river would mean for his countrymen he had no conception.

VIII

Prelude

LISTEN to a voice in the firelight, "An old man—eighty-three years—it is a long time to live;—eighty-three years. . . ." An old man talking in the warm flickering light of a night's fire: "That is a long time to live. I have seen all the Injun varmints of the Rocky Mountains—have fout them—lived with them. I have many children—I don't know how many—they are scattered; but my wife was a Crow. . . . I can't see jist now as well as I did fifty years ago, but I can always bring the game or the slinking and skulking Injun. I have jist come over the mountains from Sweetwater with the emigrators as pilot, living upon bacon, bread, milk

97

and sich like mushy stuff. It don't agree with me; it never will agree with a man of my age, eighty-three last—; that is a long time to live. . . . The grisly bear, fat deer, and poultry and fish—them are such things as a man should eat."

Squatting by the fire, blinking his sore eyes, this old man is a tall, rawboned, spare-fleshed, muscular fellow whose buckskin clothing looks as though it had never been off him in all his eighty-three years. Across the fire his auditor listens respectfully to Caleb Greenwood, "Old Greenwood," perhaps most extraordinary of all the mountain men.

When with twenty-three-year-old Jedediah Smith he sailed from the wharves of St. Louis in 1822, Old Greenwood had behind him already a man's full life, threescore years of wilderness adventure. At eighteen, having inadvertently killed a sheriff, he fled to the Mississippi frontier. The record is silent about the active years until his forty-fourth birthday. He was perhaps with Manuel Lisa when that fur trader established his posts on the upper Missouri in 1807; certainly he signed with the overland Astorians in 1810, only to desert in disgust before the Astorians left the Missouri. He joined once more with Lisa, and married a Crow woman whose name he would always honor; she bore him five sons and two daughters. "Old Greenwood," Ashley's men called him, this remarkable man of threescore years.

Old Greenwood eventually returned to the Crows. At his seventieth birthday his sight began to dim. His faithful wife, Batchicka, undertook to bring him down the Yellowstone and Missouri to St. Louis. An operation returned his sight. But the hardships of the journey had been such that Batchicka died soon after.

His eightieth birthday passed in 1843. A long time to live! Yet in March, 1844, as Frémont's exhausted party was crossing the valley of the Sacramento toward Sutter's Fort, emigrants gathering at Council Grove, on the Missouri, chose Old Greenwood as their guide to California.

The Stevens-Townsend-Murphy party rendezvoused at Council Grove early enough to give them time to get over the California mountains before snow should fall. Their wagons were strong, their oxen healthy, their supplies adequate. California promised them, perhaps most of all, a healthy climate. The dreaded fever and ague (malaria), thought to be caused by the newly broken prairie soil, was unknown in California.

With Greenwood at the head of the column, the company left the Missouri River in three divisions, headed by Captain Elisha Stevens, by Martin Murphy, Sr., and by Dr. John Townsend. There was no difficulty in the passage up the plains, and the venturesome use of what came to be known as Greenwood's Cutoff, between the Big Sandy and the Green, was successful, though the trail thus broken was across sixty miles of parched desert.

West of Fort Hall the trail ran two ways: on the right, to Oregon; on the left, to California. Here was the point of decision, now and ever after. Jim Clyman, old comrade of Jedediah Smith, and Abraham Lincoln's fellow soldier in the Black Hawk War, thought this place where the trails parted "the most Barren Sterril region" seen anywhere along the trail—"nothing to disturb the monotony of the Eternal Sage plain which is covered with broken cynders much resembling Junks of pot mettal & Now and then a cliff of Black burned rock which looks like Distruction brooding over dispair." He went on to Oregon, but Old Greenwood rode off to the left, in this summer of 1844, and eleven wagons creaked and rumbled behind him.

The route, from the Snake plain, ascended crooked Raft River southwesterly to the black silent battlements of City of Rocks. Continuing on, up Goose Creek with its sage-walled canyons and occasional grassy meadows, the trail crossed a divide into Thousand Springs Valley. Here the trails-to-be branched in striking for the head of the Humboldt, but the route by Bishop's Creek was used most frequently. Bishop's Creek surges out of the Independence Mountains north and west of the Humboldt Wells, and into the sun-bright channel to the West.

Mary's River—the Humboldt. This year grass was plentiful, the water high enough to dilute the alkali, the Diggers quiescent. The company arrived at the Sink of the Humboldt in September, and rested a week for the ascent of the Sierras.

Old Greenwood talked with Paiutes who ventured into camp. From one of these Indians Frémont's "Salmon Trout River" acquired its name, "Truckee." It was toward the Truckee that Greenwood's emigrants drove their wagons. By ascending this river, they should find a pass. It was now October 1st. The snow would begin to fall in the mountain passes about the last week of the month.

As the company packed to leave the Sink, Moses Schallenberger, brother-in-law to Townsend, discovered a Paiute making off with his bridle. Townsend struck up the muzzle of Schallenberger's gun just in time to deflect the shot. An uproar broke out among the Paiutes. It was with difficulty that Old Greenwood pacified them with presents. Next year this event would have a sequel. Now, however, Old Greenwood struck out with the little company southwesterly through the alkaline desert for the mountains beyond. A hard twenty-four hours brought them to Emigrant Springs, which scalded the oxen who stampeded into them. Only a short rest was permitted here; they set out for the Truckee, another hellish 24-hour drive culminated by a fight to keep the oxen from drinking themselves to death.

There would be no more worry about water, or about feed for the animals. The cottonwoods lining the bank of the Truckee wound into the hills, a golden avenue. But there was no road, no trail even. The way was obstructed with rocks that cut the animals' hoofs to pieces; and great boulders obstinately resisted the passage of the wagons. Again and again they had to recross the river; at last they had to travel almost entirely in the river bed itself. Up some of the steep declivities the oxen pulled in vain; it was necessary to double-team, to yoke five and six teams to a single wagon.

They awoke one morning covered by a twelve-inch blanket of snow. The snow redrew the world in beauty, but their hearts were chilled. At the forks of the Truckee they halted to argue the route. A smaller stream continued west—this was the creek flowing from what was to become known as Donner Lake. The larger branch flowed out of the mountains northerly—this was the stream draining from Lake Tahoe. Argument settled nothing. Some of the party set out on horseback to find their uneventful way to Sutter's, via the main branch and Lake Tahoe. Those who kept on with the wagons pulled up the smaller creek to the beautiful mountain lake they found within a few miles. Beyond rose the summit. Only another thousand feet.

A thousand feet! To pull wagons up that goat's trail was a prospect to break a man's heart. Granite ledges were flung together as though God had not finished with creation here. The rocks were slippery, and covered now with snow. Sheer rises of four, six, and ten feet marked the trail, and the great pines of the Sierras joined to obstruct the way.

Some of the company lost heart. At the head of the lake Townsend and Schallenberger abandoned their wagons filled with valuable merchandise and supplies. Joseph Foster, Allen Montgomery, and Schallenberger volunteered to guard the wagons through the winter; they built a cabin, but the onset of winter so frightened them that they resolved to cross the mountains on foot. Schallenberger became sick and turned back to die alone. Living on foxes, he survived the winter and was rescued in the spring.

Though some had gone on without their wagons, these emigrants of 1844 were of the stubborn American breed which nowhere on the continent had found a task out-matching its strength and will. There was a way to do any-thing. Five wagons were dragged, inch by inch, toward that forbidding summit.

Finally, a point was reached where it seemed defeat must be admitted. Even if the wagons could be hoisted up this sheer rise, oxen could not climb the perpendicular barrier. Old Greenwood looked back over the hard way they had come. Then he spat and turned again to this wall. He found, finally, a crevice through which the oxen, one by one, could be hoisted—pulled by ropes from above, lifted by the men from beneath. All the animals were lifted to the better terrain above, then log chains were hooked together, and fastened to the emptied wagons. With the teams pulling from above, and the men lifting beneath, the wagons were got up the cliff; the loads were carried piecemeal through the crevice. They went on. In a place or two it was necessary to take the wagons apart; again, they were lifted by windlasses hurriedly rigged. But they reached the summit, and twenty miles' descent brought them to the head of the Yuba River. Here they en-camped and with their 81-year-old guide went grinning to Sutter's for supplies and fresh oxen. They had brought wagons across the Sierras. Even as Frémont was hastily writ-ing his report on Oregon and California, American emigrants were walking into John Sutter's fort, an accomplishment which even they could see was fateful for this golden land.

Spring, 1845. Across the American continent threads were tangling. In Washington, James K. Polk was installing a Democratic administration that had come to power because it had correctly judged the national feeling that it was time to do something about Texas and Oregon—and Mexico and England be damned!

In Washington, Frémont's report on his second expedi-tion was finished, with thousands of copies ordered printed for the Senate, and no difficulty at all about a third expedition that should take the young engineer again to California.

In Cincinnati, with proceeds from his lectures on the evils of intemperance, Lansford W. Hastings was settling with the printer for his *Emigrants' Guide to Oregon and California,* which he had returned east to write last year, and which now should herald to the world the glories of California.

In Nauvoo, with Joseph Smith nine months dead, Brigham Young was talking about migrating with the Mormons to Upper California, to the headwaters of the Rio Colorado of the West.

On the Missouri frontier, emigrant wagons whitened the prairie.

And in the Sacramento Valley John Sutter, anxious to reinforce his settlement at New Helvetia with American rifles, was proposing to Old Greenwood that he go east and divert to California through the Humboldt Valley this astonishing new emigration to Oregon.

As soon as there was hope of forcing a passage through the mountains, Old Greenwood, in company with three of his sons, rode east. When the vanguard of the 1845 emigration reached Fort Hall, this indestructible old mountain man was awaiting them. He painted to successive companies the road to Oregon—toilsome and Indian-beset. Picturesquely he described the trail to California, and spread the golden acres before their eyes. Loyal to Oregon, Joel Palmer observed sourly, "These tales, told and rehearsed, were likely to produce the effect of turning the tide of emigration thither. Mr. Greenwood, an old mountaineer, well stocked with falsehoods, had been dispatched from California to pilot the emigrants through . . . and so far succeeded as to induce thirty-five or thirty-six wagons to take that trail."

There was a virtual row among one of the emigrant companies. The captain of the train forbade any man's leaving

the company for California: it was a plunge into the unknown; there was great uncertainty about the land titles,
and Sutter probably could not make good his offer of six
sections of land to every settler; moreover, the company was
American and ought not to dwell under another flag. Some
argued that California must become American territory,
others that Mexico would fight to hold the country, and
Americans who went there might be killed in the struggle.
"The meeting nearly broke up in a mutiny," observed B. F.
Bonney, who had decided for California.

Next morning Greenwood rode up to the embattled emigrants. "All you who want to go to California drive out from
the main trail and follow me. You will find there are no Indians to kill you, the roads are better, and you will be
allowed to take up more land in California than in Oregon,
the climate is better, there is plenty of hunting and fishing,
and the rivers are full of salmon." One emigrant pulled out
of the Oregon Trail, then another, and another. Eight families in all listened to the farewells of their comrades: "Good-
bye, we will never see you again. Your bones will whiten in
the desert or be gnawed by wild animals in the mountains."

Old Greenwood took them three days south from Fort
Hall, then left his sons to guide them while he turned back
to beguile other emigrants. As young John Greenwood one
day rode in the van of the company, an Indian suddenly
arose in the sagebrush; the frightened horse reared and nearly
unseated its rider. John Greenwood's companions laughed.
Furious, John whipped his gun from its holster. The Indian
threw up his hands; and Greenwood's companions cried upon
him a second thought. He hesitated, and the whites shouted to
the Indian to run. Young Greenwood lifted his gun and fired.
Shot through the back, the Indian fell upon his face.

At this Greenwood looked around him, and suddenly
galloped off on the trail for California. His sober companions
waited till the company came up. The Indian was coughing

blood, a dreadful sound. Truman Bonney, a doctor, examined him. He had been fatally shot through the lungs.

The Indian was laid upon a quilt and left some water. The company went on. At dusk Old Greenwood rode into camp, his face dark with wrath. "The man who kilt that Injun must die." The Indian still lived when he rode up; Old Greenwood had ordered him shot through the head and buried.

Jarvis Bonney cleared his throat, knowing that Old Greenwood thought the Texan, Sam Kinney, guilty of this outrage. "Your boy John shot him."

Old Greenwood did not bat an eye. "I want the men to git together and tell all the facts." After listening, Old Greenwood stood up. "I'll act as jedge of this trial. I order that the murderer of the Injun be killed. Shoot him on sight, like a wolf."

John Greenwood knew his father; in fleeing he preserved himself for a death years later, at a Mexican's hand. He kept well ahead of the company down the Humboldt Valley and on September 25th reached Sutter's Fort with a small party on horseback. The wagon train itself reached the Sierra earlier in the year than had the emigrants of 1844; there was as yet no snow in the passes. But rather than drag them up the precipitous heights, the wagons were dismantled and hauled up piecemeal. Reassembled, these wagons carried the emigrants to New Helvetia, where Sutter welcomed them and gave them the promised land.

Two companies thus had brought wagons to California. Solomon Sublette, a few weeks behind Greenwood, brought fifteen more. Here, at Truckee Pass, a gate opened upon California at the far end of the long road down Mary's River. Toward that pass, as the snows began to fall in this autumn of 1845, rode two sons of destiny, John Charles Frémont and Lansford Warren Hastings.

Frémont had departed Washington for the third time in May, 1845.

War with Mexico seemed imminent, and in the event of war, a shorter southern route to California, and practicable routes between Oregon and northern California, might serve the nation well. Moreover, it was a strong party Frémont led west—an exploring expedition convertible into an armed force.

The expedition left Bent's Fort on the Arkansas on August 16th, "equal to any emergency likely to occur and willing to meet it." By a route up the Arkansas and across the Rockies, Frémont reached in October the south shore of Great Salt Lake. Two weeks were spent taking observations, and then Frémont felt his investigations completed in the vicinity of the lake. In 1843 he had journeyed west by the Oregon route; in 1844 he had returned east by the Spanish Trail. Now he should penetrate the heart of this unknown land by a central course to the Sierras.

For almost the first time in all his adventurings, Frémont blazed a trail. Years of western journeying rarely had taken him out of the footprints of the mountain men. But the desert west of Great Salt Lake was known to the trappers only by fearful repute. Smith had skirted its southern verge in 1827, and Walker its northern reaches in 1833, but it "had never before been crossed by white man," Kit Carson says. Perhaps Carson could have told Frémont the tale George Ruxton heard next year, that two trappers who once got into this country had had to subsist on steaks cut from squaws. But Frémont, in Carson's phrase, "was bound to cross. Nothing was impossible for him."

It was not an inviting prospect. "The route I wished to take," Frémont explains, "lay over a flat plain covered with sage brush. The country looked dry and of my own men none knew anything of it: neither Walker nor Carson. The Indians declared to us that no one had ever been known to cross the plain, which was desert; so far as any of them had ventured no water had been found." But in the northwest, perhaps fifty or sixty miles distant, a peak glinted in the sunlight. There might be water of some kind—springs—at the base of such a mountain. Frémont decided that the company should undertake the passage of the desert. It was a decision of ominous import, because Lansford W. Hastings, that other son of destiny, had hazarded the opinion that some such route could be found, and even now was riding west toward the Humboldt.

Carson, in company with Auguste Archambeau and Lucien Maxwell, set out by night for the mountain. Two hours before sundown next afternoon, Frémont followed with his company. The plain flattened, and the sagebrush disappeared. As night fell, the party rode into a world of the dead. There was no bird song, no cricket rasp, no coyote howl, not even the rustle of wind in grasses. The moon rose on a pallid world of unshifting horizons; the very stars were strange. The quaking Indian guide became useless; paid his wage, he scuttled into the dark. The company rode throughout the night and finally encamped to light signal fires for Carson's party. With a jingle of spurs, Archambeau rode into camp just before daybreak with news of water, grass, and wood. Drinking long from their canteens, the company mounted once more, and as the sun rose they rode confidently toward the peak rising grandly before them. By afternoon they reached its foothills, "where a cheerful little stream broke out and lost itself in the valley." To this friendly mountain Frémont gave the name it bears in history, Pilot Peak. It was four years since John Bidwell and his companions had reached this point around the northern rim of the salt desert.

The horses and mules were given a day's rest and then the company turned west again. A winding course across short ranges brought them in two days to Flowery Springs. Here the party was divided to reunite at Walker's Lake. If it occurred to Frémont that a company of exploration might more profitably winter in the Great Basin than hastily cross into California, doubtless it also occurred to him that his sixty well-armed men ought soon to be in the valley of the Sacramento.

The main company he placed in charge of Theodore Talbot, to be guided by Joe Walker to Mary's River, thence to its sink and on to the rendezvous at Walker's Lake. In following Mary's River, this company would have water and grass throughout the journey, and so keep the majority of animals in the best possible condition. Frémont himself, with ten selected men, set out directly westward across the basin.

Dutifully Talbot turned northwest to Mary's River, his horses trampling into the seared November earth a trail of fatal consequence. With his own ten men Frémont crossed the Ruby Mountains to camp on a creek tributary to the south fork of Mary's River. Contemplating this great range he had just crossed, and the creeks that ran southward to the river whose sink he had sought two years ago, Frémont decided that he should name these mountains and that river. Humboldt, he named them, for the great German natural scientist. "Both the river and mountain to which I gave his name are conspicuous objects; the river stretching across the Basin to the foot of the Sierra Nevada, and the mountain standing out in greater bulk and length than its neighbors, and being one of those which I have named fertile mountains, having on it abundant water and grass, and woods."

So the river was named by an adventurer who in two years had not yet seen it, who even now was encamped only on the branch of a tributary.

Humboldt. A round, honest, solid name, a name good on the ear. . . . Yet Joseph Paul still slept in his quiet grave and the marks of Ogden's lodges still scarred the trail down the Little Humboldt. Mary's was a name of trapper legend, a light and graceful name; not, perhaps, a name for this sinuous, obstinate, desert river that flowed in the track of the sun. Ogden's was, surely, a sinewy man's name. No longer Unknown River, yet still, certainly, Barren River, it was now become the Humboldt. Frémont rode west toward glory and disgrace, but he left behind an invincible idea.

Using "just such passes as the mountains gave," trending more to the south than he would have liked but aided immeasurably by faint Indian trails that always disclosed the presence of water when water was anywhere to be had, Frémont in nineteen days reached the rendezvous on Walker's Lake. The condition of Indian existence in the country he had traversed depressed him. The Indians were really wild men. They lived to get food. The Indian dwelt amid the sagebrush, "the men living alone, the women living alone, but all after food. Sometimes one man cooking by his solitary fire in the sage-brush which was his home, his bow and arrows and a bunch of squirrels by his side; sometimes on the shore of a lake or river where food was more abundant, a little band of men might be found occupied in fishing; miles away a few women might be met gathering seeds and insects, or huddled up in a shelter of sage-brush to keep off the snow. . . . The labor of their lives was to get something to eat."

Three days after Frémont reached Walker's Lake, Talbot arrived with the main company. Guided by Walker they struck the Humboldt on November 8th and the fateful twin ruts of the emigrant route to California—no tenuous trail now; a virtual traveled road. The tired animals displayed more spirit as they followed the emigrant road. Indians said that three emigrant companies had passed during the autumn.

The trail crossed and recrossed the river, as the hills marched in on one side or the other; the topographer Kern noted that the stream presented but little variety, "always the same winding, crooked stream." Kern thought that for all the barrenness the river must become important: "Forming as it does a long line of travel of the emigrant parties, this river will soon become an interesting and noted point in this now great wilderness. Portions of its immediate bottoms may be capable of cultivation; but the bare, sandy bluffs that surround or border it, produce little save bunch-grass, and no timber. Great numbers of ducks and geese are to be found in this region."

Reaching the sink of the Humboldt, Talbot brought the detachment to encampment on a stream sluggish and not especially palatable. Walker pointed out Indian skulls strewing the ground, somber memorials of his own past. They parted reluctantly from the emigrant trail which here struck out direct for the Sierra, and made their way toward the Carson River, with its straggling cottonwood foliage. Next day, crossing plains and low ridges of sand and burnt rock, Talbot rode with his company into Frémont's camp.

Frémont now again divided his company. Talbot was to go south, by Owens Valley, "around the Point of the California Mountain into the head of the San Joaquin Valley"; Walker was well-acquainted with the route. Frémont himself, with fifteen selected men, was to attempt the immediate crossing of the more lofty pass at the head of the Truckee. They should reunite on the Lake Fork of the Tulare River.

Talbot rested his company ten days, and did not set out for the south until December 8th. Water and grass, says Edward Kern, were scarce and of wretched quality; the cook, "in order to improve the already horrid taste given to our coffee by the bad water, added some greasewood, or other noxious weed, giving it a flavor too unsavory even for appetites as keen set as our's." They were, Walker reported, a few miles west of his route with the emigrants of 1843; in that year he had found good grass and springs. They crossed into Owens Valley, obtaining "a fine view of the great Sierra Nevada from the far north till it faded on the distant horizon far to the south of us. This bold and rocky barrier, with its rugged peaks, separates us from the valley of California."

From Owens Valley they crossed by Walker's Pass into the valley of the San Joaquin and went in search of Frémont.

"The Pathfinder" himself had proceeded north until he struck the Truckee and the trail emigrants had found sooner than he. Although it was now the first week of December, snow had not yet fallen in the passes. He arrived on December 8th at Sutter's Fort. Here he remained long enough to obtain supplies and fresh horses, and to report the trail he had blazed west from the salt lake. Then he turned southeast in search of his comrades. There was some difficulty and delay in the reunion, which was not effected until February. In March Frémont set out northerly, toward Oregon, but he could not bring himself to leave California, for momentarily he expected news from the East to transform his company from an exploring expedition into an armed force. By halfhearted stages he moved as far north as Klamath Lake, in Oregon, but at the end of May he turned back. War with Mexico had broken out; the news had not reached here, but the fears and antipathies of native Californians and American emigrants were crystallizing into open conflict. In June the Americans raised their Bear Flag standard, to fight for a Republic of California, and after a period of hesitation, Frémont joined his fortunes to theirs. News arriving of events along the Rio Grande, Frémont's ragged army automatically became an army of the United States. In the winter, in southern California, he received the capitulation of the Californians who had resisted his forces and those of Commodore Robert F. Stockton and General Stephen W. Kearny. So much was glory. But after quarrels over authority Frémont was arrested and, in the summer of 1847, taken east for court-martial.

Irony attends that eastward passage. For Frémont, who fixed upon the Humboldt River its name in history, first saw the desert river as he journeyed up it like a captive barbarian chained to Kearny's chariot wheels; the certain knowledge that enabled him to publish his celebrated map of 1848, first to depict a highroad for emigrants across the Unknown Land, was born of this bitter eastward passage. American history would know Frémont again, as California senator, as Path-finder once more, as Republican presidential candidate of 1856, as unlucky or inept Civil War general . . . but he passes from the story of the Humboldt as the dust clouds eddy about this eastward-marching company.

And what of that other son of destiny? On December 25th, with nine companions, Lansford W. Hastings dis-mounted at Sutter's doorstep. The luck of the foolhardy had brought him down the Humboldt and across the mountains. Had they been delayed by so much as a day, Sutter told them, they would have been cut off by the snow. Hastings nodded, his mind busy with other things. Frémont might ride from Sutter's down into California, his nerves pregnant with the imminence of war. But Hastings in his mind's eye looked east, beyond the mountains. Whatever developed in California this year would not immediately matter to him. In his saddlebags were copies of his *Emigrants' Guide*. Already it was being read everywhere by men whose hearts traveled the western trails. There had come west with him this year only nine of the twenty-two who had originally proposed accompanying him, but there would be others next year, and next . . . .

He was a man of ideas.

IX

Hastings and His Cutoff

THE spring sun ate at the snows blanketing the continent. In the Pacific valleys there had been no snow, and now the earth was ripening with summer. In the great valleys of the Mississippi, Ohio, and Missouri the sun reached down through the gray slush to the first green shoots of the spring, and glinted from the rising waters of a thousand feeding creeks. In the Rockies, the Sierras, and the Blue Mountains the snow crunched and slid in the passes, yielding to the sun, though stubbornly. The winterbound continent stirred under this spring of 1846.

In Texas Zachary Taylor was settling down opposite Matamoras, prepared to defend the country against Mexican

claims to the land east of the Rio Grande; although instructed
to refrain from battle unless attacked, his very entrance into
the disputed territory was, in Mexican eyes, an affront to
national honor. Within six weeks an American reconnaissance
force would be cut to pieces by Mexican cavalry—news to
be taken by Polk to Congress with a war declaration.

In Washington the Oregon question was about to be
settled on the compromise line of the 49th degree of latitude.

In Iowa the Mormons, with a desperate energy that
somehow kept their wagons rolling through the mud, already
were evacuating Nauvoo in anticipation of last autumn's
agreement to migrate as soon as grass should grow and water
run. Another company of Saints led by Sam Brannan had
sailed in the *Brooklyn* from New York, and now was on the
high seas en route for California. Nauvoo resounded night
and day with the bustle of preparations to depart. Rejected
by this wicked world, the Saints of the latter days, like Israel
of old, would journey into the wilderness.

And across the state a few miles, other Illinoians pursued in Lansford Hastings' book a glowing image of California: "There is no country in the known world possessing
a soil so fertile, with such varied and inexhaustible resources,
and a climate of such mildness, uniformity and salubrity;
nor is there a country now known which is so eminently
calculated by nature herself in all respects to promote the
unbounded happiness and prosperity of civilized and enlight-
ened man."

That was a country, thought George Donner, that he
would like to see. With his third wife, Tamsen, and the five
children of his second and third marriages, he would like to
go to California. "Even in the months of December and
January, vegetation is in full bloom, and all nature wears a
most cheering and enlivening aspect. It may be truly said that
'December is as pleasant as May.'" And then, also, his fellow
townsman, James Frazier Reed, was going to California. Irish

born, of noble Polish ancestry, Mr. Reed was a man of spirit, a veteran of the Black Hawk War, and for years a successful merchant, a railroad contractor, and manufacturer of furniture. Lately, however, he had met with some business reverses.

There were others in Springfield who liked the thought of California—in all, more than thirty. Nor in Illinois alone did the spring sunshine light the way to the plains.

In California's Napa Valley Jim Clyman, back from a b'ar hunt, lifted his eyes to the white Sierras and calculated that he might soon be able to set out for the east. It was rumored that Captain Frémont had raised the American flag in Monterey, and that the Mexican authorities had called for armed volunteers to defend their rights. Dismissing the kind of reports that might be carried verbally a hundred miles or two by "an ignorant supersticious people," he nevertheless wrote Frémont offering the aid of an armed company of American emigrants now gathering around him. The captain, however, replied dubiously, "I have received information to the effect that a declaration of war between our Government and Mexico is probable, but so far this news has not been confirmed. . . . If peace is preserved I have no right or business here; if war ensues I shall be out numbered ten to one and be compelled to make good my retreat pressed by a pursuing enemy." An addition to his ranks would only complicate his problem. He had therefore to "gratefully decline your offer of a company of hardy warriors."

The captain, then, could be left to fry his own fish. Clyman set out eastward, and on April 16th, with a few companions, was courteously received into the Bear Creek encampment of that busy gentleman, Lansford W. Hastings.

No grass had grown under Hastings' feet since his arrival at Sutter's. To Thomas Larkin, United States consul here, he had intimated that a company organized at Washington with the sub rosa approval of the American government

planned to dispatch two ships yearly, transporting immigrants
to California free of charge. Larkin heard, moreover, that
Hastings was laying out a town near New Helvetia for the
Mormons who, rumor said, were about to migrate from Illinois. Since leaving California in 1843 Hastings had deter-
minedly followed his star. California now seemed ripe for the
plucking. Bring here a great company of American emigrants,
long rifles ready to their hand, and a man would need nothing
but the spirit to act. He might yet be president of California.

To publish his lyrical picture of California he had traveled
the length and breadth of Ohio, lecturing upon the evils of
intemperance. A mean sort of life, but it paid for his book.
During this winter, all along the frontier, men would have
read that book. There would be those along the overland
trail this year who were definitely bound for California; and
persuasion would divert much of the Oregon emigration.
When Jim Clyman rode into camp on April 16th, Hastings
cordially agreed to pilot his company as far as the Oregon
Trail.

Something of his plans was seeping out. Even now, men
were riding north with alarming tales of his activities. The
settlers in the Willamette Valley, who this spring had determined to find another route to Oregon than the difficult
trail across the Blue and Cascade Mountains, received this
news by June and resolved in mass meeting to send an express
to meet the westbound emigration, "in order to prevent their
being deceived and led astray by the misrepresentation of
L. W. Hastings, who is now on his way from California for
that object."

The last week of April the Clyman-Hastings company
set out for the east. With them went 83-year-old Caleb
Greenwood and two of his sons, hoping, perhaps, to pick up
some money guiding the California trains. As they set out,
the first trains were leaving Independence for the west,
alarmed by rumors that five Englishmen, ahead of them along

the trail, were stirring up the Indians against them; and dismayed by rumors that an army of Mormons would be found on the trail to murder and plunder; but stubborn in their determination, laughing at the extravagant stories told about California but half-believing them, too.

On April 29th the Clyman-Hastings company rode up into "the region of all most Eternal snow and ice." For three days they floundered through the snow before reaching the bare ground at the head of Truckee Lake. Below the lake their half-starved animals were given a chance to graze, and then they followed down the Truckee to where it turned northwardly too much, and struck out across the white desolate sink of the Humboldt: "a singular road," Clyman thought, "mostly over a bear salt plain which had a few years since been covered in water and costituted Ogdens Lake which no doubt when Mr Ogden visited this region . . . was Quit a large Lak but shallow now nearly dried up and from appearances will in a few years more intirely disappear and become the most dry thirsty imaginable"

The company rode north up the broad valley of the Humboldt, "the mountains . . . all of vitrified rock of various hues but mostly of dark red and brown," the valley floor "composed of whiteish volcanic mud" and bearing "no vegitation except a hard thorny shub called by voyagers grease wood." They proceeded up the river over "one of the most Steril Barren countys," says Clyman, "I ever traversed the hills and mountains producing no kind of vegitation and the more elevated part of the vally bearing nothing but a small shrubby thorn and not even moist enough to poduce the much dispised wild sage . . . the willows have not yet buded and the earth is so parched that we are all day covered in a cloud of dust allmost sufficating to pass through and the water is Likewise poor when obtained as there is none at all Except in the river . . . the sun arose as usual without a

speck of cloud or mist for bothe appear to be allmost unknown to this region."

The water freshened and the spring sun was coaxing out
the grass. They proceeded up the river valley between black
slag mountains—"So perfectly Barren and sterile . . . that
scarcely a bird is heard to chirp to the rising Sun and not
even the signe of an animal Except Rabbits ever ventures to
make a precarious subsistance on these plains." As cheerlesss
was the country above the Big Bend of the Humboldt, the
mountains apparently formed of slag and scoria, the valleys
of volcanic mud, salt, and soda, grown with dry greasewood
and sage. The river course was crooked, but the earth too dry
for the company to venture a cutoff; they moved, indeed,
through a dust cloud like thin gray fog.

On May 16th the company divided. Old Greenwood
piloted the slower division, while Clyman and five others rode
on ahead. The Ruby Mountains rose as white-capped peaks
above the eastern horizon, and there were occasional clear
brooks to feed the sullen river. On May 21st, at Bishop's
Creek, they reached the place where the Talbot-Kern party
of last autumn had intersected the emigrant trail. Hastings
had watched for this trail from the south, and now he halted
the company to argue its advantages. "Mr. Hastings our
pilot," Clyman observed, "was anxious to try this rout but
my beleef is that it verry little nearer and not so good a
road as that by fort Hall." After two days of argument,
the little company finally took the Frémont trail by way
of the salt lake.

By a winding course across the mountains, following the
trail only with difficulty, the company reached the summit
of the Toano Range. To the eastward, beyond the range of
vision, spread a "great salt plain." They set out northeast-
ward toward Pilot Peak and camped at its base. Next
morning they embarked upon the passage of the great salt
desert, two days' travel without water to Redlum Spring in

Skull Valley. When, next day, Clyman heard the many-noted song of a mockingbird, he mentioned it gratefully as the only singing bird heard in ten days—"in fact this desolation afords subsistance to nothing but Lizards, and scorpions which move like Lightning ove the parched Earthe in all directions as we pass along."

Hastings had other things to occupy his mind than the song of mockingbirds. He could feel vindicated the opinion hazarded in his book: *The most direct route, for the California emigrants, would be to leave the Oregon route, about two hundred miles east from Fort Hall; thence bearing west southwest, to the Salt Lake; and thence continuing to the bay of St. Francisco.* He had now demonstrated that a direct route south of the salt lake was practicable; although the crossing of the white desert had been waterless, they had accomplished this in twenty hours of hard driving.

Crossing the Jordan River, a little apprehensive at news from the Utes that the Snakes had lately killed two whites in the country through which they must pass, they made their way through the Wasatch Mountains to Bear River and went on to Bridger's Fort. But the fort was deserted, with no evidence of any human habitation in a month.

What was to be done? "In our weak and deffenceless state it was not easy to fix on any safe plan of procedure," Clyman noted. "Some proposed to return to Bear River and risk the hostility of the Snake Indians others proposed to take the trail Travel slowly and risk the Sioux[s] which ware supposed to be on our rout to Fort Larrimie so that the day was taken up in discussing what would be the most safe way of disposing ourselves a sufficient time to await the company from oregon to the states which was generally supposed would be Quite large this season." The company was gloomy and oppressed: "nothing can be mor desolate and discouraging than a deserted fort whare you expect relief in a dangerous Indian country and every imaginary Idea was started as to

what had been the caus of Bridgers leaving his establishment
But nothing satisfactory could possibly be started and we
ware still as far in the dark as ever."

Next day Hastings, his man James Hudspeth, and their
Indian servant parted from the rest of the small company
to go some miles eastward to await the arrival of the emigration. Clyman's companions, learning themselves too late
to intercept a company coming east from Oregon, finally
elected to await the others from California, guided by Old
Greenwood via the Fort Hall trail. On June 11th this company arrived. Twelve days later, on the North Platte, the re-
united party encountered the vanguard of the emigration.

Thereafter there was hardly a day that they did not
pass an Oregon- or California-bound emigrant party. "It is
remarkable," Clyman reflected, "how anxious thes people are
to hear from the Pacific country and strange that so many
of all kinds and classes of People should sell out comfortable
homes in Missouri and Elsewhare pack up and start across
such an emmence Barren waste to settle in some new Place
of which they have at most so uncertain information." But,
he realized, this was the character of his countrymen.

At Laramie, Clyman encountered old friends. Encamped
here was Lilburn W. Boggs, of hated Mormon memory, ex-
governor of Missouri now bound for California. And here
also was James Frazier Reed, with whom he had campaigned
in the Black Hawk War.

"Take the regular wagon track," Clyman advised Reed,
"and never leave it. It is barely possible to get through if
you follow it, and it may be impossible if you don't."

"There's a nigher route," Reed objected. "There's no
use taking such a roundabout course."

Remembering the mountains and the cruel white desert,
Jim Clyman shook his head. But nothing daunted Reed's
assurance. Clyman said farewell, and continued down the
plains. Three days east of Independence, he heard that war

with Mexico had broken out. Reaching Independence, Clyman disposed of his mules and made his appearance at Noland's Tavern, "and a Rough appearance it was But such things are not atall strange in Independance as it the first place all the Parties rach from the Mountains from St A Fe California and Oregon."

Clyman was to spend eighteen months visiting in Wisconsin, and then return to California in 1848, to marry and live out the quiet years to 1881. He had frankly told emigrants of his unfavorable impression of Oregon and California; he had warned Reed and others against the new cutoff south of Great Salt Lake. Those warnings availed nothing. Behind him on the trail he had left the eloquent voice of Lansford W. Hastings.

Waiting with Hudspeth for the emigration, Hastings was astonished, one day, to see a solitary horseman ride up. His name was Wales B. Bonney; he had left Oregon on May 13th, and had come by way of Fort Hall; he was returning to Oxford, Ohio, to bring his family west. Mostly he traveled by night, concealing himself by day in the ravines. Even Hastings was astonished at the mixture of courage and foolhardiness that could lead a man, alone, to make the long journey. Nevertheless, he hastily wrote a letter "To all California Emigrants now on the Road," which he induced the lone traveler to carry east to the emigrant trains.[1] As the

---

[1] This lone traveler who carried Hastings' open letter east is here fully identified for the first time. Edwin Bryant, who met him July 10th on the Sweetwater, said that he had come alone from Oregon by way of Fort Hall. "There must have been a powerful motive to induce an experienced man to risk the hazards of such a journey; and whether he ever reached the end of it or not I can scarcely conceive to be doubtful." West of Fort Laramie Bonney was robbed by Indians of his horses, provisions, and clothing, but on foot he continued another 75 miles before being overtaken by a party headed by Solomon P. Sublette, which Bryant also had encountered, on July 11th. From Fort Laramie Bonney went south to Pueblo, in the track of the "Mississippi Saints" led by John Brown, and then went with Brown and a small company of Mormons

California government, Hastings intimated, might oppose the
American emigration, for their safety the California-bound
companies should unite; they were invited to take a new
cutoff explored by the writer, via Fort Bridger and the south
end of Great Salt Lake. Although there were those among
the emigrants who would look upon this letter with suspicion, others would be impressed at the opportunity of
securing as pilot the author of the renowned *Emigrants'
Guide*.

Among the first companies to reach Hastings' encampment near Fort Bridger was that with which Edwin Bryant
rode. Although Hastings told a good story, Bryant listened
doubtfully; there seemed much to discredit the route, especially for wagons and families. That famous mountain man,
Joe Walker, now running east some horses stolen in California, had no high opinion of the new cutoff. Nevertheless,
many of the emigrants at Bridger were determined to try it,
and were only waiting for some of the rear companies to
arrive.

Persuaded by his companions, Bryant decided to try the
Hastings Cutoff—but not with wagons. He and eight others
sold their wagons for mules; thus lightly encumbered, Bryant
thought they should make out all right. But to his friends in
the rear he wrote letters—never delivered—advising them
not to take the new road, but to continue by way of Fort
Hall. With families and wagons, they should not take chances.

On July 20th, accompanied by Hudspeth, Bryant and
his fellows left Fort Bridger's circles of white-tented wagons,
its feeding cattle and horses, and its white-pluming campfires.
Spring had come late to the mountains, and only now were
the strawberries and all the bright mountain flowers blooming

to Independence, arriving September 30th and delivering 125 letters from the
emigration. His arrival was noted in the Independence *Expositor*, October 3,
1846, the news being picked up by the St. Louis *Weekly American* on October
9th and the St. Louis *Daily New Era* on October 8th. See also the *Autobiography
of Pioneer John Brown*, pp. 70-71.

along the creekbanks. Summer was short; autumn followed
hard upon spring. There was a corollary to that: the wagons
must be over the Sierra by the end of October.

Hudspeth seemed inclined to further explorations.
Instead of taking the company west to the salt lake by the
route he had come with Hastings and Clyman, he veered to
the north. Crossing Bear River, Bryant's company was led
into a maze of precipitous canyons. It was five days before
they reached the Weber between its upper and lower canyons.

They had seen nothing like a wagon road. Next morning, as the party went on down through Devils Gate into
Great Salt Lake Valley, grateful for safe release from "this
natural prison house," Hudspeth with two companions rode
up the Weber to see whether axmen could hew a road through.
It was four days before he returned. He and his companions
had forced a way through the upper canyon, and on going
up the Weber had met Hastings with a train of some forty
wagons. Hudspeth thought that a passage through the canyon
was practicable, by making a road in the stream bed in places,
and by cutting out timber and brush in other places, but
Bryant thought that the difficulties to be encountered by the
emigrants would be serious.

On the morning of July 29th the little mounted company rode south along the east shore of the lake, whose waters
seemed dark and sullen, too heavy to ripple with the wind
like other lakes or the ocean. Passing the sulphurous warm
springs at the north end of Salt Lake Valley, and with an
approving word for this valley where, less than a year later,
the Mormons would locate, the company crossed the Utah
Outlet and circled the lake to Skull Valley. They had now to
part from Hudspeth, who with three others proposed to
explore southward in hope of finding another route across the
salt desert. Hudspeth cried his parting advice: "Put spurs
to your mules and ride like hell!" "From this time forward,"
Bryant told his journal, "we are without a guide, or any

reliable index to our destination, except our course westward, until we strike Mary's river."

This salt desert lying so inimically athwart one flank of the Humboldt was, as far as the eye could see, "of a snowy whiteness, and resembled a scene of wintry frosts and icy desolation. Not a shrub or object of any kind rose above the surface for the eye to rest upon. . . . It was a scene which excited mingled emotions of admiration and apprehension." Almost at once they saw before them what looked like an arm of Great Salt Lake. Alarmed lest they had taken the wrong trail, looking about for a way out of their difficulties, they realized that the waters were moveless and made no sound—the first of the illusions abounding in this otherworldly country. Other mirages were encountered at once. Now they saw lakes dotted with islands and bordered by green trees that swayed in the wind; now they saw beautiful houses with spacious parks and stately avenues; now they saw vast, many-towered cities: "The whole distant view around . . . seemed like the creations of a sublime and gorgeous dream, or the effect of enchantment."

Late in the morning they entered upon a vast, level, lifeless white plain, "so frightfully forbidding and unearthly in its aspects, that all of us, I believe, though impressed with its sublimity, felt a slight shudder of apprehension." Even the mules seemed afraid. The sun glittered everywhere, to the horizons that met the unearthly blue sky—a baleful white glare. A windstorm whipped up particles of salt that burned their eyes, stung their flesh, embittered their mouths. Ghostly reflections of their own image accompanied them in their march. The sun went down, and they straggled upon the interminable white plain, buoyed now by the belief that they approached the springs at the base of the mountain—Pilot Peak—of which they had been told. Some seventeen hours after embarking upon the salt desert, worried by the scarlet flicker of Indian fires on the distant mountains, they reached water. Day's travel: "75 miles."

It was an experience to remember, an experience none cared to repeat. Here the hand of God had been set to creation of a cruel beauty. All were glad, after a day's rest, to set out upon Hastings' trail to Mary's River.

Four days it took, across jumbled dry country, to reach that river. On August 9th, just as Bryant with a companion was crossing, he saw at a distance some ten or fifteen horsemen riding north from the river up the stream known as Bishop's Creek. Spurring to intercept them, confident that they were a party from California, he was surprised to find them road makers from Oregon. They had left the Willamette Valley on May 10th seeking a route to intersect Mary's River at its Big Bend. Dust-begrimed and trailworn, they had established the Applegate Cutoff to Oregon.

Which of the two parties, Bryant wondered, presented the more jaded and ragged aspect? "None of us, within the settlements of the United States, would have been recognized by our nearest kindred as civilized and christianized men. Both parties had been in the wilderness nearly three months, the Oregon party, as we learned, having started on the tenth of May, and our party on the fifth of the same month; they from the shores of the Pacific travelling east, we from the waters of the Missouri travelling west. A singularity of the incident was, that after having travelled across a desert by a new route some three or four hundred miles, we should have met them just at the moment when they were passing the point of our junction with the old trail. Had we been ten minutes later, we should not have seen them."

It had been a hard three months for Jesse and Lindsay Applegate. Ten men, led by Levi Scott and guided by "Black" Harris, an old mountain man, had commenced their search for a road in May. The desertion of four of the company had forced them to return for aid, but reinforced by ten men, including the Applegates, they had set out again on June 22nd, "with a firm determination never to retrace their steps—never to abandon the noble and philanthropic enterprise," until they should have found a good wagon road. Taking the California trail as far as the canyon of the Umpqua, they made their way to the Rogue River Valley and thence southeasterly through unexplored country. Surmounting the Cascade Mountains, they proceeded into Klamath Valley. A devious way through the mountains brought them over the dividing ridge of the Great Basin, and down to the deserts Frémont had traversed in 1843. Suffering from heat and lack of water, they reached the Humboldt near its Bend. They searched for a better route across the desert west of the Humboldt, but their great problem was over, for they had found a practicable way to this river, and the river itself was a safe, sure trail almost to the intersection with the old Oregon Trail. Provisions were low, however, and Jesse Applegate and four others were dispatched to Fort Hall for supplies; the others had followed up the Humboldt, and so desperate was their need of provisions, Bryant observed on meeting them, that unless they came upon an emigrant company they should have to slaughter one of their horses.

Saluting these worn adventurers, Bryant's company rode down the river with soaring spirits. They were done with cutoffs, with question marks and the cloudy ambitions of adventurers. Again they were in the wagon trail to California; although it was in places blind and overgrown, there would be no real difficulty in searching it out, and less anxiety about their course. It was a happy sign, too, that the valley appeared to teem with antelope, even though exceedingly timid and wild.

Though unencumbered by wagons, Bryant's company was not first on the California trail this year. On August

18th, Bryant on his jaded mule was thrilled to see far ahead two white specks on a gentle swell of the plain.

The sight, in this wilderness, was like coming upon a hospitable cottage or mansion. Or more so, as the white tent-cloth of the wagons was always, in this country, the sure sign of hospitality, to the limitation of the traveler; and this was not always the case amid civilization. The wagons belonged to Messrs. Craig and Stanley, Missourians who had left Fort Hall July 23rd, and who now were two weeks in advance of all other California trains. Presenting Bryant and his company with provisions from their own slender stock, the Missourians waved cheerfully as their wagons fell behind.

Now ahead of all the emigration, the party reached the Sink on August 19th, the Truckee next day, and Truckee Lake on the 25th. On the following day they crossed the summit. They could descend into California—go first to Sutter's and then to the excitement of the war. They had left the United States for a foreign country, only to find themselves again, pridefully, under the American flag. Now they could scatter to diverse adventures. But their companions of two months ago, a thousand miles behind across mountains and deserts, were plodding west toward a grimmer destiny.

On the same day Bryant departed, Hastings set into motion the wagons which had gathered near Fort Bridger. The company proceeded to the Little Muddy and the Bear River and then, climbing a divide and descending narrow, crooked Echo Canyon, reached the Weber just as Hudspeth came up its choked canyon.

Hastings may from the first have intended going down the Weber instead of following the difficult trail across the Wasatch Mountains by which he had come east; or he may now have been persuaded by Hudspeth's report on the canyon. But the way down the Weber was obstructed by narrow canyon walls, by great boulders, by thick growths of

willows and scrub oak. They could count themselves fortunate to progress a mile in a day. Thrice they crossed spurs
of the mountains only by rigging windlasses and lifting the
wagons bodily; toward the end, as they were hoisting a yoke
of oxen and a wagon over such an eminence, the rope broke
near the windlass. The men who were lifting at the wheels
and sides of the wagon scattered to save themselves. The
oxen held their ground for a few seconds, and then plunged
over a 75-foot precipice and were crushed in a tangled mass
with the wagon on the rocks far below.

This was no route for wagons. When the party was got
out upon the benchlands above Great Salt Lake, Hastings
rode back up the canyon to post a notice above the upper
canyon. Emigrants who followed should cut across the mountains, he advised, and not attempt this route.

Returning to the tired members of his company,
Hastings led them south around the lake, in Edwin Bryant's
track. At Black Rock they buried a member of their party
who had come down with pneumonia. They would now have
to cross the Salt Plain. Encouragingly Hastings assured them
it was only forty miles across, but he saw that they filled all
receptacles with water and cut grass for the animals. At
nightfall they embarked upon the desert. The sun rose upon
a frightening prospect, the world as white as snow, no green
thing anywhere, not even the pale-emerald greasewood. The
livestock was very tired, but revived a little on being given
hay and some water. The company had made slower progress
than Hastings had anticipated; oxen and heavy wagons must
proceed more laboriously than horses and mules with light
packs. However, he told the company that they should reach
water about noon.

There was no water at noon, nor at nightfall. Through
the afternoon the wagons straggled northwest across the
still, vast, white plain, oxen giving out mile by mile, some
lying down to die and others rising after a time to struggle

on toward the salvation of the distant shining peak. Wagons were abandoned; women and children got out and walked. Nightfall, by relieving them of the dreadful sun, let them hope again, but the sun rose in the east once more, and a night's constant labor had not brought them to the end of this desert. Now the stock failed swiftly; had they not reached the Pilot Peak springs at nightfall, all the animals might have been lost.

The men went back with water and grass; some of the stock was saved, and the wagons brought in. But bones of livestock were left to bleach upon the desert.

Perhaps there was some bitterness toward the rash young man who had led them into such tribulation. But whether a good guide or no, Hastings was their only guide. And now, instead of taking the trail by which he had come east, around the north face of the Ruby Mountains, Hastings turned south in quest of a pass which might offer quicker access to the California trail. Perhaps he doubted the practicability of Humboldt Canyon. But the formidable peaks of the Rubies offered no encouragement; south they went, day after day, and could only turn west when they reached the southern end of the range. Even then, no way opened westward through the hills, and Hastings had to turn back north to Mary's River. When the worn company at last reached the California trail, they could see the fresh-cut, deep tracks of the wagons from which they had parted at Fort Bridger. This cutoff extolled in such glowing terms, this Hastings Cutoff, had brought them nothing but delay, suffering, and loss. . . . It was September now, and the fear of the Sierran snows was strong. Down Mary's River they pushed their teams. Safely they followed Hastings across the Sink and up the Truckee.

But when Hastings rode with his company into New Helvetia, the place was invested by the soldiery of the United States. His ambitions, his Republic of California, were vanished in the air that whipped the Stars and Stripes above the fort.

Lansford W. Hastings was persistent. He would try again. He would fight under Frémont; he would be a realtor, a lawyer, a secessionist in Arizona. In later years he would organize filibustering expeditions into Mexico; he would die, some thirty years later, in the midst of a Brazilian colonizing scheme. But this was his high-water mark in American history, here in his crumbled dreams. He volunteered now, in this autumn of 1846, for service in Frémont's army. In the mountains winter was at hand. Eastward, across the mountains, an emigrant company that had relied upon his professions and followed in his track by desperate forced marches was pressing down the Humboldt toward the cloud-wreathed Sierras. But what had he to do with that?

X

The Epic of Starvation

A T THE Little Sandy the Donners parted with those bound to Oregon and those unshakable in their belief in the Fort Hall route. Jessy Quinn Thornton, on July 20, 1846, made note of the farewell: "The Californians were much elated and in fine spirits, with the prospect of better and nearer road to the country of their destination. Mrs. George Donner, however, was an exception. She was gloomy, sad, and dispirited in view of the fact that her husband and others could think of leaving the old road, and confide in the statement of a man of whom they knew nothing, but was probably some selfish adventurer."

The Donner company arrived at Bridger's Fort on the

28th. Hastings had left, and three days later they set out on his trail.

To the Weber canyon the route was not unduly hard; Hastings had opened the trail. But above Devils Slide they found Hastings' note advising a cutoff across the mountains. James Frazier Reed, C. T. Stanton, and William McCutchen set out down the canyon and overtook Hastings at Black Rock. Obtaining a fresh horse from the emigrant company, Reed rode back with Hastings, leaving Stanton and McCutchen to follow as they might be able. Hastings rode a distance east and pointed the way to follow. At evening Reed returned to his company, and his recommendation was accepted, to cut their way up and over the mountains rather than attempt the Weber.

At sunrise they commenced the work. It was backbreaking labor—hewing out brush, dislodging boulders, struggling up the ravine almost yard by yard. The Mormons who followed this trail next year groaned at the labor, and tried to imagine what it had cost those who had come before them. Fifteen full days it took to climb the mountain summits and penetrate the canyons; it was August 27th before their teams pulled the Donner wagons out upon the open benchlands of Salt Lake Valley. In twenty-one days they had come thirty-six miles. They had seven or eight hundred miles still to go to reach the Sierras, upon which the snows might begin to fall at any time after mid-October.

There were eighty-six in the company after the death at Black Rock of a consumptive, and on September 3rd, with misgivings, they embarked upon the crossing of the great salt desert. Two days and two nights of hard driving, Hastings had warned them.

During the first day, Thursday, the wagons kept fairly close together. But the company began to straggle; teams failed and wagons grew heavier. Through the second day they pressed on, Reed and the Donners with their heavily laden wagons a mile or more in the rear. Night fell on the second day, and again the sun flooded the salt plain with its cruel splendor. Still the dry drive was not ended. In places the salt was crusted hard, but more often the narrow iron wagon wheels cut through the thin crust into an oozy, clinging mud. The animals bawled their thirst; the men, women, and children were in no better case. The dry drive continued through the third day, and now oxen were cut loose, wagons abandoned, everything sacrificed to the terrible imperative of reaching the springs. It was Tuesday before the last of the company staggered from the parched desert into the grassy meadows at the foot of Pilot Peak.

The crossing was disastrous; it cost them dozens of oxen and cattle; uncounted wealth in goods and wagons; it took something from their spirit. Some, like Reed, had been stripped almost of everything. All knew that this westward trek had become a struggle for survival.

A week was spent, salvaging from the desert what could be brought to the springs, while the livestock recuperated.

The last night in camp at Pilot Peak a light snow fell, ominous precursor of winter. They were terribly late, and already short of provisions. It was decided that two men should be sent ahead to California for provisions. McCutchen and Stanton volunteered. The company watched their departure apprehensively. McCutchen might return, because he left his family behind. But Stanton was a bachelor. There was nothing to bring him back. This was a company, "the Donner company," only in name. Nothing held them together, really, but self-interest.

Their only guide was Hastings' wheel tracks. Those tracks went south and south, and then at last west and north. They whipped along their oxen, cursing Hastings and this fool's route, grateful to reach at last, on the final day of September, the California trail and Mary's River.

Those who had gone by Fort Hall were far ahead, even

Hastings' train. There was no succor behind. Each day had
ground at their spirit: the hard crossing of the Wasatch, the
passing of the salt desert, the long detour around the Rubies.
Now, on the Humboldt, disintegration began.

There was something too fine about Reed to sit well on
everybody: a distinction, a hallmark of aristocracy: "just too
damned good for this world." His friend, easygoing Uncle
George Donner, had perhaps for that reason been accorded,
instead of Reed, the captaincy of the company. And the
latent dislike had festered.

On a day in the first week of October the company
arrived at the foot of a steep, sandy hill up which the wagons
must be got by double-teaming. F. W. Graves was leading,
with Jay Fosdick second, John Snyder third, and Reed
fourth. Milt Elliott, driving Reed's team, got into an argument with Snyder. Wrathfully Snyder declared he would
get his wagons up the hill without any help from Elliott's
teams; while they wrangled, Graves's wagons were drawn
over the summit by his own and Fosdick's teams. Perhaps
Elliott thought Snyder would stay put until Graves's oxen
returned; he pulled out of line and tried to pass. The trail
was narrow and the oxen became entangled. Enraged, Snyder
laid about with his whip, and when Reed rushed forward,
Snyder promised him a rawhiding for himself. Reed drew
his hunting knife to defend himself. Alarmed, Snyder lashed
out with the butt of his whip, laying open an ugly gash
along Reed's head. Reed struck out desperately and sank his
knife to the hilt just below Snyder's collarbone. Mrs. Reed
rushed between, but Snyder in frenzy struck at her and at
Reed twice more, felling him to his knees. It was over in
seconds. Snyder turned away. Then he staggered and fell into
Billy Graves's arms. To Patrick Breen, who came running up,
he gasped, "Uncle Patrick, I'm dead."

Within moments he was.

Reed stood for a moment, the blood running down his face. Then he tore himself from his family, flung his knife into the river, bent futilely over Snyder. It is said that Snyder choked, "I am to blame."

But Snyder had been popular in the company, Reed disliked. The emigrants debated a course of action: to bring Reed to trial on reaching California, to hang him now on an upended wagon tongue. Reed's friends, the Donners, were miles ahead; the wagons had begun to string out when the Humboldt was reached. Yet there were two, Milt Elliott and William Eddy, who stuck with Reed. By a compromise, Reed was banished from the company.

Mounting his horse, Reed rode on alone. Overtaking the Donners, he obtained scant provisions and, with a teamster, set out for Sutter's. There he could obtain food and livestock, and return over the mountains for his family.

The Snyder tragedy was the breaking point. Whatever had been retained of a community of spirit vanished with this death and this judgment on the banks of the Humboldt. As the teams pressed down the river through the shortening October days, each family began to withdraw into a world of its own, a world in which nothing counted except its own interest. One day a straggler, Hardcoop, did not reach camp at nightfall. Lewis Keseberg, in whose wagon he had been carried for some time, claimed to know nothing of him, but one who rode back to hunt for him found him by the trail and was told that Keseberg had put him out of the wagon to walk or die. . . . Three days later Hardcoop again was missing at nightfall. He had asked William Eddy for help, but the hard-pressed Eddy had been able to promise no more than to help once he got his oxen past a bad sandy stretch. Hardcoop had said he would try to make it, but others had passed him sitting amid the sage, unable to go another step. Eddy would have gone back in search of him, but Keseberg brutally declined any help; Graves and Breen refused to lend their horses to search for a dead man; and the others of the company declined even to wait when Milt Elliott, William Pike, and Eddy would have gone back on foot. Over them all hung the threat of starvation and the snows.

They went on. The river turned abruptly to the south after its long westward course; here was the Bend, and here the new road to Oregon opened by the Applegates. Jessy Quinn Thornton, who had bade them farewell at the Little Sandy, was now far on this road into the mountains. There would be much suffering upon this road, this autumn and winter; some companies would loiter by the way, find pasturage scant, toil over the Cascade summit only with the greatest difficulty, be caught in the rains, and harassed by Indians all along the way. There would be bitter words about this Applegate Cutoff; it would not become the arterial Oregon Trail. But now the company only looked dully at the wagon tracks winding west toward the distant blue mountains; and having looked, whipped their teams south in the track of Hastings.

The rear company presently overtook the Donners. There was harder going for all now. The river water was almost undrinkable, grass unnutritious and hard to find. Indians ran off some of the stock, and one of Breen's mares strangled in a sinkhole as Eddy, asked to help, coldly told the Irishman to remember Hardcoop.

The Indians stampeded the stock when they could or crept close in the darkness and shot arrows to cripple the oxen. It was a wretched, demoralized, threadbare company that left the Humboldt's Sink on October 13th to cross the saline desert to the Truckee. Disintegration was almost complete. Each family walked by itself, intent only upon its own salvation.

The Forty Mile Desert was crossed in twenty-four hours of terrible labor. One of the company, Wolfinger, did not reach camp. His two companions, Reinhardt and Spitzer, came up with a strange story that Wolfinger had been killed by Indians. . . . The oxen were given a day to rest, and then the pull up the Truckee commenced. Only fifteen wagons remained, pulled by half-starved teams of oxen and cows. Eddy was almost completely destitute, with nothing but the clothes his family carried on their backs, and three pounds of sugar for provisions. They toiled up the canyon of the Truckee—almost as bad as their road through the Wasatch. And on the third day, unbelievably, there rode into camp three men with seven pack mules laden with provisions.

Against all belief, it was Stanton, on whom they had no claim, who had returned. McCutchen had fallen ill at Sutter's, and Stanton, aided by two of Sutter's Indian vaqueros, had undertaken to get the supplies back to the company. Stanton brought word of Reed, too. With the teamster, he had just managed to get through. Like skeletons, they were. Reed would soon be on the back trail, though some snow had fallen in the passes.

So the revivified company came up into the Truckee Meadows. It was October 20th, and clouds threatened snow, but they were exhausted, and for five days they camped to gather strength for the final struggle to the summit.

At the Meadows William Pike was accidentally shot with his own gun; he was laid in a hastily dug grave. From that grave the emigrants began the hard pull up the Truckee. Out ahead were the Breens and their friends; in a second section followed the Reed, Graves, and Murphy families, accompanied by Stanton. Last of all came the Donners.

The Breens almost made it. On the night of October 31st they encamped just below the cabin in which Moses Schallenberger had wintered two years before. Snow lay on the ground, but only an inch or so. Next day, through deepening snow, they pulled toward the summit, but the trail was lost under five feet of snow. . . . They turned back to the lone cabin.

It began to rain, a torrential downpour. The Breens retreated to their wagons. At dark next day the second section came up, but the Donners were still behind, delayed by a broken axle. They never reached the lake that came to bear their name; they stopped, finally, on Alder Creek some five miles below.

There was a final effort to get over the snowy summit. Stanton and one of the Indians actually reached the pass. But in exhaustion the others who had made the effort gave up. Stanton came back to them. The party returned to hole up at Truckee Lake.

Reed had arrived at Sutter's on October 28th, as the wagons were toiling up the Truckee. He obtained pack horses and provisions, and on the 31st, in company with McCutchen, he took the back trail. When they reached the foothills it had begun to rain. The rain mixed with sleet, and when they reached lower Bear Valley, the snow was a foot and a half deep. It was deeper at the head of the valley, where they stumbled on a lone emigrant and his wife who had thought to winter here, whose cattle were already swallowed up by the snow.

The two fathers fought upward through the snow. It deepened to four feet, five, seven. Even such desperate men finally had to admit defeat. They were perhaps within a dozen miles of the summit. But the animals could go no higher. If the animals were abandoned, and they somehow won through on foot, they should have brought nothing but two more mouths to feed. Beaten, they returned to the fort, bringing the emigrant and his wife. Sutter gave them such consolation as he could. If the emigrants killed their cattle and preserved the meat in the snow, they might have enough provisions to last out the winter. Something had to be left to hope. For until the snows hardened in February, nothing could be done for their relief.

Reed set out for Yerba Buena, the embryo San Francisco, to seek help from the naval officers there. Around Sutter's the country had been swept clean of men, who had gathered to Frémont to quell insurrection. He found the way to Yerba Buena blockaded, and men at San Jose unwilling to leave their families amid such turmoil. Nothing, it seemed, could be done until the "war" was settled. Forthwith he enlisted, and marched and countermarched until the almost bloodless struggle ended on January 2nd. With peace restored, Reed set out for Yerba Buena, arriving toward the end of January. A meeting attended by most of the male population of the town was held, and $700 raised on the spot, a sum subsequently almost doubled; volunteers also offered to aid. By the night of February 5th an expedition was ready to leave. On that night a launch arrived from Sutter's. It had news of the company in the mountains. On January 17th two men and five women had reached Johnson's Ranch northeast of Sutter's. In the mountains the emigrants were starving.

In the two camps at Donner Lake and Alder Creek the emigrants did what they could, building rough cabins and lean-tos, gathering firewood. They had clothing. Shelter was not their problem.

Many of their cattle were slaughtered, though not all—a thaw might spoil the meat. It was plain that they must exist on starvation rations. Some of the company went out to fish and hunt. But they had no luck at the fishing, and even Eddy, the best hunter among them, brought in almost nothing—a coyote, an owl, two ducks, a gray squirrel; once, by great fortitude, a grizzly.

On November 12th thirteen of the strongest among the men, and two women, made the first effort to get over the mountains on foot. They hardly got beyond the head of the lake. The snow was soft and ten feet deep. Nine days later growing desperation led to a second effort, this time by sixteen men and six women, who took with them Sutter's seven mules. The snow was more solid underfoot, and they managed to climb to the pass, and to encamp just beyond the summit. The mules had been brought to here only with difficulty. Evidently they should have to be abandoned. But Stanton and Sutter's Indians refused to go on without them. Eddy argued in vain. Only Stanton and the Indians knew the way to be followed. The party plodded back to the cabins.

Stubborn and self-reliant, Eddy began to plan another onslaught on the pass. On the night of November 25th, however, it began to snow again. It snowed eight days. Some of the cattle and horses, and Sutter's mules, strayed off into the storm and were forever lost. The snow drifted eight feet deep and all but buried the cabins.

The snowshoes were Graves's idea. Reared in Vermont, he had learned their uses. Stanton also knew something about them, and on December 6th, between two storms, Stanton and Graves began to manufacture snowshoes from oxbows and rawhide. On the morning of December 16th seventeen of the company—virtually all who were physically able—set off toward the sheer white wall of the pass. They might die in the effort. But probably they would die if they remained. And in leaving they reduced the drain upon the provisions.

There were snowshoes enough for only fourteen, but two of the Murphy boys and "Dutch Charley" Burger thought they might be able to follow in the footsteps of the snowshoers. Dutch Charley and Bill Murphy soon turned back, but Lem Murphy kept on, and eventually snowshoes were improvised for him. Altogether, fifteen crossed the pass toward nightfall of the second day, weak from starvation, shuddering with cold, trembling with exhaustion, but determined not to turn back.

West of the pass the glare of the sun on the snow was intolerable. Stanton became snowblind almost at once; he was the weakest and he gradually fell behind. Yet on the fourth day, and the fifth, he managed to reach camp, an hour behind the others. On the sixth morning, when the others stirred from camp, he sat with his back against a tree, smoking. "Are you coming?" asked Mary Graves. "Yes," he said; "I'm coming soon." So they could go on while he sat against the tree, puffing at first upon his pipe, feeling the cold filling his veins, his flesh . . . then no feeling at all.

That sixth day, that day Stanton did not reach camp, finished their rations. Eddy alone had something—a half pound of bear meat found in his pack with a note from his wife. It was a pitiful resource to sustain him in a final extremity.

Stanton perhaps had thought the Indians could find the way. But they had come this way only once, at another season and in the opposite direction. That sixth day the party strayed from the trail, south away from the Bear Valley. Next morning they went only a mile, and then camped in a snowstorm, still hoping that Stanton might come up. There was no certain way to go, and when they stumbled downward again they strayed farther to the south. They fought their way on through the mounting snowstorm, two days utterly without food.

There was no food except . . . .

Patrick Dolan put it into words—draw lots to see who should be sacrificed. But Will Foster objected; besides, how should the thing be done? Eddy presently proposed that two men should take six-guns and fight to the death. But this also was objected to. There was no alternative but to go on until one should die of exhaustion.

Antonio, the Mexican herder, died that night as they huddled about the campfire. But before they could avail themselves of his flesh, disaster beset them. They had been able

to build fires on the snow by the mountain man's device—
cutting green logs and building fires of dry wood on that
foundation. On this night, however, the green logs were of
diminished size, and as they piled wood upon the fire in
answer to the ferocity of the storm, the fire ate through the
logs. The snow began to melt; the fire upon its platform
began to settle into the depression created by its heat. And
the axhead was lost as one of the party sought to find new
wood in the storm.

The fire sank visibly; at midnight they were eight feet
deep in a circular well in which snow water was rising. But
the fire was maintained for a time; the logs were sunk on
end into the snow, and the fire built on top. By crowning
misfortune, one of the half-frozen Indians then upset the
fire. It hissed out in the water about their feet.

Eddy forced them to climb out of the snow well into
the raging storm. Under a blanket of tents he arranged
them in a circle. They were covered at once by the snow, and
thus insulated, and huddled together, their starved bodies
provided enough warmth to keep them from freezing. So
they lay through the night. The gray light that filtered down
through the snow at daybreak was that of Christmas Day.

Uncle Billy Graves died while Eddy was building the
shelter. Now it was Dolan's turn. He began to talk wildly
of setting out in the snow toward the settlements. He
threshed about in the shelter of blankets, then burst out
into the storm, cajoling Eddy: come out, come with him.
Then he began to pull off his boots and clothing. It would
take only a few hours to reach the settlements. Eddy laid hold
of him, and tried to drag him back into the shelter, but could
do nothing with him. After a while, however, Dolan came
back to lie down outside the shelter and was dragged under
the blankets again. Through the afternoon hours he lay quiet,
and as the gray light began to fail he died.

There were now eleven left of the fifteen. The storm

raged throughout the night, and they huddled in their shelter. Thirteen-year-old Lem Murphy became violent in his turn; in his delirium he could hardly be held. Still it snowed when morning brought the gray light again. They had been thirty hours under the blankets. Eddy tried to kindle a fire in the shelter, and was badly burned about the face when his powder horn exploded. But during the afternoon, at last, the clouds broke. They crawled from the blankets into the sterile snowy world. Taking some cotton from Mrs. Pike's mantle, Eddy struck sparks into it which he nursed into a blaze and set fire to a tall, dead pine tree. The fire roared in the branches, and they stood within the circle of heat, heedless of the limbs that fell to the snow and blazed about them. They might all have been brained. But except for Lem Murphy, who now was dying, all of them lived to eat for the first time in five days. The food was cut from the body of Patrick Dolan.

The ten who still lived remained three days in camp, gathering strength for the ordeal before them. Systematically the flesh was stripped from the bones of the dead, and what was not eaten at once was dried to be carried with them.

They recommenced on the 30th the trek down through the bewildering, snow-mantled hills. There were five men— Eddy, Foster, Fosdick, and Sutter's two Indians—and the five women who had set out from the cabins—Mary Graves, Mrs. Foster, Mrs. Pike, Mrs. Fosdick, and Mrs. McCutchen. Fosdick was weakest of them all, and Foster in not much better case. The women and Eddy had shown themselves finally the toughest of the company.

On the night of the 31st they encamped within sight of the green Sacramento Valley—but far, far off, and separated by a 2,000-foot canyon into which they must descend and climb out. The dried flesh on which they had lived for a week was gone. Though they found, on New Year's Day, that the snow was sufficiently packed for travel without their half-rotted snowshoes, they were held back by Fosdick, and they had no food.

The rawhide was taken from their snowshoes, roasted in the fire, and eaten. It was better than nothing. They got two miles farther next day, the only food their worn boots and shoes. The starved whites furtively eyed the Indians. These Indians had come to these straits in their behalf, but in the frontiersman's view the Indian was a kind of animal. . . . The Indians disappeared from camp.

Fosdick could not travel; neither would he send on the company as had Stanton. Eddy proposed going ahead with the gun; they had reached bare ground, and there was some hope of finding game. The women wept. Losing Eddy seemed the end of them all.

Mary Graves went with him; the others followed behind, the Fosters, Mrs. McCutchen, and Mrs. Pike ahead of Fosdick and his wife, far in the rear. The feet of the two Indians had left a bloody trail which deepened its scarlet as the others passed.

Eddy and Mary Graves had gone only two miles when they saw a place where a deer had lain during the night. Suddenly they saw the deer, less than a hundred yards off. For a moment it seemed that Eddy was too weak to level the rifle. But the shot went true. They fell upon the carcass, drinking the warm blood as it flowed from the rent made in the deer's throat. They rested a little, then built a fire and roasted the liver and other of the innards.

Those who followed heard the shots Eddy fired during the night to hearten them. Far behind, Fosdick roused up: "If only I can get to him, I shall live." But he died during the night. His wife wrapped his body in their only blanket, and lay down alongside, yet lived through the night. At daybreak she set out to find the others. Two who had come back to avail themselves of the bodies they expected to find, met her on the way, and went with her to their camp. Eddy was there with some parts of the deer when they arrived.

All ate of the deer's flesh, and then Mrs. Fosdick with Mrs. Foster returned to the dead man. Over the wife's resistance, Mrs. Foster cut from the body the heart, liver, arms, and legs. One deer would not long sustain seven people.

This day was spent in camp, resting and drying the human and deer flesh. Next morning they set out again. They found themselves finally in the bottom of another canyon, and all the third day was spent in climbing up its precipitous western bank. At nightfall, after they encamped at the summit, Foster drew Eddy aside. He had been gradually going to pieces. Now he proposed, as they were once more out of food, that Mrs. McCutchen be killed. Or Mary Graves, or Mrs. Fosdick. "No!" Eddy snarled. He left Foster to tell the women of their danger. Foster followed surlily. He could handle Eddy, he said. Hardly more sane than Foster, Eddy flung him a club to defend himself, then pulled his knife to make an end of him. But the women threw him to the ground and took his knife from him.

In the morning the seven went on, staggering with weakness. Crossing a stretch of snow, they suddenly saw the bloody track of two men. It was the trail of the Indians, who somehow had got this far. A mile farther on, they came upon the Indians, lying upon the ground, utterly spent but not yet dead. One Indian Foster shot through the head and then the other. Here was food. . . .

As they went on, there was game to be seen at intervals, but Eddy was too weak to kill it. He and the three women with him chewed grass and at night kept watch, camping apart from Foster. Another storm broke upon them, after the two weeks of fair weather. They were below the snow line, but the rain was an added horror. Somehow they kept going.

Toward evening of January 12th they stumbled on an Indian trail.

The trail brought them to a Digger village in the chaparral. The Indians fled at this apparition of starvation, then attempted to minister to the grisly things that had come from out of the brush. But they had nothing except a bread of acorns. Though the others could eat this, Eddy could not, and as they staggered down through a succession of villages, he drew sustenance only from the grass he plucked along the trail. On the morning of the 17th, however, he obtained from an Indian a handful of pine nuts which returned to him some measure of strength. It seemed almost as though this strength was drawn from the last vitality of his companions. The five women and Foster lay down to die by the side of the trail.

Eddy shook his head dazedly and went on. Five miles he got almost without help; then with the aid of two Indians he got another five miles, half walking, half dragged. And so it was, toward sunset, that he reached an emigrant cabin near Johnson's Ranch. Harriet Ritchie opened the door to see something suspended between two Indians, something that asked for food. It was human. It was a man. Harriet began to cry. She helped carry Eddy to a bed. The Ritchies prepared some food, and aroused the neighbors. By midnight four men with packs reached Foster and the starving women. They were brought in next day. Seven lived of the fifteen who, thirty-three days earlier, had climbed from the head of Truckee Lake.

Thirty-six hours in bed sufficiently revived Eddy to enable him to write a letter to be carried to John Sinclair's ranch, near New Helvetia. Mrs. Sinclair immediately dispatched clothing for the women, and sent the letter to Captain E. M. Kern, in command at Sutter's.

There were not many able-bodied men at the fort, as Reed had found two months ago, but Kern called a meeting and asked for volunteers, pledging three dollars a day to those who would go. This was a munificent wage on this frontier; but the men to whom he talked were no mountain men; they were, themselves, dismayed by western snows. There were only three volunteers, Aquilla Glover, Sept Moultry, and Joseph Sels, but when John Sinclair returned from Yerba Buena within a day or two and offered with Sutter to guarantee the payment of the wages, four more men were persuaded to go. On January 31st, having made their preparations, the seven men set out from Sutter's. More aid would be needed, and Sutter's launch was dispatched to Yerba Buena to summon it.

Glover's party reached Johnson's Ranch on February 2nd. Here they made their preparations. On the morning of February 4th the relief party set out for the hills.

Their number had been augmented to fourteen, including William Eddy, who though still weak was drawn by the terrible need of his wife and children. Not all the fourteen, however, proposed to go into the snows; they came along to help with the pack animals, as far as these could be taken.

The rains made the going miry, and the lowering skies promised no relief; indeed, the seventh of the year's great storms already had commenced in the mountains. There was no snow here in the valley, but by the morning of the 5th the rain was so torrential that Glover's men had no choice but to wait for the weather to better, though every hour counted now. It was not until the 7th that the sun broke through the clouds, and that day also was wasted, drying the soaked meat and flour to keep it from spoiling.

Through mud, across creeks become raging rivers, up steep ridges and into the snow, the men of Glover's party fought their way to Mule Springs. The animals could be got no farther. Two men were detached to guard the provisions, while two others, including Eddy (who, it was seen, could not possibly cope with the snow), were sent back with the animals. Shouldering packs consisting mostly of food, ten men on the morning of the 10th began the fifty-mile trek. It was desperately hard going, and they did not reach Bear

Valley until the 12th. That night it snowed again, and rained, and all the day of the 13th had to be spent in drying out; a cache was made in preparation for a final push to the cabins.

On the morning of the 14th three of the men refused to go on. For a moment it seemed that all would abandon the grueling effort, but "Dan" Tucker, one of those gallant spirits who had been recruited at Johnson's, pledged to every man who stuck it out five dollars a day, from the time they had entered the snow.

Perhaps it was not the money that counted. A man's values changed here. More likely it was what George Stewart has called "stubborn male courage and that deep-seated sense of honor that a man should not flinch in a task to which he has set himself." The three went back, but Glover, Moultry, Sels, Tucker, Ned Coffeemeyer, and John and Daniel Rhoads shouldered their packs and went on. Taking turns at the trailbreaking, they crossed from the Bear to the Yuba and made a dozen miles before nightfall. That they might not mistake the way in returning, they set fire to dead pine trees, leaving charred spires to mark their course. But on the 15th, as they climbed toward the pass, it began to snow. They had to stop and make snowshoes, and the whole day's travel was only five miles. The storm ceased the next day, but on this day also they made only five miles. On the 17th they crossed Summit Valley and camped just under the pass. The snow under them was thirty feet deep.

The 500-foot climb of the last mile was a desperate endeavor. Glover and Daniel Rhoads were almost done, and the others had to carry their packs. But now they were not to be denied. Soon after noon they surmounted the pass and could look eastward into the wilderness of snow that held those for whom they had come. Through the short winter afternoon they worked their dangerous way downward. Just at dusk they came through the trees to where Eddy had said the cabins would be found. There was only snow to be seen. They hallooed.

Like an animal from its burrow a woman emerged from a hole in the snow. Then there were others, ghastly caricatures of humanity, weakly crying salutation, deathly voices strange over the snow. This could not be relief?

The going of the snowshoers on December 16th was marked by the first death at Truckee Lake. Baylis Williams died in the hours just before their departure. Death climbed with the snowshoers beyond the summit, but death remained in the cabins too, a dweller beside the fire. The storms drifted the snow about the cabins—two feet, six, eight. The cabins were buried, and the families lived as in caves, venturing out rarely, husbanding their slender resources. The storms of November had cost them many cattle; these lay buried under the snow God knew where. There was little food of any kind; in December, even, many of the families began to boil the hides with which they had covered their cabins; hours of boiling reduced the strips of hide to a nauseous, unseasoned, gluelike jelly barely more nutritious than nothing at all. Bones thrown to the dogs in an earlier day were retrieved and boiled again, boiled until they fell apart and could be crunched between hungry teeth. The dogs themselves went into the kettles. The days were a monotone, the cabins verminous and foul, the fires always burning under the kettles. Now and then the men ventured out in search of firewood, but they were weak and did not go far.

Christmas was as all other days, except perhaps for the Breens and the Reeds. Breen had been more fortunate with his cattle than the others, and still had some beef, as he had had the foresight to begin eating hides early. Mrs. Reed had hoarded a cupful of white beans, half a cup of rice, some dried apples, a two-inch square of bacon, and some tripe; from these she fashioned a Christmas dinner more poignant for her children than any they would ever know again; they stood about the kettle and, as it boiled, hailed with delight the occasional appearance of a bean or piece of tripe.

There was little intercourse among the cabins, and hardly any at all between those at the lake and those of the Donners on Alder Creek. On December 9th Milt Elliott and Noah James left the lake cabins to look in on the Donners, but because of the storm it was December 20th before Milt got back. Uncle Jake Donner, Sam Shoemaker, James Smith, and Reinhardt all had died. It wasn't starvation. They still had hides. They just got weaker and died. Things were worse down below because there were no cabins, just brush shelters and tents; and there was less food. Uncle George Donner, who had cut his hand in that accident with his wagon on the lower Truckee, was failing rapidly; his hand had got no better, and his whole arm looked bad. Noah James stayed down there to help Jean Baptiste and Uncle Jake's young stepsons, Sol and Bill Hook, with the man's work.

At the lake Dutch Charley Burger died on December 29th. His possessions were taken over by Keseberg. Milt had heard at the Donner camp that Reinhardt, before dying, had confessed that he and Spitzer, who had stayed behind at the Sink to help Wolfinger cache his goods, and who had come up alone, had killed the man for his goods. On the last day of December Patrick Breen wrote in the laconic diary he had begun to keep: "Thursday 31st Last of the year, may we with Gods help spend the comeing year better than the past which we purpose to do if Almighty God will deliver us from our present dredful situation which is our prayer if the will of God sees it fiting for us Amen."

January finished the Reed provisions. The children's pet, the dog Cash, was sacrificed to the kettle, but though no ounce of the carcass was wasted, the little dog's body sustained the family for only a week. Under the spur of terrible necessity, Mrs. Reed decided, with her daughter Virginia, Eliza

Williams, and Milt Elliott, to attempt to cross the mountains on foot. Three-year-old Tommy she left with the Breens, Patty with the Kesebergs, and Jim with the Graveses.

On January 4th she set out. Eliza had to turn back after only one night; the others got actually as far as the pass, and on improvised snowshoes struggled on another day. But they seemed to wander hopelessly, and when on the third night Virginia's feet were frostbitten, they turned back. They returned January 8th, just ahead of the fifth great storm of the winter, in which inevitably they must have died. Before the storm was ended, Breen found the snow thirteen feet deep at his cabin, "dredful to look at."

The Reeds moved in with the Breens, who had a little to eat and were more charitable than they had been. But they got little food from the Irish family except their leavings—the discarded bones. This, with such hides as they could find, kept them alive. Those in the other cabins, they found when the storm let them investigate, were very badly off, too. Mrs. Murphy had gone blind, and her boy, Landrum, was failing fast. Keseberg was sick and his baby, Lewis, died on January 24th.

As February came to the cabins near the lake, even the hides began to go. As Glover's courageous relief party came up into the mountains from Johnson's, Eddy's little daughter died, and Mrs. Eddy three nights later. There was death in the McCutchen family, death in the Murphy family. Spitzer died, and Milt Elliott.

And so the relief party reached the lake at evening on February 18, 1847.

Three of them set out at once for the Donner encampment. It was decided that those who had the strength should be taken over the pass on Monday, the 22nd. To delay even so long was dangerous, as another storm might set in, but rest was essential.

Six were brought back from the Donner cabins, Noah

James, Mrs. Wolfinger, and four of the older children. There had been no more deaths, but George Donner had grown steadily worse. Tamsen Donner was strong enough to come along, but refused to leave her husband. Jean Baptiste wanted to come, but was forced to stay and take care of the women and children.

Twenty-three, in all, set out with Glover's party. Seventeen were left at the lake besides the twelve who remained on Alder Creek. Of the twenty-three who went, seventeen were children, of which three were three years old, one five, and one eight. One of the three-year-olds, Naomi Pike, John Rhoads carried on his back. Mrs. Keseberg carried her Ada. But all the other children had to walk for themselves; the men already were dangerously overloaded. The risk in going was as great as the risk in staying. Everything depended on the weather.

Heroic three-year-old Tommy Reed got along for two miles through the snow before he gave out. His eight-year-old sister, Patty, was little better off. They would have to be sent back. There had been many hard dilemmas for Mrs. Reed, but none harder than this. Go on with her other two children toward her husband, or turn back with the youngsters? Glover urged her to go on. He would come back himself, he pledged, to rescue the children. At last Mrs. Reed was persuaded. Glover and Sept Moultry turned back, and carried the children to the cabins; Patty expected never to see her mother again but was willing to return and take care of her brother. They were left with the Breens, accepted by them with bad grace. Twenty-eight, in all, on the 23rd began the ascent toward the pass. Their rations amounted to one ounce of smoked beef and a spoonful of flour twice daily; this could not be much increased even when they reached the first cache.

The company got across the summit, and followed the relief party's trail to the cache at the head of the Yuba. But that cache had been rifled by wild animals. They were almost without food, and four days' journey to the next cache.

These seven men of the relief company had already shown of what high courage they were constituted. Three of them were named to shepherd the refugees forward while the other four set out with all speed to bring back from the next cache all the food to be found . . . if this cache had not been rifled too.

Soon after the journey was resumed, John Denton failed. Yesterday he had barely been roused from a coma in the snow. A mile's travel this morning told him he could go no farther. Like Stanton he met his end with fortitude. The others could do nothing for him, and therefore they should go on, he said. If a relief party were at hand, help might be sent back. If not—

The three men of the relief party wrapped him in Tucker's quilt, gathered him a pile of wood, and left him virtually all their remaining food. He was a man of a breed they recognized.

It was three days before Moultry and Coffeemeyer got back to the straggling column. No relief party had been found in Bear Valley, and Glover and Daniel Rhoads had gone on toward Mule Springs and the stores left there while the other two turned back with loaded packs to feed those following in their trail. The food permitted everyone to hope again. But the children were giving out. Ada Keseberg had died, and four of the starved children who had come so valiantly thus far had to be carried. They *were* carried. Doggedly the five men got the company down through the snows.

On the sixth day, as they toiled over the hard-crusted snow in the early morning sunlight, they saw ahead a column of men approaching in single file on the trail. It might be Indians. But it was not. It was the Second Relief. Bent under his pack, James Frazier Reed came up to gather into his arms his wife and his daughter Virginia.

The relief expedition organized in Yerba Buena three weeks ago had come up. Relief now was no venture solely dependent on man's high courage and the vagaries of the weather. Here was the spearhead of organized effort.

The party from the cabins continued down the trail, after they had been fed. All would be safe except young Bill Hook, who in his ravenous hunger would steal food and kill himself in overeating. But Reed's job was not done. Still at the lake were the other starving emigrants . . . and two of his own children among them.

With his nine companions, McCutchen among them, Reed climbed on toward the summit. Stronger and more experienced, and able to travel at night without fear of losing their way, they made better time than the First Relief. On March 1st they arrived at the cabins; Patty was sitting on a corner of the cabin roof, her feet in the snow, as Reed came up. Gathering her into his arms, he asked for Tommy. The boy was inside the cabin, asleep. So Reed, who had been dogged by misfortune since entering upon the salt desert, was supremely fortunate: all of his family preserved to him.

It had been only a week since Glover started the climb up from Truckee Lake with his twenty-three charges, but that week had begun a grim new chapter in the life at the lake. On February 26th Breen wrote in his journal: "Mrs. Murphy said here yesterday that she thought she would commence on Milt. & eat him. I dont think that she has done so yet, it is distressing." Going to the Murphy cabin after their arrival, Reed and McCutchen found, lying just without the door, the body of Milt Elliott. The dead features were still composed, the head untouched. But from his arms, his legs, and his body, the flesh was largely gone. Within the cabin, bones were scattered amid half-eaten parts and tufts of vari-colored hair.

Things were worse at the encampment on Alder Creek. As two of the relief party approached, they met Jean Baptiste carrying a man's leg severed at the thigh. The George Donners had sent him to "borrow" from the other family this part of the carcass of Jacob Donner. The body, indeed, lay close by, the arms and legs removed, and the heart and liver taken from the opened trunk. The head was cut off, but the frozen features regarded this scene with terrible impassivity. The two men had hurried on to the encampment, where they found some of the children tearing at half-roasted heart and liver. Elizabeth Donner was found, far gone; she had determined that her children should live, but would herself touch nothing of the flesh of her husband.

Reed set about clearing things up, sickened by four open, empty graves. Then he went on to George Donner's tent. Uncle George was still alive, though dreadfully emaciated and his arm very bad; his family had lived through the winter on meat, tallow, hides, bones, mice, anything they could find. Their last hide had sustained them only until the arrival of Glover's party; the food left them by the First Relief had not lasted long. . . .

Two of the relief company were left here, together with Baptiste. George and Elizabeth Donner were obviously incapable of crossing the mountains, and Tamsen resisted all entreaties to leave her husband. As a larger relief party might be expected at any moment, the younger children were best left here also. But Sol Hook and Mary and Isaac Donner set out from Alder Creek with Reed. Meanwhile others were gathered at the lake cabins. In all there were seventeen, including the Breens. In the cabin Eddy and Foster had built so long ago were left Keseberg, Mrs. Murphy, Simon Murphy, and the two boys, James Eddy and George Foster. These five would be taken care of by the relief party that must be coming up. A week's provisions were left for all, and three of the Second Relief were left to take care of things. On

March 3rd Reed began to shepherd his feeble company up toward the pass.

Progress was heartbreakingly slow. They were burdened by many children; and none of the refugees seemed capable of realizing the urgent danger in which they still stood; Breen's fiddling at night was all the more exasperating because of his heedless disinterest in getting to safety. Moreover, the Third Relief, hourly expected, did not put in its appearance.

On the third day, with the pass not yet scaled, food low, and clouds piling up threateningly above the peaks, Reed sent three of his men ahead to the first cache; one was to return with food, and the others to proceed to the next cache. With the three men who remained, he spurred his seventeen refugees up the shoulder of the pass. Perhaps the emigrants put more into it this day; at noon they had achieved the summit, and by three in the afternoon reached the head of the Yuba where the First Relief had encamped on its outward journey. None of the men who had gone ahead without food returned; and at night it began to storm. There was no question of breaking camp next morning; Reed doled out the last of the flour—a spoonful each—and tried to keep the fires going. At nightfall Reed wrote in his journal: "There is a great crying among the children, and even with the parents there is praying, crying, and lamentation on account of the cold and the dread of death from hunger and the howling storm. . . . Night closing fast, and with it the hurricane increases."

Worn out, Reed dozed in the night. The fire died down and almost went out; except for McCutchen, all must have frozen to death before dawn. The storm continued throughout the next day and again through the night while little Isaac Donner died in his sleep. It was not until about noon of March 8th that the storm blew itself out, when the company had been twenty-four hours without food. Their case

was desperate. All must push on who were able, and those
who were not must wait here hoping for the Third Relief.

He would rather die in camp than on the way, said
Patrick Breen; and after solemnly warning him that the
blood of his children would be on his own head, Reed ceased
to argue with him. Altogether, twelve remained behind,
seven Breens and five Graveses. Mary Donner, with a burned
foot, found that she could not go on, and came back to the
others. Without any food at all, the four men and the three
remaining children set out for Bear Valley.

Meanwhile one of the three men left behind with the
emigrants, Nicholas Clark, went bear hunting; the other two
sought out Tamsen Donner. Perhaps she offered them $500
to carry her three children to safety, and gave them the
money at once. The men seemed willing to carry such strange
things as silver spoons and other valuable keepsakes. They
set out with the children, but before they had gone far, they
laid the children on the snow and went off to talk together.
Finally they came back and took the frightened children to
the Murphy cabin. Thereupon they disappeared, just before
the onset of the storm.

If they had ever had any intention of carrying out the
children, they abandoned it while the storm raged. When it
cleared, they set out. Strong and unencumbered, except with
Tamsen Donner's silverware and other valuables, they plowed
rapidly through the snow, and shortly overtook Reed's company. If Reed and the others had questions, they kept them
to themselves. In this country a man early learned to mind
his own business.

They went on together, the six men and the three
children. There was no telling what had happened to the three
who went ahead to the caches; caught in such a storm, an
experienced mountain man might come out no better than
any greenhorn. . . . Actually, as they were to find, it had
been as bad as that for the three who had gone ahead. They

had found the first cache rifled by martens, and had been caught by the storm short of the second cache, lacking even the wood that had sustained Reed through the storm. One of their number, John Turner, who had come to California in '26 with Jedediah Smith, had been so badly frozen that he could go on only with the help of the other two. They arrived at the cache, and one of the men took some of the food back a distance on the trail and hung it on a tree for Reed to find. In search of help, they then proceeded on as best they could. And during the day, indeed, they met a small company coming up from Bear Valley, Eddy and Foster among them. At nightfall Reed and his companions likewise came up, badly frostbitten and exhausted, but safe.

So Reed passed on down to the Sacramento Valley, and the responsibility for rescue passed into fresh hands.

Where had been the Third Relief? Unluckily, it had been under the command of Passed Midshipman Selim Woodworth. Nursing his fears of frostbite, he had not ventured beyond Bear Valley until on March 8th the two fathers, Eddy and Foster, fought their way up to the advance base from Johnson's Ranch. Under the sting of their scorn, he and his five men had been induced to go a little farther, but when, after meeting Reed, volunteers were asked to go with Eddy and Foster to the cabins, none, including Woodworth, was to be found. None, that is, save the giant John Starks.

Three was not enough. Reed persuaded the fathers to turn back to Bear Valley, to obtain more aid from among Woodworth's men. Four men finally were found for the job. Eddy, Foster, and two others were to go to the cabins while Starks and the other two were to bring in the Breens and Graveses—if any still lived. They set out on the morning of the 11th.

On the afternoon of the second day they reached the encampment of the Breens. The fire had melted through the snow, and now burned on bare ground in a strange subterranean chamber. Mrs. Graves had died during these six days, and her five-year-old son. On the fourth day, they had commenced to eat the dead; they had begun with the children, and had eaten most of the flesh from Mrs. Graves' arms and legs. When the Third Relief came up, they found boiling in a kettle the woman's breasts, her heart, and her liver. Eleven still lived.

Nightmare unending! It had not been expected that so many could live through the storm. For three men to undertake to get eleven helpless people down through these snows seemed out of all reason. Besides, nobody had much sympathy for Breen. But though the others were willing to carry out the three Graves orphans and little Mary Donner, leaving the others to shift for themselves, John Starks flatly refused. He had come here to bring these people out. Accordingly, his two companions took Mary Donner and the youngest of the Graves children, and Starks himself began the job of shepherding the others out of the mountains. The other four, Eddy, Foster, and their companions, continued east to the pass.

They left Starved Camp at daybreak, and soon after sunrise surmounted the pass. Driven by terrible anxiety, they pushed on to the cabin they had built four months ago. Four months! Years had never been so long. And somehow it was the most terrible story of all to which they returned.

James Eddy, of course, was dead. Yes, and eaten too, Keseberg said. And as the little Donner children told the story, something more horrible had happened to little George Foster. One night Keseberg had taken him to bed with him; in the morning he was dead. Old Mrs. Murphy wept over the dead body; Keseberg had strangled her grandchild, she said. Keseberg had hung up the child's body, Georgia Donner said, inside the cabin, on the wall. It did not remain there long.

In their anguish the two fathers looked at each other.

Perhaps for a moment they considered killing Keseberg with their hands. He was a starved, shambling, pitiable thing, standing before them in his filth. They shuddered and turned away. Here at the cabins, in addition to Keseberg, Mrs. Murphy, Simon Murphy, and the three Donner girls, was Mrs. Donner. From Clark, he of Reed's relief party who had remained here in the mountains, she had learned of something disquieting at the upper cabins. Leaving her husband in the care of Clark and Jean Baptiste, she had come up only the day before to see what could be done for her children. Now she offered Eddy $1,500 in silver if he would take out the children. He would not burden himself with any such weight, he told her, not even with a hundred dollars. But he intended to take out the children.

What of her? Tamsen's wiry vitality had sustained her through all the winter, though she had weighed less than a hundred pounds to begin with. She was capable of making her way out. Tamsen Donner smiled. Yes. But there was her husband, George, hanging between life and death. While he lived, she would never be separated from him. Besides, there was her little Sammie, still living at the camp on Alder Creek. She asked that they wait a day, while she returned to the lower camp. Clark and Baptiste could bring the boy and go out with the others.

Even a day's delay was too much. At any hour a storm might wreck this final endeavor. Eddy could not wait. And so Tamsen Donner shook his hand, saying good-bye, and walked off into the trees.

By noon the four men, carrying the three Donner children and Simon Murphy, started on the back trail. They reached the foot of the pass at evening, and there were overtaken by Baptiste and Clark. These men had deserted dying George Donner and five-year-old Sammie, stealing what they could bring with them. The boy's weight had been too burdensome, but Clark willingly shouldered forty pounds of booty.

Next morning they crossed the pass for the last time. It was March 14th, almost three months since William Eddy, with the other fourteen snowshoers of the Forlorn Hope, had crossed this pass in the hope of reaching Sutter's.

At midday of the second day, they overtook Starks, who indomitably had moved along the nine in his charge—packing all the provisions, most of the blankets, and sometimes a child or two into the bargain. A few hours after this junction of the parties, they encountered a new relief expedition from below. That hero of the First Relief, Aquilla Glover, had returned to the fight; he had met Woodworth and shamed him into turning back toward the mountains.

It was proposed to bring out the five who remained at the cabins. But when Woodworth said he could spend no more time on this matter, and would return to Mule Springs and make ready the horses to take everyone out, the others were too discouraged to go on. A few weeks later Glover's report and Sheriff George McKinstry's acid letter persuaded Woodworth to make a final effort. But this also came to nothing. There was little incentive now. The Donner affair had dragged on too long. Relief was no longer heroics. It was just plain, slogging, profitless hard work. Those at the cabins were left to their own devices.

So it was that no one else went into the mountains until spring rolled back the snow belt. Then a company of six men set out under William Fallon, an old mountain man called Le Gros. Relief was in part the aim but as much so was loot. In two days they reached the lower end of Bear Valley, from Johnson's Ranch. The horses could be taken no farther. On April 18th they crossed the pass, and by noon were at the cabins. Conditions were more horrible than before: filth and mutilated corpses. Even Fallon's flesh crawled. They went on to the Donner tents, and there came upon a large iron kettle containing human flesh. A dead horse and a dead ox, disclosed by the melting snow, still frozen and in good condition, were seen near by, but with little evidence that the flesh had been used for food. The body of George Donner was found. He had probably not been dead more than four days. The body was wrapped in a sheet; but flesh had been taken from the body, and the head had been split open and the brains removed. Tamsen Donner was nowhere to be seen.

Next day Fallon's men hunted for valuables, disquieted by tracks they had seen in the snow and by their failure to find the silver Tamsen had offered to William Eddy. On the following day three of the company climbed to the lake cabins again. And here they found Keseberg. Human bones were scattered around, and in a large pan were liver and other entrails taken freshly from a human body. . . .

Mrs. Murphy, Keseberg said, had lived about a week after the departure of Eddy and Foster. Then at an indefinite later time Tamsen Donner had come to say that her husband was dead. She seemed exhausted and crazed, obsessed with the idea of going to her children. She had wanted to start over the pass at once, at midnight. He had dissuaded her and put her to bed. Next morning she was dead.

And so, the relief party reported, "He eat her body and found her flesh the best he had ever tasted! He further stated that he obtained from her body at least four pounds of fat!"

It seemed to the three who listened that there stood before them one of the most noisome monsters that ever lived. Tamsen Donner only a month ago had appeared still strong. Foster himself had seen and talked with her. Was it logical that the life should run out of her in an hour? Moreover, they found in the cabin two kettles filled with something that seemed to be human blood. Was blood to be obtained, as Keseberg said, from dead bodies?

Questioning him closely, they became more dissatisfied with his replies. They searched him and the cabin, and turned up several hundred dollars in gold and other valuables— things that had belonged to the Donners. Unless he made a clean breast of things, and told also what he had done with the loot from the Donner encampment, they told him, they would string him up.

They left him protesting his innocence, and went on down to Alder Creek. Next morning the seven men returned to the lake cabins. When Keseberg protested to Fallon his ignorance of where the Donner money was to be found, Fallon Le Gros grinned in his rage. "Keseberg," he said, "you know well where Donner's money is, and damn you, you shall tell me! I am not going to multiply words with you, nor say but little about it."

Alarmed, Keseberg denied knowledge of the money or goods; what was found on him, he said, was the property of others. Fallon choked him off with a rope; at last Keseberg led the way back to the Donner camp, where he disclosed $273 which he said he had hidden for Tamsen. Making ready to leave, the men found in the Murphy cabin the body of one of the Murphy boys, with body opened and skull split; the "brains, liver and lights" found in Keseberg's cabin evidently had come from here. Keseberg made a final meal on the grisly food in his cabin, and then, on April 21st, the Fourth Relief turned back for Bear Valley. On the 25th they reached their horses. With them they brought Keseberg. Eighty-seven had taken the Hastings trail to the Humboldt in July. Forty-seven reached their destination. It is like a signature of the river.

XI

Kingdom of God

*C*ome on, oh Israel, intoned Sam Brannan to the
Saints, *it is time to go!* In December, 1845, it was time, indeed. Westward, half across the continent, the city of the
Saints resounded to the furious hammering of the smiths
and the wheelwrights. In September, to a hard-lipped general
of the Illinois state militia, Brigham had announced his purpose to remove from Nauvoo in the spring. Some ten days
earlier he had written to Sam: "I wish you together with your
press, paper, and ten thousand of the brethren, were now in
California at the Bay of San Francisco, and if you can clear
yourself and go there, do so."

Young Sam Brannan was not surprised. Disfellowshiped

166

in April for indiscretions, he had gone to Nauvoo to plead his case, returning successful to New York to resume publication of *The Prophet* as the *New York Messenger*. With his second issue, on July 12, 1845, he printed a verse, "Hurra for California!" and began to serialize a work lately published by a gentleman, a Mr. Hastings, who recently had been lecturing in New York on the Pacific paradise. In an August issue his paper observed mysteriously, to readers who might wonder at all this commotion, that it was a part of the Saints' religion to learn everything possible of every country, and additionally, as California was a portion of that new world God had made choice above all others, it was sufficiently worthy the attention of the Saints.

This young man with the bushy dark beard, heavy-lidded eyes, and resolute lips had been a printer's apprentice, an elder laboring in the vineyard, publisher of a paper for the Saints. In his twenty-sixth year, he was asked to lay his hands on destiny.

It was time to go! In mid-December the *Messenger* summoned the Saints to sail around the Horn to the Bay of San Francisco. In February the little *Brooklyn* sailed with 238 passengers, all under the immediate care of Elder Samuel Brannan. There was one severe storm in each ocean, but the ship anchored safe at the Bay of San Francisco the final day of July. The Stars and Stripes, from which they had sailed in February, now floated above the rolling peninsular hills. "There's that damned flag again!" legend credits Sam with saying.

Not all the *Brooklyn's* company arrived in good standing. Four of the passengers, during the voyage, were excommunicated for conduct Sam found "wicked and licentious"; two, indeed, had behaved so disgracefully, swore Elder Brannan, that had their doctrines gained ascendancy, the company should every soul of them have perished.

About the town of Yerba Buena, situated between blue

sky and bluer sea, the company set to work at lumbering, at farming, and at other useful occupations. They took time off, however, to quarrel with each other and with Sam. In some exasperation at the spirit among his followers, Sam announced in a New Year's Day extra of his *California Star,* that they had "gone astray after strange gods, serving their bellies and their own lusts," and refused to prepare for the coming of their brethren overland. Such, he prophesied darkly, would have their reward. This region had its disadvantages, common to any new country, but it was a beautiful land where the Saints might find peace and prosperity. The brethren now were laying out a settlement on the San Joaquin. As soon as the snow was off the mountains, men might be sent overland to meet the Saints from Nauvoo. He, Elder Brannan, might even go himself.

The snow was not yet off the mountains at the end of January. . . . A company of emigrants who had been caught in the snows had reached Captain Johnson's after the most horrifying experiences. Terrifying news came out of the mountains at intervals during the next two months. Why, it was said, one of the emigrants took a child of about four years of age in bed with him, and devoured the whole before morning; and the next day ate another about the same age before noon!

From the south there were other stories—echoes of the battles in Mexico, and of the marchings of Frémont, Kearny, and Stockton. And there was news of the arrival of a Mormon Battalion at San Diego.

But as the snows melted through April, Sam stowed into his pack the sixteen published issues of his strangely secular paper, and set out with three companions for Sutter's. Fallon's Fourth Relief was in the mountains; it was said they had not been able to get horses through to Truckee Lake. Sam was told that it would be two months before he could get through the mountains, but even as Fallon's men were bringing in Keseberg, he set out with three men and eleven horses and mules.

The sun had consolidated the snow; going on foot and driving the animals before them in a 26-hour drive, they reached the bare ground near the Donner cabins—"a heart rending picture," Sam moralized, "and what is still worse it was the fruit of their idleness, covetousness, ugliness, and low mindedness, that brought them to such a fate. Men must reap the fruit of their folly and own labors."

He proceeded down the Truckee and across to the Humboldt. The melting snows flooded the trail, but on June 9th Sam came to Fort Hall.

Somewhere ahead, he could be sure, were the Twelve Apostles. The trails were opening. He would find them, and guide them to Fort Hall, down Mary's River, and across the California Mountains to the shores of the San Joaquin. Next year, perhaps, he would even travel all the way to the States. Why, he would think no more of traveling across the continent than of taking his breakfast!

At Fort Hall Sam rested ten days, and then set out again, taking two of his men and leaving the other at the fort with some of his animals. Eleven days later, he rode up to the west bank of the Green River to find the Saints, beset by clouds of mosquitoes, building two rafts to ferry their wagons across the river.

Strange wilderness rendezvous! Sunburned horsemen from the west eyed sunburned brethren who had brought wagons so laboriously to the tops of the mountains. Sam was received with singularly little enthusiasm. Though he described eloquently the valley of the San Joaquin, where the Saints awaited the coming of their brethren, Brigham's mind's eye envisaged another haven. Only yesterday he had parted from Jim Bridger. Old Gabe had filled in the picture that had shaped in his mind when he read Frémont's report in '45. He wanted a look at the valley of the Great Salt Lake.

Finally Sam held his tongue. When Brigham got a look at this God-forsaken place in the mountains, he might be more amenable to reason.

It took three days for the Mormon pioneer company to cross the Green, and then they set out west again, accompanied by an army of mosquitoes. On the night of July 3rd Brother Brigham named five men to turn back with a wagon to meet the Sick Detachment of the Mormon Battalion. Sam had heard of the arrival of the battalion in southern California, but none had got so far north as San Francisco before his departure. He learned now that the government had enlisted 536 volunteers from the Mormon encampment at Council Bluffs the previous summer, that these had marched first to Fort Leavenworth and thence to Santa Fe, the jumping-off place for the Pacific. The lame, the halt, and the sick had been weeded out from the battalion, and Captain James Brown and Lieutenant W. W. Willis had taken detachments north to winter at Pueblo. The Sick Detachment had been instructed, when the trails opened, to go north to Laramie. Now they must be somewhere on the trail behind.

On July 4th twelve of these brethren in the service of the country rode up, joyful in this reunion. Brother Brigham decided that Sergeant Tom Williams should turn back upon the trail, accompanied by Sam, to meet the others from Pueblo. Since the battalion members had not received their formal discharge, least of all their pay, Brannan should offer to pilot some of the men to San Francisco, where they might try to collect their pay.

Accordingly Sam turned east again, and was not with those who followed Hastings' dim track from Fort Bridger to the Weber, and thence by the Donner trail into the great calm valley where the lake glinted at the edge of the sky. It was not until three days after Brigham reached the encampment in Salt Lake Valley that Sam arrived.

Appraisingly Sam looked over Brigham's Zion. He

couldn't feel that it amounted to much. A brine pond stinking under the sun. Creeks hardly deep enough to baptize a
man in. The soil so dry a man thirsted to look at it. And, a
mile above sea level, the frosts would stay late and come
early. Altogether, a hell of a place to locate the Saints!

However, he gave them the benefit of his experience.
In the public meeting on August 1st he added his weight to
the recommendations of those who had seen adobe houses
at Pueblo and thought them needed here. A man could build
an adobe house, Sam agreed, quicker than a man could get
out the logs for a log house. Adobe houses were healthy, and
best for the equinoctial gales. Why, in California he had a
man who could take three men, make adobes for a 30-foot
house, build the house, and put a family in it within a week.
In fourteen days he had put up a printing house and published his first paper. Elder Brannan had learned a great deal
in the year since he had stepped ashore at Yerba Buena.

It had been agreed that Captain Brown should take a
company to California guided by Brannan. Sam was glad to
climb on his horse, on the morning of August 9th, and set
out for Fort Hall. After the Saints had starved and frozen
here a year or so, he would not lack for company in California.

Among the ten named to escort Captain Brown was
strapping young Abner Blackburn. Happy-go-lucky and
boisterous, Abner loved wine, a good story, and seeing the
country. At Fort Hall the company bought supplies for the
trip and set out for the Humboldt up which Sam Brannan
had come ten weeks ago. Beyond City of Rocks, that desert
metropolis inhabited only by owls and bats, they met Commodore Robert F. Stockton of the Pacific Squadron, en route
east with an escort of marines to testify in the Frémont court-
martial.

Stockton's men had been attacked by the Indians on the
Truckee. Some of the horses had been killed and some of the

men wounded, including Stockton himself. A party of such smaller size as this should keep its eye open. They climbed Goose Creek and crossed into Thousand Springs Valley, "a few wild naked savages with no fig leaves to cover them" coming up close to gawp. They were fat, on crickets and other things, though it was said that in the spring they were so poor the skin on their bellies stuck to their backs.

They rode to Mary's River, and, says Abner, "we travled down this stream until we wear tired of it. the scenery is not verry strikeing unles one is desirous to be struck it appeared like some fervent heat had taken the life out of it. Brannan and cap Brown could not agree on anny subject Brannan thought he knew it all and Brown thought he new his share of it. they felt snuffy at each other and kept apart."

Down the long course of the Humboldt Sam managed to keep the peace. Scorched by the summer, the Humboldt seared a remembrance into Abner's mind: "the mountains looked like they had been burnt with some great heat the rocks would ring like crockery ware with no timber in sight only willows on the river. the alkily covered the plains come to the long sink of the river it had run so long through salt and the alkily the watter was brackish and stinking. could hardly drink it. made coffe with it and was no better. filled the canteens with it and started a cross a forty five mile desert deep with sand. . . . come to the trucky river about sun down. the animals nearly worn out this is a fine large rushing stream of cold watter from the Siere Nevada mountains." As Stockton here had been attacked by the Indians, they kept a good watch as they moved up the canyon of the Truckee.

Not three months ago Elder Brannan had gone down this very stream moralizing upon the quarrelsomeness of the winterbound emigrants. But now, as Abner tells the tale, "cap Brown wanted travel on several miles before breakfast.

Brannan said he would eat breakfast first. Brown sayes the horses would goe anny how. for they belonged to the government and wear in his care they both went for the horses. and a fight commenced they pounded each other with fists and clubs. until they wear sepperated. they both ran for their guns we parted them again. Started on and left Branan with his own horse. after we stopt Brannan went past we thought the savages would get him certain."

Shortly after seven o'clock next morning, however, Elder Brannan rode suddenly into the midst of a company marching down the rugged canyon of the Truckee. They were brethren of the Mormon Battalion, discharged in July and en route to the new Zion.

For an hour Sam halted to let his horses feed and to eat a little himself. The Salt Lake country, he said, was a fine country but no place to live; the Saints would presently be moving on to California. He was going on across the mountains to Sutter's, and thence down to San Francisco and its rippling blue bay. Cap Brown would be up presently with letters for the battalion boys.

Waving his hat in farewell, Sam rode on toward San Francisco. Here, he was sure, was to rise "one of the greatest cities of the present age." Hardly more than a year ago there had been only three families in this sleepy, wind-swept little village. Already the improvements were beyond all conception, houses in every direction, business very brisk, money plentiful. Sam looked on San Francisco, and found it good. When Brigham and the Saints should join him here, his cup would be filled to overflowing. To Brigham he wrote in October: "I want your confidense, faith and prayers, feeling that I will discharge my duties under all circumstances, and then I am happy; no undertaking will then be too great nor any burden too heavy. . . . My whole soul, might and strength is bent on laboring for you night and day." And again in December he wrote that there was the greatest

anxiety arising here for Brigham to settle in California. "The
gospel can be preached in every town and village of this
country without the least opposition and the Kingdom be
the Lord's."

But was it the shadow of approaching events that lay
over him as he brought the letter to a close? "I am surrounded
by the allurements of the World and need your prayers and
blessings."

In the mail brought up the Truckee by Captain Brown
was a letter to the battalion boys from Brigham. *When you
receive this and learn of this location, it will be wisdom for
you all, if you have got your discharge as we suppose, to come
directly to this place. . . . If there are any men who have
not families among your number, who desire to stop in California for a season, we do not feel to object.*

Here was permission, if only halfhearted, for some of
the brethren to stay in California and gather means before
journeying on to Zion. The battalion camp on the Truckee
divided. Some, like Henry W. Bigler and James S. Brown,
turned back into California. Others, like Robert S. Bliss and
Daniel Tyler, heeded the call of their families and Brigham's
warm words: *We want to see you, even all of you, and talk
with you, and throw our arms around you, and kill the fatted
calf and make merry; yes, brethren, we want to rejoice with
you once more.*

On September 8th the little company of battalion men
divided. "It was hard parting," Henry Bigler acknowledged
to his journal, "but we knew it was best to obey the Servants
of God. It was stated that the Lord would be with us, and
one dollar earned and brought to Salt Lake would be worth
five times its value." They arrived at Sutter's on the 14th.
Sutter wanted to build a mill. A three-mile race would have
to be dug, and mill timbers got out. After thinking it over,
a number of the brethren accepted employment. They were

introduced to a fellow, James W. Marshall, who had come down from Oregon two years ago with a man by the name of Clyman. The sawmill was to be built on the south fork of the American River, and Marshall was Sutter's partner in the business. Late on the 27th Henry Bigler and four others set out for the millsite, where brethren already were at work.

The mill-building battalion boys left Sutter's just in advance of Captain Brown's return to the place, his saddle-bags bulging with golden doubloons received from the army paymaster. California was no place for him to tarry. William Squires had concluded to stay here "with a dashing young widdow who lost her husband while comeing around the Horn." That, says Abner, "come near breaking up the company. but we promised to return according to agreement. our Boss thought best to return soon or the dark eyed sinueretos would capture his whole outfitt. their was great inducements to stay in the beautiful land."

Concerning Captain Brown's return up the Humboldt to Zion, laden with the wealth of Babylon, Abner is graphic: "we started the 5 of October 1847 on the biggest tom fool erant that ever was known. a whole band of half broke animals to pack and drive through a rough mountain country and hostile indians tribes. . . . my consience smote me but would not back out at this stage of the game with our pot gutted horses we packed and unpacked a dozen times a day. and then herd them at night in this camp their came verry near being a mutiny. and nothing but fair promises and extra pay kept us from it." Indians chased the five of them down the Truckee and out upon the desert. The captain was missing, and his men finally located him praying: "O Lord, save us from those red Devils." "We broke in on his devotions," Abner says shamelessly, "and had a good laugh on him the rest of the trip." They reached the Humboldt and moved up the river, Indians underfoot, packs falling off, "and nothing but the everlasting greece wood and stinking

alkly to look at." They elected to take Lansford Hastings'
cutoff to the salt lake. Provisions were so short that there was
"an awful goneness" in their stomachs all the time. They
crossed a salt plain, the ground, grass, and bushes stiff with
salt: "we wear affraid" Abner avers, "to look behind for fear
of being turned into a pillar of salt, lik lots wife. i am sure
we wear no better than she was." They crossed the great salt
desert; the captain could cry, "Toot your horn, Gabriel, we
are almost there!" And in fact, in the late afternoon of November 16, 1847, they rode into the young Great Salt Lake
City. The Saints had built a fort there for safety, Abner explains, "when a few women could have run the whole band
of goshutes out of the country with mop sticks."

On the American River Henry Bigler, James S. Brown,
Azariah Smith, Israel Evans, and others of the battalion
worked faithfully throughout the winter. Henry Bigler himself spent much of his time hunting, for oftentimes Sutter
was neglectful in supplying the camp with provisions. But
on the morning of January 24th he was in camp to scrawl
in his journal an entry for history:

Monday 24th this day some kind of mettle was found in the
tail race that that looks like goald. And six busy days later there
was another entry: Sunday 30 clear & has been all the last week
our metal has been tride and prooves to be goald it is thought to be
rich we have pict up more than a hundred dollars woth last week

There was an effort to keep the secret, though Marshall
brought Sutter to have a look. The battalion boys went on
with their mill building, but went gold hunting on the side,
and found the metal all up and down the river. Gradually
the news leaked out. On March 15th the *Californian* mod-
estly announced that in the new raceway of Sutter's sawmill
on the American Fork gold had been found in considerable
quantities. "California no doubt is rich in mineral wealth;

great chances here for scientific capitalists." A week later the *California Star* also observed that gold had been found forty miles above Sutter's Fort.

But the news had not yet really sunk in. Sam Brannan was much more preoccupied with dissension among his followers than with the news from the American River. On March 29th he wrote Brigham a troubled letter: "You may rely upon my pushing every nerve to assist you and sustain you to the last and when any man comes to you with his fears that Bro Brannan's carried away with the world, which no doubt there will be some, that I don't preach my business to every night and morning you will confer a great favor upon your unworthy friend; by informing them that you are fully able to look after him without their assistance."

Such humility would not be found in Sam again. Hardly had his paper, on May 29th, pronounced the gold news "all sham—a supurb take in, as was ever got up to guzzle the gullible," than Sam himself arrived back in San Francisco from the gold fields, swinging his hat and bellowing, *"Gold,* GOLD, *GOLD from the American River!"*

He almost evacuated the town. The field was left "half planted, the house half built, and everything neglected but the manufacture of shovels and pickaxes, and the means of transportation to the spot." The news would spread, widening in ripples that would crash as waves on the seven shores of the world.

For Sam the "allurements of the World" were altogether too overwhelming. All Brigham's prayers and blessings now could avail nothing. In April of 1849, a year late, Brigham wrote to him: "The man who is always doing right has no occasion to fear any complaints that can be made against him, and I hope you have no occasion to fear." He was glad to hear that he might rely on Sam's pushing every nerve to assist and sustain him: he should expect $10,000, at least, on Sam's tithing, and if Sam had accumulated a million, so as to tithe $100,000, "so much the better, and may you get 2 millions next year. If you want to continue to prosper, do not forget the Lord's treasury, lest he forget you.

"Now, Bro. Brannan," Brigham admonished, "if you will deal justly with your fellows, and deal out with liberal heart and open hands, making a righteous use of all your money, the Lord is willing you should accumulate the rich treasures of the earth and the good things of time in abundance; but should you withhold, when the Lord says give, your hope and pleasing prospects will be blasted in an hour, you think not of, and no arm to save. But I am persuaded better things of Bro. Brannan."

This letter came, during the summer, to the lost soul. Not content with making money hand over fist on his own, he had been tithing the Saints. To Apostle Amasa Lyman, who came around to collect, Sam revealed his utter abandonment to Babylon. "You go back and tell Brigham," said he, "that I'll give up the Lord's money when he sends me a receipt signed by the Lord!"

What, finally, was the fruit of this "covetousness, ugliness, and low-mindedness"? Wealth, power, might in a drunken world! Ten years later fortune forsook Sam, his money, his friends, and his wife. He lapsed into rum-soaked poverty. At the end, an old investment returned to him $49,000. A miracle, really! But here, says Sam's biographer, is the greater miracle: "Sam Brannan, renegade adventurer—drunkard, spendthrift, rake—Sam took every dollar of that money and paid his debts with it, quit drinking, got rid of his paralysis, and died, on the rounding of his seventieth milestone, redeemed through the power of his will." The Lord who giveth and taketh away struck his own curious balance with Sam.

As for the Saints who labored at Sutter's Mill and with Marshall loosed Sam's destiny upon him—these could not be tempted to stay. In June, 1848, they rendezvoused in Pleasant

Valley, where Hangtown soon was to rise. Here, between 11 A.M. and sundown, James S. Brown washed out $49.50 in gold. Yet next day with his brethren he took his way eastward toward the Humboldt without regret, never to see the spot again. "People said, 'Here is gold on the bedrock, gold on the hills, gold in the rills, gold everywhere, gold to spend, gold to lend, gold for all that will delve, and soon you can make an independent fortune.' We could realize all that. Still duty called, our honor was at stake, we had covenanted with each other, there was a principle involved; for with us it was God and His kingdom first." And the Kingdom of God did not extend so far west as the Humboldt.

XII

The Golden Army

THE New York *Herald* published the news in August. Nobody believed it. But by September the cities along the eastern seaboard began to quicken with excitement. The President's Message to Congress, on December 5th, authenticating the news with gold actually received from California, touched off delirium. Through December and January ship after ship sailed south out of ports burning with gold fever.

The fever spread inland, to the farms and the towns. Those who had the money embarked at once down the long rivers to the ports fronting the sea. Others who could not go so soon or who looked instinctively, within the nation's pioneer heritage, to overland routes, turned their eyes to watch the sun carry its own flaming gold below the horizon.

With the spring, trails would open into the west. *Oh, Su-sannah, don't you cry for me! I'm gone to Californy with my washbowl on my knee!*

The hosts began to gather in the Missouri Valley early in April. It was America in revolution. Frontiersmen had wrought with the frontier, men who knew the uses of rifle and ax, who rode horses with confident thighs, and cracked superbly expert long whips above their teams. But now the white-handed gentry were here equally, determined to master the crafts of the trail. Here were the banker's son, the farm hand, the grocery clerk, the lawyer, the pimp. Here were William Kelly from distant London, Dr. Amos Batchelder from Pelham, New Hampshire, Alonzo Delano from Ottawa, Illinois, Bennett Clark from Boonville, Missouri . . . and plain Hank Jones from anywhere. They came by twos and tens. They came by scores and hundreds.

They united in companies at the frontier. Provisions had to be got, and horses and mules. "A mule's natural disposition," Amos Batchelder found, "is not the most amiable, and his disposition not to go the way you want him to is proverbial. . . . The Mexicans charged 5 dollars for breaking a mule to the saddle, and I thought well earned their money." Only a month ago he had been in a quiet New England town. These scenes were exciting and surpassing strange, yet no less strange to men who had lived all their lives on this frontier.

About Independence, in every direction, were oxen, mules, and horses, tied to trees or running at large. The "forest" resounded with the unearthly braying of the mules. Wives and children wandered about, and ladies of uneasy virtue. "Long trains of wagons," observed Amos Batchelder, "are almost continuously passing, drawn, in some cases, by as many as eight yoke of oxen, under the direction of numerous drivers who are continually yelling and cracking their long whips, making much confusion, and altogether an exciting scene."

Out of Independence and St. Joseph the Golden Army marched for California. Some eight thousand took the southern trail through Santa Fe. But the Road to California was that through South Pass to the Humboldt. Twenty-five thousand and more took the California Trail. They rode on horses and mules; they rode in wagons behind oxen; they walked beside wagons that carried their goods. There were those who set out trundling all they owned in wheelbarrows.

It was not until May that emigration out of Independence began to move in force. A lesser army had crushed the armies of Mexico. The white covers of their wagons glittered in the sunlight, like the sails of ships upon the sea.

William Kelly felt strongly the simile of the sea. His company's departure was like "a small fleet leaving a roadstead for the vast and trackless ocean." The prairies and plains were both awe-inspiring and depressing— "a series of immense undulations, like the huge lazy swells of the Atlantic in a calm." But this was no swelling sea. The Golden Army moved under the dust of its own passage—a dust cloud that lengthened as the army marched out of Independence and St. Joseph. At the end there was a dust cloud half across the continent, from the Sierra Nevada to the mud-swirling Missouri River.

At the beginning there was novelty, and the gratification arising out of pure physical action. But monotony invaded the days. The routine began at dawn, when the night guards called out the men delegated to move the picketed animals to better feed. As the sky whitened, all the camp began to stir, breakfasting and making ready for the day's travel. Tents struck, packing completed, and animals harnessed, the march began at six. A noonday halt gave the stock a chance to feed, and then the march was resumed until five, when camp was made for the night, the respective companies corralling their wagons for protection from the Indians. Supper over, there was a chance to think, to write in journals, to roar the songs of the gold trail, the firelight flickering bright orange against the settling darkness, while overhead the stars winked in their thousands.

The unearthly howling of the coyotes was inexpressibly chilling and sad, a lament for everything left behind and an uncanny prophecy for the future. But they had come expecting to have to have "a peep at the elephant," ready for the hardships of the trail. Some must fall along the way, unlucky victims of circumstance—drowned in the crossing of a creek, caught under the wheels of a wagon, shot by an unwitting gun. That was the price to be paid. If there were those, disheartened, who turned back to report with a sardonic self-abasement that they had seen the elephant, "yes, and eaten its ears," why, so much the worse for them! The riches of the earth belonged to him who had the strength and courage to take them. A man might be one-armed or goateed, card shark or plow hand, Mormon or abolitionist . . . but if there was guts in him and some horse-sense, he stood a chance of getting through.

Well, then!

> Miss Ella she is twenty-nine,
>   Has taken two degrees;
> And torn her shirt tail off behind
>   So she can show her knees!
>
> So take your time, Miss Ella!
>   Take your time, Miss Ella, do!
> And I will rock the cradle,
>   Give the ORO all to you!

With the latecomers, up the Mississippi and Missouri rivers, came that most dreaded of scourges—cholera. A man might rouse up at dawn as usual, and lie dead upon the ground before breakfast was finished. Agonizing cramps seized upon the legs, feet, and belly; the body grew cold, the skin bluish,

wrinkled and dry. The strength drained out of a man, his
voice reduced to a hoarse whisper, eyes sunken, the features
pinched out of all recognition. Suddenly, the man was dead
before your eyes!

The destroyer followed along the trail. The Golden Army
fled it, hardly pausing to bury its own dead. Perhaps a fifth
as many as got through to California died along the way
through the summer of '49.

Nearly everyone who left the frontier tried to take too
much with him. As the livestock failed, the emigrants climbed
into their wagons and pitched out the stuff into the night.
Captain Howard Stansbury, en route to Utah, in July picked
his way west through "bar-iron and steel, large blacksmiths'
anvils and bellows, crow-bars, drills, augers, gold-washers,
chisels, axes, lead, trunks, spades, ploughs, large grindstones,
baking ovens, cooking-stoves without number, kegs, barrels,
harness, clothing, bacon, and beans." On a single day he
passed seventeen abandoned wagons, and twenty-seven dead
oxen stinking in the sun.

But the Golden Army went on. Out ahead were the
"packers," traveling light on horses and mules, moving as
fast as they dared press their animals. More slowly came the
wagons with their yoked oxen, but the dust rose in the sky
ever more westerly—up the Platte and the Sweetwater to
South Pass, that great, open valley in which, like a promise,
welled "Pacific Springs."

Here, like many another, Alonzo Delano ascended a hill
"to take a parting look at the Atlantic waters, which flowed
towards all I held most dear on earth. . . . As I turned my
eye eastward, home, wife, and children, rushed to my mind
with uncontrolled feeling, and in the full yearnings of my
heart, I involuntarily stretched out my arms as if I would
clasp them to my bosom; but no answering look of affection,
no fond embrace met me in return . . . in its place there
lay extended before me barren reaches of table land, the bare

hills, and desert plains of the Sweetwater, while long trains of wagons, with their white covers, were turning the last curve of the dividing ridge, their way-worn occupants bidding a long, perhaps a last adieu to eastern associations, to mingle in new scenes on the Pacific Coast. Sad, but not dispirited, I descended the hill."

At South Pass is most manifest the meaning the rivers of America have had for adventuring Americans. The brightness of water trickling east or west from springs. . . . It flowed upon the imagination, so near to the heart's fullness. Whether of home and all things past or of the shining hope, South Pass and its springs had an eloquence for the heart. America was a land of dwellers by the river; that of one's self which went into the flowing water was forever free, changeless and glad. Here was companionship, the murmur of the water a beloved voice of the earth, ever familiar and comforting. By the rivers of America all things returned unto themselves, and time and space and separation and death had no permanence or power.

All who surmounted the imperceptible summit and camped at Pacific Springs knew that the past was done with, and that the labor must endure to the end. The wind rustling in the sage and lifting the dust bitterly to their cracked lips could speak of hardship to come. But beyond South Pass there was no turning back.

Through the sage plains and the sand the Golden Army marched for the Green. Greenwood's Cutoff struck directly across country toward Bear River; a more southerly trail made for Fort Bridger, where the forty-niner might choose whether to follow the track of the Saints to Great Salt Lake City or turn immediately north to regain the main trail at the Bear. William Kelly was one who went by Bridger's post to the valley of the Great Salt Lake, reaching the city June 15th. Others would follow, bartering their wagons and useless goods for delectable vegetables and fresh horses, oxen, and

mules, anxious at any price to be off. From Great Salt Lake
City they struck for the Humboldt trail—a few by the ill-
omened desert of salt, but most by a route north to Fort Hall
or north around the Great Salt Lake to intersection with the
California Trail at City of Rocks.

Over the dry drive on the main trail, the Golden Army
came to Bear River with its incredible green meadows. Peg-
leg Smith, old mountain man, accomplished horse thief, whom
his new neighbors were beginning to suspect of unchristianlike
conduct, watched in stupefaction the cavalcade that passed
his lodge. The old days were done in the West; the trap trail
was no more, and he had retreated into the Bear River Mountains with his squaws; first a passel of saints come to roost
in his back yard, and now this!

On to Fort Hall, then, with its scarlet banner and
whitewashed walls, and down the Snake to thunderous American Falls. Up writhing Raft River and across jumbled country to City of Rocks.

So now the trails had all come together again. "We saw
the dust ascending to the skies," Bennett Clark's journal
says, "shewing that every avenue to the golden region was
crowded with eager travellors to the Great El Dorada." The
forty-niners thumbed their copies of Ware's *Guide*, published
in St. Louis by a young man who had read Frémont and
Bryant and Hastings and turned out this book for the trade:
"You strike the HUMBOLDT RIVER at its head, from thence
your course is down its valley for three hundred miles . . .
principal river of the great basin . . . valley is rich and
beautifully clothed with blue grass, herds grass, clover, and
other nutritious grasses . . . course marked by a line of timber, mostly cotton wood and willow trees . . . unobstructed
for three hundred miles. . . . Indians of the most thievish
propensities, requiring, on the part of the emigrant, untiring
vigilance, to prevent their stealing and killing their teams,
&c. . . . Be always prepared to resist their attacks. The

road being level, and generally hard, enables you to travel over it with comparative ease . . . soil is light and porous in many places, making the travel bad on account of the continual clouds of dust arising . . . had better be on the road at a very early hour; the great heat of the sun, and continued clouds of dust, render it unendurable in the middle of the day. —Rain seldom falls here."

By golly, not so bad! They'd seen worse, a hell of a lot worse.

A pull across country brought them to Goose Creek, with its mica that glittered like gold in the stream bed. Goose Creek was climbed to its head, and now the trail wound through Thousand Springs Valley. Alonzo Delano wrote of his company's great desire "to reach the great River of the Mysterious Basin"; they felt a curiosity to see a river that flowed three hundred miles yet had no outlet. Out of the canyons, at last, the Golden Army marched into the great valley of the Humboldt, delivered from "the frightful barrenness" of this sage-stricken land east of the Humboldt.

There was grass for the firstcomers, and indeed more grass this summer than in most years before or since, from the heavy winter snows and slow spring, but as the dust began to rise all down the valley, the grass became more scant, the valley sterile and hostile. Bennett Clark's company, reaching the river in mid-July, congratulated itself on having reached pretty safe ground, their stock in good traveling order and the only danger now from overdriving. But the good grass soon disappeared, and the trail was through country "rough mountainous barren & destitute of grass & water," with "no vegitation to be seen on the hills and mountains around except the wild sage a growth which has become most sickening to us." The Golden Army was beating the dust out of the earth in clouds; they marched through a stifling ashy haze hourly more unendurable. "Grazing again very short. What will the emigrants behind us do?"

Water alone was not everything, a secure trail not everything. "Nothing but the hot sterrile lands & dust immediately around us & naught in the distance to releave the eye, but bare rugged hills of basalt. Our feelings just now is that if we once get safely out of this great Basin we will not be cought here again in a hurry."

Amos Batchelder was one of those behind. Six weeks after Clark he reached the Humboldt. The day was darkened by the dust that hung in the atmosphere; he could hardly make out the mountains across the valley. The river was muddy, in many places standing in stagnant pools saturated with alkaline matter. "This part of the country is more mountainous than we expected to find it. It is very barren, and almost uninhabitable. There is not a particle of wood except dwarf willow, wild sage, and greasewood. . . . The sky has been perfectly cloudless for many days, with one exception. . . . Everything is as dry as ashes. Our hands are full of cracks, and the more we wash them in the alkaline water, the worse they crack. The men are remarkably healthy, and have a great appetite. The table is thoroughly cleared at every meal, but we cannot make up our faces to kiss the cook, who has not been shaved for the last four months. . . . As we go along we see some of the most grotesque figures I ever saw—living caricatures of the human species. We see a great many strangers every day, bound for the gold region. Some of them are mounted on poor, dusty looking mules, others on poor, miserable looking worn down horses, dressed in dusty, ragged clothes, as most of us are. Some with their pantaloons pulled on too far, or with one leg of them gone as far as the knee, others with both legs of their pants entirely worn and torn off to the same altitude, with things on their heads that look as much like almost anything else as a hat. White broad brimmed, round topped hats, are the most fashionable in this region. Dead carcasses are seen everywhere on the road."

William Kelly, with the vanguard far down the Humboldt, wrote of other troubles: "The water of the river, now clearly shrinking, both by evaporation and absorption, was positively bitter of alkali, preparing us for an increasing deterioration as we proceeded. . . . The only cure left us, and one which we resolved pushing to the extreme, was despatch." Nearing the Sink, he thought that the company he now commanded "was in a very seedy and unsound state, more nearly resembling a batch of invalids crawling in search of an hospital, than a band of adventurous travellers charging the Great Sierra Nevada to jump into the golden valley of the Sacramento. But this lodestar . . . kept up the flagging spirits."

The grueling passage of the Humboldt erased any memory of earlier hardship. The toil up the Platte in retrospect seemed almost to have been happy.

> I crawled out and started on,
>   And managed very well,
> Until I struck the Humboldt
>   Which I thought was nearly Hell.
> I traveled till I struck the Sink
>   Where outlet can't be found;
> The Lord got through late Saturday night—
>   He'd finished all around,
> But would not work on Sunday,
>   So he run it in the ground.

The humor was grim enough to be comforting. Provisions more scant, the stock failing day by day, dust filling the valley like a gray terrible pall, alkali water an ever-present danger to the stock (even the flowing water not always safe), the 300-mile trek west and always west had the cloudy horror of a nightmare. Alkalied stock fell in its tracks, sometimes in the very water from which it was drinking, and men must wade out amid the rotting carcasses to slosh a blanket in the water and wring from the wool into kettles a wetness that strong stomachs could keep down.

The Diggers were not so bad this year as they would be later, but arrows from the sagebrush or the darkness buried themselves in the stock to set the bright blood flowing; the forty-niners fired into any likely clumps of bushes, careless for the innocent or the guilty, content to blast their own passage through, and hell take the careless or the unlucky who might follow behind to answer to the Diggers.

Struck by an idea, a half dozen Argonauts took to the river. Swimming was less arduous than eating dust and roasting their feet on the trail. But the trail and the river parted company. G. W. Thissell tells the story: "The train had taken a cut-off and left the river. The heat was intense. The sun was almost blistering our backs, which were now as red as lobsters. It was ten o'clock and no train could be seen. We left the water and heeled it down the river through the willows, like so many wild men. One o'clock and the train came in sight, but many miles away. In the willows we came upon a band of friendly Indians who gave us old moccasins to put on our feet. At two o'clock, when the train came back to the river and camped, we were still two miles away. Two of our company on horseback brought us our clothes. Our backs were so blistered we could scarcely wear our shirts. At six o'clock we were only twelve hours older, but many years wiser."

Farther down the river, toward the Sink, the milky water would not have invited them at all. William Kelly observed it with distaste: "The porous banks were fast diminishing the river into a paltry stream, now nearly the consistence of thin gruel, so fully was it impregnated with alkali, and nearly at a blood heat." There was little incentive even for the "sheep scrape"—the Saturday night cleanup.

This was the way to California, the Road to Samarkand! In the gold fields a man might or might not be lucky. That was within the keeping of the blind god Chance. But it was not luck that brought a man through to the gold fields: it was a stubborn courage, male strength and purpose, the granite structure of a man's spirit. Scum might ship by sea, but a man who came through the valley of the Humboldt to the High Sierra and thence through the great pine forests to the sun-bright land of his seeking came with a consciousness of his stature as a man.

So the legions of the Golden Army rounded the Big Bend of the Humboldt and made for the Sink, the road "toilsome as hell," a wasteland of parched grass and sand and foul water—"O Barrenness!" Frightful tales of what lay ahead drifted back along the trail. Bennett Clark made a journal entry on August 4th:

"We found the water in holes here that had been dug by those before us, and such water we never remember to have drank. It was cool but most horrible to the taste—a mixture of alkali and Sulpher & no doubt all coming from the sink. This was however all the water we could get. We had not more than watered our animals before ox teams commenced coming in & in 3 hours there were at least 150 or 200 wagons assembled at this point. In watering our stock we mixed flour with the water so as to sustain them. Here we stoped until 5 oclock this evening. The heat was excessive. Our animals were tied up to keep them from straying. We saw a man here who had just returned by the left hand road & he gave us a horrid account of the teams that had gone that way. A general panic now seezed upon all & doubt & fear prevailed every where. There is yet a stretch of 45 miles ahead of us without grass or water except at the boiling spring 25 miles from this point."

Already the destruction was appalling. The trail was lighted at night by the murky flames of wagons abandoned by those who had gone before and chopped now into firewood. "The light of the fires lit up our pathway and revealed the awful loss of stock." So littered was the trail with rotting carcasses that it often forced wagon trains out of their course. A traveler who came next year and saw another such scene could not forget the picture: ". . . a number of ox teams of five and six pairs each, lying down in their yokes—some of them dead, some of them with their swollen tongues lying extended out in the dust, and moaning and groaning as pitifully as one of our kind—unable to avoid the almost perpendicular rays of the sun now beating upon this spot with a fury almost indescribable. . . . A myriad of buzzards hovered around, alighting now and then to pick out the eyes of the prostrate whether dead or alive."

Here at the Sink the trails began to fan out, the ironic service of the Humboldt done. The old trail struck more westerly to the Truckee. Many went this way; but the fate of the Donner party, retold all along the trail, was associated with this route. More struck southerly across the Sink to the Carson with its incredible green trees and grass. From the Truckee and the Carson the trails split and split again, as the companies of the Golden Army rode into the Sierras in reckless quest of cutoffs and new ways. But before the Sierras could be climbed, the Forty Mile Desert must be crossed.

Preparation was made by soaking the wheels of the wagons in the river. The constant dry driving had shrunk the wood until it seemed that the will of God alone held the wheels together. In the water they swelled again to a semblance of tightness. Grass was cut for the stock, and every receptacle filled with the nauseous water. On either route bad water could be found halfway across the desert. To escape the murderous sun, the trek began just before nightfall.

William Kelly, who got to the Forty Mile Desert among the earliest, tells of the crossing to the Carson. "At one o'clock we had our wheels on, mules to, and everything ready for the

Desert march. The wheels were all the better for the immersion, being braced as tight as drums, and free from the slightest rattle—a compliment I am unable to pay the men and animals. . . . We soon left the greenish confines of the Sink in a southwesterly course, and got out on the shores of the sandy ocean, calculating to reach the sulphur springs before dark; but we got in amongst the still billows of the light ashy earth . . . the mules being literally obliged to breast through them, making the dust arise in such dense clouds it well-nigh nearly suffocated us, completely blinding us to the track. We had near three miles of this nuisance, and by the time we got through the mules were panting from exhaustion, and snorting or sneezing convulsively. . . . It was ten o'clock when we reached the neighborhood of the sulphur springs, which we would have undoubtedly overrun, only that the mules set up a most discordant braying, which warned us of their proximity."

The company marched through the night, hoping after sunup for a glimpse of the Sierras, but haze veiled everything except sand. Not even a stunted sagebrush was to be seen. "The sun fired up with great intensity, and so very early as eight o'clock struck with a glow that made us quail at the idea of its meridian vigour." They managed to make about three miles an hour until ten, when they struck soft sand that exhausted even the faithful mules. A wonderful mirage of lake and city enchanted them and disappeared. After two hours they reached a hard plain, "a great relief to the draught animals; but the direct flames of the solar fire seemed absolutely to curl around us, creating a wavy visible sort of atmosphere, as if we were moving through transparent smoke; and this at length produced a state of insensibility in some and madness in others, four of the men coming up to me and demanding water in a most peremptory tone, as if I had a supply and denied them access to it. About twelve o'clock we halted, to administer the gruel to the animals, but there were only seven men out of the entire [company] able to lend a hand. Some were howling for water, and some threw themselves in a fainting fit under the shade of the waggons." The animals having received a meager drink, the march was resumed, but two men who had quite lost their minds had to be tied in a wagon, and a helpless teamster stowed in with them. Those who were under the wagons paid no heed to the order to move, "nor could they be got to heed its iteration until the waggons were moved on, and they were left exposed to the sun, when they arose, but in a dreadfully enervated state"; deaf and insensible, they could be argued into nothing; it was necessary to hoist them into their saddles. A dust storm assailed them, in clouds and waves as high as the wagons, but they were fortunate in a few drops of rain that fell upon them. Late in the day they reached the Carson Valley slope. The loose stock, at the scent of water, stampeded for the stream, and even the mules in harness could hardly be controlled. The men exhibited as little self-control as the animals; Kelly feared they would burst with drinking. Luckily, no one died.

Kelly's company had come fast across the Forty Mile Desert, and they had taken the precaution of lightening their loads and bringing water. Yet he felt that they had barely escaped with their lives. Those who came after broiled in the desert, the animals sobbing for water and lurching to the ground. The desert stank with the passing of the Golden Army, the men fallen amid their animals, scores and hundreds obliterated at the very end of this long, hard way.

Yet there was courage, here and on the march to the Truckee; men who escaped from the inferno went back carrying water to their teams. Not for property alone: the love a man can know for a good and faithful animal that has served him to death.

As frightful was the trail across the Forty Mile Desert to the Truckee—this way went Bennett Clark. His company

set out in late afternoon, and reached the hot springs in the
middle of the desert just at daylight, "the most dreary desolate looking place we ever saw . . . the water bubbles & boils
up from the fissures in the rocks & forms into a small lake
quite clear but so hot that it scalds. We dipped up the water
& pourd it into some holes in the earth & cooled it & then
watered our animals, again mixed flour with it. The mules
were so hungry that they ate dust & gravel & chewed up
whativer came in their way—gearing, wagon covers or any
thing they could reach." Soon after 7 A.M. they resumed the
labor—twenty miles to go through the blazing August day;
they could not broil at these hot springs until nightfall.
Heavy sand forced them to rest the stock every few yards,
but somehow they got through to the Truckee by nightfall.

"All along the desert road from the very start even the
way side was strewed with the dead bodies of oxen, mules &
horses & the stench was horrible. All our travelling experience furnishes no parallel to this. Many persons suffered
greatly for water during the last 8 or 10 miles, and many instances of noble generosity were developed on these occasions.
Some trains that got over before us sent water back in kegs
& left them on the road marked for the benefit of the feeble."
Resting several days here on the green banks of the Truckee,
Clark turned to look out again upon the desert. "The evening
was warm & still and the sky without a cloud & nothing in
sight but the arid barren ashy plain. Occasionally we could
see some poor old horse or steer deserted by his master &
unable to bear up longer against the urgent necessity for food
& drink, come stalking along towards the wagons, their hoofs
breaking thru the crusty earth with a noise similar to the
dead crakling sound caused by walking thru frozen snow, as
if to ask us for relief. . . . Taking the general aspect of this
desert into view, and the fact that there is an absence of
every thing desirable and an abundance of every thing per-
nicious here coupled with what we saw, we cannot conceive

a hell more full of horrors. It realises all that such a mind as
Dante's could imagine."

Bennett Clark turned to the Sierras, and, by one of
those ironies that beset men's lives, fell ill as he reached the
summit; he was taken by his friends to San Francisco, and
there took ship back home, never seeing the "bright red gold
for dearie," to round out his life as court clerk and probate
judge in Missouri.

Recoiling from these tales of the Sink and the Forty Mile
Desert that filtered back upon the trail, some left the Humboldt at its Big Bend, persuaded that by the Applegate Cutoff they might reach the gold mines sooner and with less
suffering. Alonzo Delano took this trail, and Amos Batchelder. But the Black Rock Desert proved almost as trying, and
the passage of the mountains infinitely more difficult.

The Trail to California in the end clung to the valley of
the Humboldt. Dust, alkali, dryness—a daunted gray world
—the Humboldt was not of a kind with the other rivers
of America. But the Humboldt ran in the path of the sun.
By the Golden Army that trampled twenty-five thousand
strong through a region which Frémont only four years
earlier had explored as an unknown land, the valley of the
Humboldt was fixed in the American epic.

XIII

Outpost of Zion

THERE was not the proper fear of God in Abner, and he loved wine too well, the wine of action more heady than any. A man who could say so insouciantly of the laying on of hands for a gunshot wound that "Brigham and Kimball were there and prayed me out of danger"—clearly such a man was deficient in saintliness. So the gold fields appealed much more strongly to Abner Blackburn than building up the Kingdom of God with irrigation ditches.

In the spring of 1849 he departed Zion. After "the usual amount of quarreling and swearing that all such companies have," his party reached the Sink of the Humboldt. There was a new route since he had gone this way with

Cap Brown and Sam Brannan—the returning battalion members last year had come east through the Sierras into Carson Valley, and across the Forty Mile Desert by what the Golden Army this year was calling "the new route."

Taking this trail, Abner's company crossed to Carson Valley in two days, and stopped to recuperate in the good blue shade of the cottonwood trees. Why, Abner presently demanded of the company, was gold not found east as well as west of the mountains? He was given the sage reply that no one had looked for it. While his companions loafed about the camp playing cards, Abner wandered off with a bread pan and butcher knife.

In a side ravine he scratched up some color, and in a larger gulch did even better. When he strolled back to camp, all hands "grabbed up pans knives and kettles and started out." Until nearly sundown, Abner says, they "scrached scraped and paned." Among them they found nine or ten dollars' worth of the stuff. But lacking tools and provisions, they abandoned the place, promising to return when they got around to it. In California, however, they found gold and riotous excitement. With his brother Abner worked the summer through, making "a respectable pile of the needful."

As autumn drew on, he and his brother rode east across the mountains looking for relatives who ought to be somewhere on the trail. On reaching the Humboldt, they learned that the folks had stopped to winter at Salt Lake. Abner was all for turning back to Babylon but there was a girl his brother wanted to see, and so they rode on to the Valley—"just as good as the elders of Israel, at least our gold was." His brother got married on Christmas Day, and Abner went a few miles south to winter in Utah Valley with his uncle.

With spring he wanted to be off to California, however Brigham might thunder in the pulpit that the business of a Saint was making green his fields. There were others with like ideas, and some eighty souls set out for Fort Hall late in April.

Nothing of note happened down the Humboldt, "only camping hitching up going on and stoping again." Arriving in
Carson Valley, Abner went to have a look at his gold mine.
But some enterprising persons had worked out the best
places. Discovering gold here seemed, anyway, a dubious sort
of distinction.

. . . And Abner and history might have shaken hands
on this, except that the place where he had seen his first
color within a decade blazed in the mind of the West as
Gold Canyon. The hills might even now have quivered under
the vision of the Comstock. But no ghosts of the future
stalked this summer afternoon of 1850.

As they prepared to go on over the mountains, the vanguard of the emigration overtook them. Thousands and thousands, they said, were behind them on the trail. And because
last year the Golden Army had wasted its substance so recklessly, the Argonauts this year had come too lightly pro-
visioned. Companies on the trail were practically starving.

Abner and others of the party looked at one another.
Why not pick out the best possible location here in Carson
Valley and run a supply station? It might pay better than
mining. Abner and his brother accordingly picked out the
site for "Mormon Station." There was, Abner says, no better
place on the river, "cold watter comeing out of the mountain.
and pine trees weare plenty on the edge of the valley. their
was oceans of good feed for stock, it was choice place for our
business built the first house for our stasion out of pine logs
and a large lot coral for stock and fixt for traffic." Roof and
floors were deemed superfluous for the double-logged, two-
roomed cabin, which in size was about 20 by 60 feet. (Nevada history, accepting the somewhat vague dates of H. S.
Beatie in his manuscript, *The First in Nevada,* has always
dated for 1849 the establishment of Mormon Station. Abner
Blackburn's reliable reminiscences establish 1850 as correct. Beatie says that he came to Utah "in C. T. Benson's

company arriving here on the 26th of October," the year
being assigned as 1848 from his saying subsequently that he
arrived in Carson Valley in June, 1849. However, E. T. Benson did not come to Utah in 1848; he stayed in Iowa to
oversee Mormon affairs with his co-apostles George A. Smith
and Orson Hyde. He led to Utah a large company of the
Mormon immigration of 1849, arriving in Salt Lake Valley
October 28th. Beatie's information was given from memory
in 1884.)

With a couple of teams Abner and a companion set out
over the mountains for provisions to stock the place. Learning that in Sacramento snow was fetching $80 a ton, they
filled their wagons, covered the snow with pine boughs and
wagon sheets, and "killed two birds with one stone hauling
down snow and carying back provisions."

Mormon Station was a fabulous success. Although James
Abbey, speaking for the emigration, called the place "a perfect skinning post," Abner observes that it was hard to keep
supplies on hand, and Hampden S. Beatie, while acknowledg-
ing that flour was worth $2 a pound, fresh beef $1 and bacon
$2, says that since they had insufficient flour to sell in large
quantities, they "used to deal it out in small quantities thereby
benefitting more people."

Business was too good to remain a monopoly long, and
other traders packed in supplies across the mountains. The
miners' truth was already sinking in: you could make your
pile quicker out of the miners than out of the ground. The
only risk was that the miners might tear you root from
branch. At Mormon Station the principal danger was from
companies that abandoned their wagons, now that the Carson
was reached, to pack on over the mountains. The boys, says
Abner, "would get on a spree at the station. cut up harness
bend guns around trees. run a lot of waggons togeather set
them on fire. and run amuch gnerly their was no law or gospel
to hinder them."

As autumn wore on, the owners of Mormon Station split up. The place was sold to a man named Moore, and the partners departed in various directions, heavily laden with their new wealth. Abner decided that Fort Hall was a likely place to convert his horses into something he could carry in a sack, and as others of the company had wives they wanted to see at Salt Lake, most of them crossed the desert and set out up the Humboldt.

This had been a bad year along the Humboldt, grass burned to a crisp, and Indians harassing the passage of the emigrants. At night they attacked the stock, killing and crippling it or running it off; they could drive their arrows clear through a man, a worse wound than a bullet, and often their arrowheads were poisoned. Usually they kept from sight, but sometimes they moved boldly along the trail, "quite impudent and ferocious."

Vigilance usually sufficed with the Diggers, but Abner and his companions had the bad luck to run into a band of marauding Bannocks. Pursued up the river, they lost almost all their horses and pack animals, and made for Salt Lake by the cutoff around the north shore of Great Salt Lake. By "traveling at night and dodging the indians" they came through all right. Abner had never seen the Indians on the Humboldt worse . . . and the fighting spirit of the company was not all it could have been. Too many men had wives they wanted to see.

So Abner came back to the Saints, "and they wear real good while our money lasted." But gay Spanish dress and the Spanish custom of riding girls on horseback within the circle of a man's arms did not square with saintly ideas of decorum. As the sun warmed the spring days, Abner prepared to depart the Saints once and for all. Trying to live perfect before the Lord was too trying.

A company fitted out by John and Enoch Reese, Salt Lake merchants, to trade in Carson Valley with the gold diggers, set out from the city of the Saints on April 10, 1851, the flour-laden wagons and the cattle following behind while Abner and some companions ran the gantlet to the Sink. Arrived in Carson Valley, Abner soon forced a passage of the Sierras, and yielded himself up to Babylon. John Reese, however, set about the permanent location of an outpost for Zion. Buying out the claim to Mormon Station, he soon had a respectable establishment—a two-story building, boasting kitchen, dining room, storeroom, and two large rooms upstairs, surrounded by scattered log houses and fields that soon were green with wheat, barley, corn, and even watermelons. Although down the river other traders located what was beginning to be known as Ragtown, Reese felt himself to have found by far the best place for a settlement, and to seal his claim to the land, he bought out Captain Jim of the Washoe Indians for two sacks of flour.

Emigration fell off this year, but Reese fenced off his lands, brought in some pigs from California, and traded off his provisions and goods for cattle and horses which fattened wonderfully on the wild hay of the Carson bottoms. During the year others filtered into the region, not only straggling placer miners but men with livestock, and farmers who were tiring of digging in the gravel along California rivers. Zion, adulterated, no doubt, and hardly of the best blood of Israel in any case, gave prospect of flourishing here as well as in the valley of the Great Salt Lake. The emigration of 1852, greater than any that had gone before, brought actual boom times. Enough could not be raised to supply the demand, Colonel Reese remembered. Turnips proved almost worth their weight in gold; a bunch that cost him a dime he sold for a dollar— all he could raise. And the watermelons were large and luscious, their great red hearts dripping savory juice.

There were neighbors, like this man John Redding, over in Jack's Valley, and Lucky Bill Thorrington, up the river, about whom doubtful stories were told, but others who came in were good and substantial men—the blacksmith Van Sickles, for instance.

In the fall of '51 the settlers in Carson Valley, numbering perhaps a hundred, got together and resolved that Congress should be petitioned for a territorial government, that land claims be surveyed, and that a governing committee of seven men be established. Later meetings provided further land laws and a judicial machinery. Altogether, this outpost of Zion exhibited a fine disregard for the proprieties, for Congress had created the Territory of Utah, with Brigham Young, the Lord's Anointed, as governor and ex officio superintendent of Indian affairs; the boundaries of Utah extended west to the Sierra Nevada, and Carson Valley lay within the august jurisdiction of the authorities in Great Salt Lake City.

As an outpost of Zion, the settlement in Carson Valley from the beginning had a doubtful reputation. Saints might go there, but there was no organized mission; none had been "called" to settle Carson Valley. Besides, that valley was too near the gold mines. The Utah legislature early in 1852 took the counties down the center of Utah, drew long east and west parallels across the map to allocate quite definitely all the lands of Utah Territory, and considered it had performed its full duty by western Utah.

In June, 1852, Tom Williams arrived in Carson Valley with a herd of cattle bound for the California markets. Abner Blackburn said of him in his battalion days that he "made his brag that he had stolen from a hen on her roost to a steamboat engine," but Tom Williams was now well on the way to becoming the eminently respectable Thomas S. Williams, Esq., merchant and lawyer. The citizens of Carson Valley, he advised Brigham Young, "declare in language too strong to utter that they will no longer be governed or tried by Mormon laws, that they are chiefly organized here to redress the wrongs inflicted on United States citizens who had the good luck, or were fortunate enough to escape with life and limb from Utah. . . . Col. Reese and his nephew Mr. Kinsey who are both so good and accommodating while in Salt Lake have been the ringleaders in opposing the organization of the territory of Utah and declare they will pay no taxes what are levied on them from that source and advise others to hold out in like manner untill they get this valley annexed to California."

He went on to California, there to be "awfully shocked although not very much surprised" at the depraved condition of society.

Next year Carson Valley had another visitor from the city of the Saints; this earnest brother, Edwin D. Woolley, advised an old acquaintance, "This is a great country when we get it all fenced in, whether it has changed much for better or worse since you were here I cannot say, but if for the worse it must have changed very fast, and if for the better it must have been very slow, it is the most God forsaken place that ever I was in, and as to Mormonism, I can't find it here. If the name remains, the Spirit has fled. I have my doubts whether Mormonism can exist in the country as far as I have been."

Brother Woolley might have found in Carson Valley enthusiastic amens about the perils to Mormonism if not about the God-forsakenness; more and more miners were drifting over the mountains to prospect the hills and canyons, and these were quite indisposed to meet on Sundays and sing "The Spirit of God Like a Fire Is Burning." Their taste for Mormon song, indeed, ran rather on this wise:

> The Mormon girls were fat as hogs,
>   The chief production cats and dogs;
> Some had ten wives, others none,
>   Thirty-six had Brigham Young.

The damned old fool, like all the rest,
Supposed his thirty-six the best;
He soon found out his virgin dears
Had all been Mormons thirteen years.

Forty-three of these obstreperous citizens took it on themselves to petition the California legislature for annexation of Carson Valley. Hearkening to this rumble from afar, the legislature of Utah in January, 1854, created the county of Carson, and sixteen months later dispatched, to rule over the region as probate judge, Apostle Orson Hyde, whose experience among the wicked and ungodly on the Iowa frontier eminently qualified him for the job.

In May, 1855, in company with United States Justice George P. Stiles, United States Marshal Joseph L. Heywood, Enoch Reese, and some thirty-five others, Orson Hyde set out for the western frontier of Zion. The country between Bear River and the head of the Humboldt did not impress him. "I think," he reported to the *Deseret News*, "that I should be unwilling to exchange my garden of one and a half acres in Salt Lake City, for all the land that I have seen." The Humboldt bottoms were rather more satisfactory, with rich grass and clear-flowing streams, but here were white alkali flats and sloughs. As for his companions, Judge Stiles was beginning to get accustomed to the western life: "I think that he will pass in this country where we have to sleep with one eye open, one foot out of bed, a rifle in one hand and a revolver in the other." Everything was going excellently. No profanity was heard among the boys. All were attentive to prayers. "I feel that the Lord is with us, and on him we rely for aid, for wisdom, and for strength."

He proceeded down the Humboldt to the scene of his labors. The cattle of the emigration were dying at an appalling rate. It was heart-sickening to see and smell the dead carcasses on the road. The fuel was good enough, but the road and the hills he thought "too monstrous for a Christian train of wagons to traverse." Nevertheless, in mid-June he came safe to the Reese ranch in Carson Valley. The crops looked fine despite the destructive grasshoppers, which here as in eastern Utah were laying waste the earth this year. The brothers Reese had "a most splendid mill and ranch." Altogether, he liked the look of what he saw.

The "Olive Branch of Israel," as the Saints called him, decided that he had better begin by settling once and for all the boundary question. By September a commission had established the fact that the California boundary bisected Lake Tahoe, some miles to the west, and Judge Hyde could therefore set about his business.

An election was held at which Mormon candidates were elected to every office save that of prosecuting attorney. Far from pleased with this, or even with the very presence of the Mormons, the Gentiles promptly petitioned California anew for annexation; and for good measure fired a shot in Hyde's direction. It was unendurable that he should bring among them his "spiritual wife"; they could only "look with disgust upon the prospect of raising up their daughters among such associates, and they ardently desired that their homes in their pleasant valley [should] not be 'defiled' by the horrible favoritism and deception of Mormonism."

The *Deseret News* laughed. "The idea of the 'ladies' of that Valley, of the class represented, petitioning Congress and exhibiting their wrath and indignation, is quite amusing. . . . A gentleman of veracity, who spent the winter of 1855-56 in that country, asserted in our hearing not long since, that at a party got up during the winter, an unusual effort was made to secure the attendance of as many females as possible, to give interest to the occasion; and that in searching the valley from the Humboldt to the Sierra Nevada only *three* were found and one of those was a 'lady of color.'"

Obviously, Zion here was not far advanced toward a

state of grace. But Hyde was not lacking in energy. In the spring he set about building up this corner of Zion. Mormon Station was dignified as "Genoa," and its streets were laid out and lots surveyed. Franktown was laid out in Washoe Valley to the north. A splendid sawmill, worth perhaps $10,000, was commenced by the apostle, who himself located in Franktown.

In view of the ornery miners and Mormon-haters, it was decided that the Carson Mission should be strengthened. Several score settlers were "called" to migrate to Carson; they arrived in June, 1856, and soon were locating on likely farm lands in Carson, Washoe, and Eagle valleys. With their entrance into these western valleys, Mormons could breathe more easily, their political supremacy reinforced. As for the others, for the time being they must content themselves with hard, sour words: "Damned Mormons!"

So was established a perilous outpost for Zion at the far end of the Humboldt trail, a fact of running water and ripening fields realized under the great rampart of the Sierra Nevada. Was there reason for disquiet? Was anything to be apprehended from the agitators who wanted a severance from Utah? The *Deseret News* hearkened to an eastern report that Congress was not disposed to make California more unwieldy than it already was, and that relief could be afforded the moral outrage of Washoe memorialists by properly enforcing laws contemplated to be enacted against polygamy: "All right. Hush my dear, lie still and slumber."

XIV

Variations on the Theme of Murder

THE tramplings had been westward, but now began
the interlocking eastward movement. East and west through
the Humboldt Valley flowed the restless blood of America.
In all the long course of the barrenness there was no station
of civilization. Men embarked as upon the trade routes of a
sea in riding eastward from Carson Valley or westward from
Fort Hall or the Mormon settlements. It was a sea made dangerous by raiders white and red, a sea on which law was the
superior might of a man or a company.

A few scattering traders established temporary posts up
and down the long river valley. But the occupation was hazardous; and the traders were looked on with suspicion by

208

the emigrants, for there were dark rumors abroad that white men and red were leagued along the Humboldt in murder and rapine. There are tales told of these years in the history of the Humboldt.

There is a story that Bill Hickman tells. In his way Bill had been a sufficiently conscientious Mormon. He did jobs that sometimes seemed necessary, though whether the necessity was Bill's idea or that of his leaders is a question not easy to settle. At the time of the Mormon migration to the Rocky Mountains he had made himself useful along the Missouri River bottoms, breaking up a gang of bogus-makers (counterfeiters), knocking off a dangerous half-breed and some Indian horse thieves. He lived on a violent frontier, and picked up a certain reputation. Finally he moved on to Salt Lake Valley.

For a while Bill was content trading with the emigrants, but in 1851 the gold fever got him and he set out for California with the last emigrant company of the year.

Bill was nominated captain. As he was not acquainted with ten men in the company, he got up and objected; "but this was of no use," says he, "they said that they had heard of me, those who did not know me, and had made up their minds to have me for their Captain; that we had to go through a country full of bad Indians, and they knew from what they had heard that I knew more about them than any other person in the company, and I had to accept."

The passage down the Humboldt was a bitter experience —mile after mile of burned wagons, and skeletons of men, women, and children, "their long and beautiful hair hanging on the brush; and sometimes a head with as beautiful locks of hair as I ever saw, and sometimes those of little children, with two or three inches of flaky hair, either lying by or near them, the wolves having eaten the flesh off their bones." All had been scalped.

This was the inevitable sequel to the inundation of '49, when through this valley had trailed thousands upon thousands, trampling under the grasses, drinking dry the springs, abandoning dead cattle in the watercourses, shooting at the fortuitous targets of Indians glimpsed in the brush. The Diggers had fought back.

Hickman's company got, as Bill puts it, "terribly riled up." They met the shattered remains of a train which had lost nearly half its stock and a dozen men, and thought there was no show to get through. "We thought differently," says Bill. And when there began a sudden yelling in the brush, instead of waiting for the attack some twenty-five of the men grabbed guns and went after the Indians like loosed mastiffs.

The surprised Indians fled like antelope, and the whites struck them down right and left, thirty-two in all. Other opportunities offered for this kind of sudden death as the company proceeded down the trail, but all this was normal to the era, and what makes memorable the westward passage of Bill Hickman's company is the happening after reaching the Carson River.

One of his men, Bill says bluntly, "got killed. He was the best man I had. His name was John Watson. He was killed by the worst man I had, a man who was said to be running away from Missouri for murdering a man there. They had a quarrel, and this man undertook to shoot Watson, but would have got killed if I had not interfered. Watson came to me, and told me he knew the man intended killing him, and thought it hard I would not let him shoot him. I then went and talked to the man, and he promised faithfully he would not touch Watson. I told Watson there was no danger. He thought different, but said he would be quiet, and not another word passed between them. That evening Watson was lying on his blankets, sleeping, when this man, Hensley, went and put his pistol to his head and blew out his brains."

Hickman, out with the horses, returned to find Hensley, with four guns on his belt, swearing there were not men enough in camp to take him. Quite coldly Bill considered shooting him down, but sat down at his campfire and said nothing.

Next morning, by the firing of thirty shots over his grave, Watson was given such military honors as the occasion afforded. Dismally, then, they rode on. At nightfall they encamped with sixteen men eastbound from California. Bill had known their captain in Illinois, and after downing a good drink of brandy, he recounted what had happened.

"Hang him up!" they shouted. "There's no law here. We have to tend to our own skunks. In the mines he'd have been hung in less than three hours."

"Well," Bill said, "I'll have him arrested. Half a dozen of you come up after dark and we'll investigate the case."

He picked out four of his best men, told them to get as close to Hensley as they could, "and then bounce upon him." When one of the men got within ten feet of him, Hensley straightened and reached for a gun, but the men were all over him at once.

After supper, the California captain came over with his six men. It was voted that Hensley should be tried. The trial ran smoothly to its end, no evidence denied. Hensley had a certain hard eloquence: "That damned son of a bitch, he insulted me by giving me the lie, and no man can do that and live. That's my motto and he knew it; so he deserved to die." He had no other defense.

The jury returned a verdict of murder in the first degree. Bill proposed, the company sanctioning by vote, that the jury be authorized to pass sentence. It required five minutes: "Hang him."

A tree was found with a suitable limb, and the prisoner was advised that he had half an hour to live. Hensley desired a man to pray for him. But after ten minutes he began to damn everyone, "acting more like a devil than a man going to die." In his last five minutes Hensley turned his attention to Bill. "If there is such a thing, I will come back and haunt you all the days of your life."

Bill smiled grimly. "I'm not much afraid of live men, much less of dead ones."

A lariat was put around Hensley's neck and thrown over a limb; he was then drawn four feet from the ground. The other end was fastened to a stake, and everyone went to bed. Next morning they rolled the corpse in a blanket and buried it under the same tree. Bill supplies an epitaph for the times: "I noticed the looks of the company that day, and all seemed to say we had done right."

There are other stories more shocking for their insight into the fortitude of the human soul than for their grisly details. There is the story of the Holloway company of 1857.

There were ten in all. They neglectfully camped in an open space too near some willows that edged the riverbank, and at daybreak Indian rifles poured a deadly volley into the camp.

Mrs. Holloway stumbled out of the tent to see about her the bodies of her companions; her husband lay across the breakfast fire. Shivering to the morning cold, she saw the Indians emerge stealthily from the willows. She seized her baby and turned to run. The Indians fired at her. She was struck by several arrows and at least one bullet, and fell to the ground.

Horribly, consciousness remained. The Indians came up to tear the clothes from her body and their arrows from her flesh. Once, when they left her for a second, she ventured to move very slightly, but at this evidence of life they took hold of the arrows still in her body and worked them about in the wounds, pushing them deeper into the flesh while they stamped upon her with their heels. With eyes closed, she lay without the twitch of a muscle, the movement of a finger, even when a knife slashed in her hair and her scalp was ripped from her head, even when her baby was taken by the heels and brained against a wagon.

Another emigrant company hove into view. The Indians ran for the willows, dropping much of their plunder as they ran. A part of that plunder the emigrants found as they came up, the long dark strands of hair matted with blood and dust. It was Mrs. Holloway's scalp.

Although at first they thought her dead, the woman was living when the emigrants reached her. She was semi-conscious even, though incapable of speech. As they carried her west to California, she recovered strength, the wounds healing. For a time she seemed to have recovered. From the hair of her recovered scalp a wig was made which she wore inconspicuously. But the agony and the terror dwelt within her mind. As the months passed, she lost her hold upon reality. Quietly mad, she died in Napa City.

Travelers along the Humboldt heard what had happened to the Holloways. And were the Indians solely to blame? There were tales told along the trail . . . of desperadoes from California who preyed upon those who traveled this highroad of the nation . . . of renegade Mormons murdering and robbing Gentile and Saint alike. Attacked trains swore that they had heard the voices of men who talked English freely. Wagonloads of ammunition, it was said, were carried by white men in league with the savages. Were these merely rumors of the sagebrush?

As early as May, 1852, Major Jacob H. Holeman, Indian agent at Great Salt Lake City, wondered about that. He scrawled a note to the Commissioner of Indian Affairs:

"I have been informed this morning that a Mr. Williams received a letter from a friend of his, a Mormon, stating that he is associated with a company of white men and Indians who are stationed near Carson Valley, and that their object is to plunder and rob the emigrants. He advises Williams, who is a Mormon also, to paint the horns of his cattle so that

he may be known, as they do not wish to molest the brethren.
. . . We ought to have troops here." Ten days later he wrote
again: "I have . . . learned that the individual who made
the communication to Mr. Williams is a notorious character
by the name of Reading; and although he was once a member
of the Mormon Church, he is now held by them in utter
contempt, and looked upon as a great scoundrel, but in consequence of some act of personal friendship which was shown
him by Mr. Williams previously he has given him this. . . .
From what I can learn there is no doubt of the existence of
the band, and that their object is to plunder the emigrants,
and all who travel that road leading from the states to California, at or near the Humboldt or Mary's River, beyond
which the principal robberies are committed."

He ended this letter on an insistent note: "We want a
few troops on this route very badly. The *white* Indians, I
apprehend, are much more dangerous than the *red*. The renegades, deserters and thieves, who have had to fly from justice
to California, have taken refuge in the mountains, and having
associated themselves with the Indians are more savage than
the Indians themselves. By their cruelty to the whites, they
have stimulated the Indians to acts of barbarity, which they
were never known to be guilty of before. . . .''

The tale of this villainy is a hidden one and Major
Holeman brought no further light to bear upon it. Renegades
from California leagued with the Indians remain murderous
presences of the night. But outcast Mormons become looters
brought to the Humboldt, ironically, the first white settlement in all its great basin.

Nauvoo, the Beautiful, had risen along the banks of the
Mississippi like a city evoked by Aladdin. In five years the
Mormons made Nauvoo the largest city in Illinois. Every boat
that came up the Mississippi brought its quota of Saints, and
many came by the overland roads. Nor was it only the right-

eous in heart who gathered to Israel. Thieves and blacklegs came also, bogus-passers and murderers. Organized gangs had long looted and murdered up and down the Mississippi Valley, and these found Nauvoo a useful cloak for their activities. If the Mormons were accounted to blame for their operations, why, so much the better!

On Devil Creek, in Iowa across the river from Nauvoo, old George Grant Redden located with his wife and their sons, William H., John, Return Jackson (Jack), and George Jr. Tales about them got around. "Not honorable," his fellow thieves judged Jack; he wouldn't share the spoils rightfully. Old Grant Redden, however, was considered "a fine old fellow. He always keeps the boys when they want to stop with him; and let's them pay up when they are a mind to." The oldest son, William, who lived at home and did not travel much, was accounted more honorable than Jack.

Some guests who stayed with the Reddens at the end of June, 1845, hatched out a robbery that turned out badly. Colonel George Davenport was killed at Rock Island, and by September a detective, Edward Bonney, had the murderers in jail. Old Grant and his son William were arrested as accessories before and after the fact, while Jack narrowly escaped arrest. At the first trial of the Reddens, the jury disagreed; at the second, in February, 1846, William Redden was sentenced to the Illinois state penitentiary for a year. His father, released for lack of evidence, "made tracks on the Mormon trail" west across Iowa.

The company that Brigham Young led out of Illinois was a motley one. God-fearing, righteous Saints rubbed elbows with bogus-passers and blacklegs of all kinds. Conscientious William Clayton and Norton Jacob were companions of Old Grant Redden . . . and Tom Williams, and Peter Haws and his sons. Peter Haws, an early Canadian convert, had been named in Joseph Smith's revelation respecting the building of the Nauvoo Temple; yet upon investigating an uproar in camp one day, Brigham learned that Peter, Tom Williams, and several others were quarreling over the proceeds of bogus-passing operations; Peter had let Tom have some bogus on shares, and he had not remitted his share of the profits. Brigham called down maledictions on their heads. "Unless you repent and forsake such dishonesty, the hand of the Lord will be against you and all who partake of such corruption." Brigham had, indeed, no patience for bogus-passers. "There are those in Camp," he had already observed, "who are passing counterfeit money and have done it all the time since the Saints left Nauvoo, and there are men among us who will steal. Some plead suffering from persecution as an excuse, and say they are justified in stealing from the enemies of the Saints because they have robbed them, but such a course tends to destroy the kingdom of God."

Jack Redden, who perhaps was a Saint only on Sunday, did not take these fulminations too seriously, for in July, 1848, Jim Bridger, aye, Old Gabe himself, had to indite a melancholy letter to the Saints in Salt Lake Valley: "A man in your valley by the name of Jack Redding . . . passed two five dollar bogos pieces upon us last fall." Old Gabe had proved himself more than a match for Blackfoot, Arapahoe, and Apache, but all this trail wisdom availed nothing with his own countrymen. Evil days had fallen upon the West when Old Gabe must bite upon coins like any country store-keeper.

The trails of the West afforded the Reddens abundant opportunity for their talents. John Redden soon located in Jack's Valley, not far from Reese's Mormon Station, and the other Reddens established themselves near Salt Lake Valley.

So stories came to the ears of Major Holeman, and letters addressed to Thomas S. Williams, Esq., advised painting the horns of cattle moving over the Humboldt trail. Now and then something went wrong, as when, for three months in 1854, Jack Redden was jailed at Great Salt Lake City for horse stealing. But the hazards experienced by the Reddens seem not to have been very disconcerting.

There is almost a genealogy in this rapine and murder along the Humboldt. The third wife of Jack Redden was a sister of Carlos Murray, who also had come West with the Pioneer Company of 1847, and in the same Company of Ten as Redden. Carlos, described as an undersized young man with ruddy complexion and fiery red beard, by no means prepossessing, did not need any tutelage in the occupations of the night; rumors soon began to accumulate about his activities along the Southern Trail as well as along the Humboldt.

And finally, ripening this unlovely genealogy, Carlos married a daughter of Peter Haws. Brigham had been by no means first to find fault with the moral development of the Haws family; Joseph Smith had told Peter roundly, in March, 1843, that he must correct his boys, for if he "did not curtail them in their wickedness, they would eventually go to prison." Eleven years later the sons had not gone to prison and neither had they been curtailed in their wickedness.

In '49 or soon thereafter Peter made the trek to Salt Lake Valley. For several years he made a livelihood at whisky-making, but it was harder all the time to get along with Brigham Young, and in the summer of 1854 Peter removed to a fertile location on a creek flowing into the South Fork of the Humboldt, below the Humboldt Wells. Here the Haws set about making the first settlement anywhere along its winding course. One son, Alpheus, and brother-in-law Carlos Murray devoted most of their time to their trading post on the river. Peter, however, was a man of sound farming instincts. While the young men cultivated the local Shoshone chiefs, Peter occupied himself with the soil. His garden grew potatoes, corn, cucumbers, watermelons, squash, pumpkins, peas, beans, turnips, and onions; and wheat soon waved near by. A corral confined the cattle and sheep at night, and the long cabin of cottonwood logs had two large chimneys. There was for perhaps 250 miles in any direction no other permanent dwelling.

Looking upon the bluff old man and this very tangible fruit of faith and hard work, men were loath to believe all that they heard about the Haws. Orson Hyde stopped off at Peter's in May, 1855, en route to Carson Valley and was frankly delighted with what he saw. "Mr. H. has managed to secure the confidence of the Indians to a great degree. He appears to apprehend no danger from them. His stock roams unherded and unguarded without molestation, unless by some strange and transient Indians. He keeps no locks upon his doors; but the strings hang out day and night. He has succeeded in restraining them to a good degree from committing depredations upon the whites as they pass. . . . Mr. Haws is very anxious that the [Indian] agent come out here with his own interpreter, and stay during the season of emigration, and make himself acquainted with things as they are, as some have felt to censure him with being colleagued with the Indians in robbing emigrants. This, so far as I can discover, is unjust and cruel."

The new Indian Agent, Dr. Garland Hurt, who came to Peter's ranch in August, 1855, to negotiate with the Indians of the upper Humboldt a treaty which the government never got around to ratifying, was quite as impressed with Peter's accomplishments. On returning to Great Salt Lake City his aide reported that this section of country was very beautiful and would afford "a settlement for five to six thousand inhabitants, there being plenty of water for irrigation, timber in abundance, and the soil inferior to none in the Territory— fine mill sites, and plenty of grazing land for stock." Alpheus had acted as Hurt's interpreter and things had gone most agreeably. It was hard to credit the doubtful tales. Jules Remy, an eastbound traveler, found Peter "worthy of admiration for the fervour he displayed in his sermons" on

Mormonism, and could not believe that so substantial a fellow knowingly harbored ruffians like Carlos Murray.

Yet Oliver B. and Clark Allen Huntington, who in the fall of 1854 ventured to explore a new route to Carson Valley south of the Humboldt, knew their venture was made in peril of their lives, for Allen and Alpheus Haws had coldly agreed in Great Salt Lake City that next time their paths crossed one or the other should die; and Indians through whose territory they passed were banded with whites by secret oaths, signs, and passwords.

For all these tales, it was November, 1855, before the long arm of the law plucked up Murray by the hair of his red head and set him down in a courtroom.

For murder of an Indian a posse was dispatched after Carlos on October 31, 1855. Bill Hickman, now returned to Zion, says that the writ was put into his hands, and with a posse of forty men he "went, found, arrested, and brought Murray to Salt Lake City," getting back in town on December 1st. In February, the case of the *United States* v. *Carlos Murray*, "for the murder of an Indian in Thousand Spring Valley," was brought up before the District Court in Great Salt Lake City. Ironically, Bill Hickman was one of the three lawyers to whom Carlos entrusted his defense. Another of the legal battery was Tom Williams, who wore a frock coat and carried into court his solidifying dignity as Thomas S. Williams, man of affairs.

The prosecution had no good evidence, and the defense did not bother to introduce any evidence whatever; the jury quickly returned a verdict of not guilty.

Carlos returned to the lonely outpost on the Humboldt. With him, evidently, went George Redden, youngest of Old Grant's sons. In May they rode east toward Great Salt Lake City, in company with Carlos' wife. As they reached Thousand Springs Valley, they were shot down by tribesmen of the Indian Carlos had slain. The howling Indians closed in to rip from the dead their clothes, jewelry, and scalps.

So ended the first settlement on the Humboldt. The Haws fled west toward California. For a while rumor told of their activities smuggling arms and ammunition to the red wolves in the Humboldt Valley. In November, 1862, a Mormon leader pronounced a valedictory upon them. "Hawes . . . has not kept the Faith—he and his sons lived some time on the Humboldt River, 200 miles from any settlement, with the reputation of adding murder and robbery of emigrants to their other enormities. We understand that Peter is dead, and his boys to be in California, the possessors of no enviable reputation, as the scene of their exploits on the Humboldt had become too dangerous for them."

Long after, in 1899, Oliver Huntington encountered Alpheus Haws once more, in Oakland.

"We visited Alpheus Haws, the man who, in 1854, had the Indians on Humboldt River and in Ruby Valley banded together with secret signs and pass word, like the robbers of old, and he laid a plan to murder me and my traveling partners . . . I could but keep thinking how the Lord delivered me from the death he had planned for me by the Indians. He told us what a sufferer he had been for 15 years, how he had been cut open 13 times for stones in the bladder, and had not made water naturally in 2 years. We chatted together like other men but he could not hold his eyes on mine—was uneasy under my gaze for he had sought my life yet I felt no bitterness towards him for he was a terrible sufferer."

No comfortable moral of retribution cloaks the Reddens. Except for Jack, they drop from history with the violent death of George in Thousand Springs Valley. A citizen of Utah the rest of his days, Jack was, once in Tooele County and thrice in Summit County, a justice of the peace. He died in 1891, revered by posterity as a monument to all the respectabilities of life.

. . . So the tales of violence along the Humboldt in the fifties, the river valley sudden with the hazards of the frontier.

XV

The Short Route

DEATH and alkali and everlasting barrenness. A river that flooded the trail in spring and choked upon its own dryness at other seasons. A river, too, that flowed west quite irresponsibly, with a great, useless elbow bend that added distance and multiplied hazards. Frontiersmen of the fifties began to question whether southern desert valleys might not offer a "central route" to Carson better than the Humboldt trail.

The Mormons, who rode in twos and threes and dozens into the desert spaces east, south, and west of Great Salt Lake City, early wondered whether trails were irrevocably bound to the Humboldt. In April, 1853, E. L. Barnard advised the

Saints that a company was soon to be sent to explore a new route, and in the same issue of the *Deseret News* Seth M. Blair intimated that explorations were already in progress. Jack Redden displayed a discouraging interest in the idea; in December, 1853, he informed the *News* that he was convinced a new road, shorter by 250 miles than that of the Humboldt, could be found west from the south shore of Great Salt Lake; he had explored in October as far as the southern reaches of the salt desert, but having heard that Indians planned to attack the settlements, he had returned to give warning. Having done his duty by the citizenry, he was about to set out anew.

No more is heard of these projected explorations. It remained for Lieutenant E. G. Beckwith, commanding an expedition dispatched by the War Department to examine Pacific railroad routes, to make the first constructive exploration of the mountain-desert south of the Humboldt.

Beckwith left Great Salt Lake City on May 5, 1854. Separating in Skull Valley from the Frémont-Hastings trail, he struck out across the salt desert almost southwesterly for the Goshute Mountains, then proceeded northwesterly to a stream flowing from the eastern slopes of the Ruby Mountains; he named it the Franklin, and found that he had fallen once more into Hastings' road. Seeing no better trail, Beckwith followed the famous cutoff to the southern end of the Rubies; then, as the Hastings road meekly descended the South Fork toward the Humboldt, he struck off into the jumbled country west.

It soon became obvious that no railroad would care to climb the innumerable short ranges; and Frémont had already enthusiastically commended the Humboldt route. Beckwith veered northwest and came out on the Humboldt at Lassen's Meadows, halfway between the Big Bend and the Sink. The journey had not been hard; streams that in late summer might be mere dry throats were filled with the spring runoff, and springs were sufficiently abundant. Encounters with the Diggers enlivened the otherwise rather dull passage; uniformly they were filthy, emaciated by starvation, apprehensive, and "very" naked. Making them happy with kettles of soup and small presents, he enlisted their services in his trail finding.

Crossing the Humboldt and adding his endorsement to the recommendation that the railroad follow its valley, Beckwith pursued his instructions west into the Sierra Nevada, leaving to others the problem of locating a route to Carson.

Lieutenant Colonel E. J. Steptoe wintered with an army detachment at Great Salt Lake City and decided to go west next spring by a new route if one could be found. Brigham Young suggested as guides Oliver B. and Clark Allen Huntington. John Reese went also with two employees. The sixth member of the party was an Indian.

They started September 18th. A couple of miles outside the city they were overtaken by eleven teamsters. The men had only a horse apiece, and half rations, but the explorers finally accepted them into the company.

It suited them to follow Beckwith's trail until Antelope Springs, where he had veered toward Franklin River. They rode directly southwest and a day's travel brought them into the Hastings road; they congratulated themselves on having saved four days' travel.

One of the company, Davis, thought that gold was to be found in these mountains. During the noon halt a little dirt was panned but instead of gold the pan yielded several "rubies"—garnets—"one very large and fine." Rations were already short and this was no time to go to mining, but the company fixed on this valley and these mountains the name Ruby.

In the afternoon two Indians tried to cut Davis off. His horse outran them to camp, which had been made early and in an open location, out of some foreboding of evil. As they were sitting down to an early supper, seven haughty Indians rode up and dismounted near the fire. All were dressed in white clothes, and their horses were well shod. Their leader, who wore a grotesque Panama hat, could talk English. "I felt," says Oliver Huntington, "that under the Panama hat was a dreadful chief for blood and plunder, and that he could talk English, and I was right in my judgment or feelings."

Drawing his uncle aside, Allen Huntington asked whether he had not observed the Indian to make a secret sign, a strange motion, as he shook hands. "I believe these are the Indians who have murdered so many men along the Humboldt. They're banded with whites by secret oaths, signs, and passwords." He was thinking of Alpheus Haws, from whom he had parted fourteen days ago in Great Salt Lake City.

"I felt a strange but bright sensation come over my mind," says Oliver, "and I could see with my heart, or my spirit could see without my eyes. I told him we would leave the horses and go quickly to camp, where he should go up to that Indian, give him the same sign he had given us, and that we would be safe among them."

The effect was astonishing. The Indian shook hands warmly and flung his arms around him. Warily, then, they talked to the Indian about Haws: "Every word had its effect as I anticipated," Oliver says, "and the chief understood that this man who lived on the Humboldt, and whom very many believed to be the cause of all the murdering done there for money and plunder, was our friend from boyhood. . . . The chief called that man his 'daddy,' meaning father."

Frankly the Huntingtons said that they were returning in a little more than one moon. It did not seem necessary to add that there would only be three of them on the back trail. Next morning the Indians escorted them eight miles, giving what information they could about the route ahead. But it was not pleasant to contemplate returning.

Alarming inroads had been made on the provisions. This was no time for cutoffs and adventures; they stuck to Beckwith's trail. Even before they reached the Humboldt, they had to kill a horse. Luckily, descending the Humboldt, they stumbled on a lame cow; the meat lasted them to Carson Valley. Altogether, it had not been a pleasant journey. "The poisonous effects of the water of the Humboldt," the Huntingtons reported later, "can hardly be believed except by sad experience. We came near losing all our animals by it, as well as our own lives, and could sensibly feel its poisonous influence within ten minutes after drinking, as we can feel the cheering influence of a cup of good strong tea."

Reese's Mormon Station was reached October 15th. Oliver had been pretty badly used up by the last stages of the trip, and he, like Allen, was glad to rest there before beginning the return journey. Their Indian disappeared, and they thought perhaps he had been killed by one of the local Indians, but a man who came up from Ragtown said he had seen the Indian, barefoot and bareheaded, footing it back to Brigham Young's wickiup. Actually, alone and on foot, he got back to Salt Lake Valley before the Huntingtons.

By November 2nd Reese had outfitted them for the return trip, and with some apprehension lest snow mask the way, six men set out from Mormon Station. Reese's partner, Stephen A. Kinsey, intended to go the whole route, while Reese himself with two men proposed to travel the first two hundred miles.

They took the emigrant road down the Carson to Ragtown, and there struck into the unknown, intending to follow the river to its sink, thence south and east to intersect the southernmost point of Beckwith's trail.

About eighty miles out, the company was augmented by a fellow named Davis who had a large herd of sheep wintering in Salt Lake Valley.

The sand desert east of the Sink promised little, but

Oliver collared two Indians who were wild enough to run from him; these finally disclosed a spring, which welled from the ground only ten feet from where Oliver had left the company to chase the Indians, and within thirty rods of where he had caught them.

It was thirty-six hours before they could water the animals again. Twice, from the trails of Indians, hares, coyotes, and antelope, they judged they must be near water, but they were not equal to finding it. It was the horses, finally, who found water, a swift-running desert brook hardly three feet wide. Next day they struggled futilely to cross a mountain range blocking their eastern path. Just at nightfall two Diggers trotted up, and with one of these Allen could talk in Snake. This Indian demonstrated his good character by leading the white men to water. That night he told them of a canyon by which to continue their travel east; by morning, however, he had vanished, and a new blanket with him.

Next morning the little company divided, after eating two boxes of sardines. Reese decided to explore a range of valleys north, which he thought might offer a trail to the Humboldt; the way he went never became important to emigration, but affixed his name to long Reese River, which flows into the Humboldt near Battle Mountain. The parting was on the west slopes of the Toiyabe Mountains. With his three companions, Oliver Huntington continued east, and a day and a half later the party came shouting into their outbound trail.

But Indians watched them from the craggy canyon. Slowly they rode toward the rocky trail they must climb, saying dolefully that a coward cornered is the worst man in the world to fight, and that they should give an account of themselves if they had to. However, by "talking and preaching to the natives half an hour or more," Allen inveigled them out of hiding. The Indians were given presents and persuaded to go on to camp, where they should be given more valuable presents.

The Diggers' bows and arrows were sequestered when camp was made at a large spring. Oliver thought the time opportune to teach these children of nature something about guns. Going into a narrow ravine, he cut from his journal a couple of leaves, doubled them, shot a hole through the center, and cut them in two. One of the leaves he secretly gave to Kinsey. Now uncle and nephew began to argue loudly. When the Indians wanted to know what all the uproar was about, Allen said that Oliver was boasting about his prowess with a gun.

Vastly edified, the Indians watched while Oliver took a leaf from his journal, folded and cut it, and put it in the cleft of a three-foot stick. Kinsey walked a third of a mile off, switching papers along the way, and planted the stick in the baked earth. Allen then pulled out his dragoon revolver, squinted expertly, and shot.

An Indian was sent for the mark. He came back on the run, gabbling his amazement. "The Indians," says Oliver, "all joined in the talk but superstitiously avoided touching the paper. I could not, of course, shoot better than that and therefore did not try."

In the morning one of the Indians who "lived over that way" volunteered to guide them, and all during the day he ran beside the galloping horses. Their respect for him, however, vanished in the middle of the night, along with two blankets.

His tracks were plain in the trail next morning, and the four whites rode on with forebodings. They were no more than a day and a half's ride from the south end of Ruby Valley, and no more than two and a half from the north end, where most of the Indians were gathered.

Next day, Oliver says, the eyes of his understanding were opened to see where he could make a very great cutoff;

he proposed to his companions that they make direct for a low ridge. Believing the Lord had taken a hand in their affairs, they made for the ridge, and encamped after nightfall "without any fire or noise," perhaps ten miles from the summit.

About midday on the 19th they made their way down into Ruby Valley. South they could see twisting columns of smoke—signal fires. Riding hard, they got across the valley to a little mountain basin through which they had come westbound. As they rode down into the basin, they suddenly saw seven Indians.

They had to have water, even if it meant fighting for it. Allen resolved upon some overtures. "If they'll smoke with us, they'll talk and if they'll talk, we can be friends and learn something."

The Indians were willing to smoke. After the oldest man had smoked tranquilly for a time, he asked with a suddenly revealed astonishment where they had come from. Allen pointed out the trail, and the wrinkled old man nodded sagely. "That is the only way you could come."

He told them that the chief in the gaudy Panama hat had called out all the fighting men, and they now lay in ambush at the south end of the valley, expecting the return of the whole seventeen men.

"Why didn't you go?" Allen demanded.

From his rags the wizened old man produced a piece of tobacco about an inch and a half square. "You gave me this tobacco," he said, "and I could not fight you as long as that lasted."

Allen looked at the dirty brown plug. "What if it had been all gone?"

The old man, according to Oliver, had as mild and pleasant eyes as any Indian ever had, and at this he raised them with as much honesty and simplicity as a child; after looking in the fire a moment, he said, "I don't know what I would have done."

The other six Indians were sons and sons-in-law of the old man, and he had kept them all from joining in the ambush. Oliver and Allen got into another impressive argument about their shooting prowess; they smoked again with the Indians, had something to eat, and listened to parting advice. By sunrise the whites must be far to the east, for the Indians here would get on their track.

No other hint was needed. The company rode until nightfall, made a false camp, and drove hard to Antelope Springs. There were no further difficulties. On November 26th they called at Brigham Young's office, made their report, and then went around to account for themselves to Colonel Steptoe. Immediately thereafter the Huntingtons made a third report, to the Mormon community in the *Deseret News:*

"This whole route is well supplied with grass—no drive over thirty miles without water in the dryest season of the year, and, in the early part of emigration, it is plenty in all the mountain rills. Wood and sage brush are abundant.

"Added to these advantages, we avoid the Humboldt, and alkali in general, and we are confident we can reach Carson Valley by this route inside of 500 miles, and that soon this will be the main thoroughfare for California immigration."

Oliver wrote up his logbook into a guidebook, and turned it over to William H. Hooper, Utah's current delegate to Congress, with the understanding he should receive half the profits resulting from publication. The guidebook apparently was never published and is lost.

The Huntingtons reported to Steptoe their entire faith in the route they had found. By spring, however, Allen's father, the noted interpreter Dimick B. Huntington, had got into an altercation with the federal officers, and their viewpoint on the Huntington family suffered somewhat from jaundice. "Steptoe with his troops," Oliver says, "left the City on the 29th April, 1855, for California by the north route having been turned from their purpose of going the desert west route, by O. P. Rockwell, and Geo Been who were sent out to explore a portion of the route and pronounced it impassable, more as enemies to our family than friends to improvements."

However, George Washington Bean, a faithful Mormon scout, says that he "found the upper end of Salt Lake Desert very wet & miry for several miles. consequently deemed it impracticable & so reported it to the Col."

The "short route," nevertheless, was an idea that drew men of adventurous blood. Mormons, alone and by twos and threes, strayed off into the deserts west of the Tooele settlements to see what they could see. Howard Egan, who has been called "the Mormon centaur" from the fact that he almost lived in the saddle, has been credited with finding an Egan trail to Carson, but Egan stuck mostly to Beckwith's trail and his pathfinding was principally confined to hunting new passes through the Ruby Mountains.

In June, 1855, Thomas Pitt and George Tyler came east from Carson Valley, like others after them, by a "short route" evidently the same as the Huntington trail; while Pitt and Tyler were riding east, other Mormons, to the south, were exploring westward into the desert valleys; their object, however, was not to find a trail to Carson but to judge whether an Indian mission should be established among the Diggers near a range the Mormons called "the White Mountains." Bishop David Evans reported to Brigham Young that the Indians they found near the White Mountains had never seen whites before. "These Indians know nothing only what they know naturally; their food is snakes, roots, locusts, and reptiles of every kind, in short every and anything that hogs will eat, and some things that hogs will not eat, such as dogs, cats, &c. We killed a large wild cat, and gave to them,

and they eat it insides and all." E. G. Williams added a post-
script for trailmakers: "I am well satisfied that no man nor
set of men have any business to travel that route without
competent guides, as the water, what little there is, is in such
by and sequestered spots, that no one would be likely to
observe it."

This was observation all too competent for the whole
of the country south of the Humboldt. It was country hard-
handed and grudging. Sage marched in the valleys up the
tangled slopes of the mountain ranges which impartially
baked one side in the morning and the other in the afternoon.
It was a beautiful country; the emigrants who toiled down
the Humboldt would gladly have made trails south into the
valleys, wrenched up the sage, and driven their plows into
the soil . . . had there been rain. But this was the country
of the Humboldt, the country of the Desert River.

Once more the Mormons tried to find a promising desert
route. Seth M. Blair was asked to take a company and lay
out a good trail to Ruby Valley. Taking with him Oliver
Huntington and some eighteen others, he explored for several
weeks in the vicinity of Deep Creek Valley, but returned to
report that he had been quite unable to find a new route to
Carson.

When, finally, a desert route was laid out in Carson
Valley, it resulted from the explorations of another army
officer. In the fall of 1858 Captain J. H. Simpson, exploring
westerly from the new military post at Camp Floyd, discovered a practicable wagon road to the Thomas Mountains,
some eighty-five miles distant. Through the winter Howard
Egan, exploring for Chorpenning's mail company, carried
that route on to Ruby Valley. Captain Simpson learned next
May, when he resumed his own explorations, that Egan had
"tried twice to get south from Ruby Valley, toward Genoa,
in Carson Valley, but was once defeated by the snow, and
once business in Salt Lake City diverted him." The mail

route had adopted Hastings' road down the South Fork of the Humboldt to reach the Humboldt at Gravelly Ford. Disliking both Hastings' and Beckwith's trails for their final reliance on the Humboldt, Simpson struck off southwesterly. John Reese, his guide, was energetic in scouting out the country, but even when the party arrived at Reese River he had to acknowledge that his memory of the country had so faded that they could put little reliance upon it.

The little company with its wagons forged ahead; water somehow always found at reasonable distances, with grass and some timber also, they reached the Carson in June. Simpson was delighted, contrasting the 565 miles of his route to the 853 miles of the City of Rocks-Humboldt trail and the 689 miles of the mail road. Here, he felt, was a logical path not only for the mail and wagons but also for the magnetic telegraph.

Simpson soon returned east. Going still more southerly, he shaved a few more miles off the route, but in the end it was largely his outbound trail that came into general use. It was not a trail without disadvantages; it was generally much drier than Simpson had found it, and feed was more scarce. But by 1859 civilization was reaching the country of the Humboldt; capital was available to prospect for wells and put up mail stations. Simpson's became, at last, the Overland Stage Route linking West with East until there could be a railroad.

XVI

Retreat to Zion

Looking out upon South Temple Street on this morning of August 15, 1857, Brigham Young saw young men galloping down toward Main Street in clouds of dust. Freighters cracked their whips above the heads of straining yoked oxen. Sisters in faded sunbonnets walked past en route to the Tithing Office store. The sun broiled the earth as usual, and reflected brightly from the running water across the street. Life had not quickened for his people in these three weeks except in their hearts.

At Silver Lake on July 24th he had announced the news of the day. The United States was sending an army to Utah to crush "rebellion" here. They had always known that it would come, the world rising in the last days to destroy Israel in the mountains. Ten years ago he had stood upon the Salt Lake plain and promised them: "Give us ten years of peace and we will ask no odds of the United States!" God had vouchsafed them the ten years.

But as the soldiers of the Saints rode up Emigration Canyon toward the Wyoming plains, the children of God must be gathered into the mountains. The missionaries in Europe and the States must come home. The San Bernardino and Carson Valley missions must end. The Lion of the Lord, ready for the climactic struggle of his life, signed a letter directing that an express be sent to Carson. Peter Conover, George Bean, and some eight or ten others should make the trip. Conover would be in charge, and Oliver Huntington and Lyman Carter would be the guides. They should go by the Desert Route.

They rendezvoused in Rush Valley on August 18th. In all there were sixteen men; and Oliver had told Brigham that it would take sixteen or eighteen days of the hardest kind of driving. They carried provisions for twenty days. The Desert Route had been chosen because the Snakes were too hostile this year on the Humboldt; and the Desert Route, though waterless for long stretches, was shortest.

The company made fifteen miles before nightfall on August 19th, and next day struck southwest across the salt desert to Granite Rock, and to springs found years ago by Jack Redden. As fast and as direct as they could travel, they made for Ruby Valley. On September 24th, as the sun went down, they camped in the Ruby Mountains. Water was getting harder to find. On the 25th they spent the entire night watering a part of their animals with four quarts each. The next day they found no water at the usual watering place, but during the night, by digging with sticks and knives, the guard found water, and all the animals got a little to drink.

This was grueling work, and all the men ate with starved appetites. The twenty days' provisions shrank so fast, Oliver Huntington says, that they curtailed their appetites and cooks.

At 2 P.M. on August 29th the company reached what they called Sardine Springs, near the site of Austin. The animals were watered and baited, "but ate nothing ourselves," Huntington says, "as we calculated to stop for the night at Allens Springs 12 miles farther but when we got there found them dry and then near sun down. We had no water to cook so shook our cracker sacks and got a single handful each, of dust which we mixed with water from our canteens and nearly drained them. It was 20 miles to the mouth of the canyon up which 2 or 3 miles was our next water to which we resolved to travel that night and started at sunset with weary animals, dry and hungry men. Traveled until about midnight and tied our animals to sage; laid ourselves down on the ground and slept until morning." Relying on Oliver's assurance that water would be found a dozen miles beyond Sardine Springs, only one man had filled his canteen. Their water was almost gone.

At dawn they set out again. At nine in the morning they reached the mouth of a canyon two or three miles up which water ought to be found; but in this year when the life seemed burnt from everything, Oliver could not be sure that this was the right canyon, and they decided to go on ten or fifteen miles farther to Brook Creek "which was unmistakable and ran down the valley."

"We kept on our course," says Peter Conover, "following our trail, the one the guide had taken years before. Then there was plenty of water." But now the men's tongues swelled until they could hardly keep them in their mouths. And the place where they expected to find water was dry. "Oh! what a sight for perishing men."

It was seventy miles to water ahead, and fifteen or twenty back. Animals and men were nearly finished. Huntington was in the worst straits of all. "He could not see, hear or make a loud sound," Conover says. "There he gave up to die."

Steve Moore and Joe Dudley, whose horses still had something left, started up the wash in search of water. Conover and G. W. Bean followed. And they actually found water. "Oh! what a draught," says Peter. "It seemed like I had never in my whole life tasted anything half so good. I rode my horse right into the water and commenced drinking, then began throwing water on myself and horse. That helped to quench our thirst." As the others came up, he threw water on them. "Dave Canfield came up and began drinking, I was going to throw some on him, when he turned and said if you throw water on me I will shoot you. I laughed at him and said, Why Dave you will kill yourself. It is none of your business if I do, he said. He drank until he could drink no more, then turned and crawled around on the ground. Oh the pain he was in. I called one of the boys to come and help me drag him to the hill. We each took a leg and started up the bank, him kicking and trying hard to get loose. We dragged him to the top of the bank, then the water commenced running out of his mouth like water running out of a hole in a barrel. Then he called for more water and I went and got him a quart, which he drank. . . . We laid him in the shade of a cedar, where he laid like a dog until night. After that he was all right."

Meanwhile Oliver Huntington and the others had waited vainly for a signal smoke. "We lay on the sand in the shade of our animals until sun an hour high in which time every one became quite overcome. I was worst of all and became quite deaf and blind, scarcely able to stand. All my faculties seemed dried up. All watched for the smoke but could see none. No one could see properly, some could not hear well and some could not talk well." Deciding that Moore and Dudley had had time enough to go to the top of the mountain, the men set out on the back trail, leaving Dudley and

Moore to follow their track should they live to see it. They
had traveled a mile when Oliver fell from his horse, "and
awoke struggling for breath and saw all standing or laying
around me. As soon as I could speak told them to bleed a
horse and give me the blood. When the horse was corded the
question was asked where is the place to stick him and it is
said that I stuck my finger in the sand and said 'there.' "

At this moment a column of smoke climbed into the
sky, perhaps a mile and a half distant. All but two left Huntington, and flew for the smoke. Presently Moore was seen
bounding over the high sage like a deer; all thought he was
riding. "Oliver is nearly gone in," the brethren cried, and
Moore rushed on with two canteens. The words "water,
water is coming" roused Oliver and he "sat up, unstopped
the canteen, blessed the water with thanksgiving then blessed
Bro Moore who seeing us turn back took 3 canteens full and
ran towards us about 3 miles when he built the fire we saw.
He had built a large smoke where they found water and there
stayed wondering what we were about. . . . I drank one
swaller at first but could not taste it then in a minute 3 or 4
and so on increasing in numbers every minute or two until
my judgment checked me. I sat and talked until I sensibly
felt my faculties fast returning then rode toward the water
praising God in my soul as I rode along."

They spent the night at the water and all the next day,
killing their poorest horse and jerking the flesh. Huntington
manufactured waterbags from horse intestines and they set
out again an hour before sundown. Some of the pack load-
ings had to be thrown away, and one horse gave out, but
at about eight on September 1st they reached the Sink of
the Carson.

As they were without a mouthful to eat, Conover and
Wesley Wheeler set out for Ragtown, bringing back twenty
pounds of flour, seven of bacon, three of sugar, and two of

coffee. All this was gone after breakfast on the morning of September 3rd, but now they had not far to go.

At Ragtown they learned that a company of Mormons planned to leave on the 5th for the Valley. Conover, Huntington, and one other man set out for Washoe Valley to stop that company. All the Saints, by Brigham's orders, were to return to Zion together.

Conover's party traveled all that day up Carson River, and at dark came to a saloon kept by a man called Dutch John, where they got some crackers and cheese. After supper they left the road to follow an Indian trail over the mountain. About midnight they lost the trail and lay down to sleep till daybreak. . . . Locating the trail, they saddled up and traveled about a mile to reach the summit. The Washoe Valley settlement was outspread below. Peter's horse squealed and from a log cabin under the hill some people came out. Inquiring how far it was to Washoe Valley, Peter was told it was six miles.

They reached the home of the mission president just as Chester Loveland was sitting down to breakfast. He read their message and smiled and asked them in to breakfast. In eighteen blazing, thirsty days they had finished their mission. They would never get a cent out of it. The animals they had lost would not be restored to them. That was all right. Of such works was the Kingdom of God.

Loveland had been instructed to rake up all the money he could find, and turn it over to Conover for ammunition. (It had always been a tenet of the Saints that the Lord helps those who help themselves.) The Saints of Washoe had contributed a considerable sum in tithing, which Loveland had expected to turn over to the Presiding Bishop; this was given to Peter Conover to use as he saw fit. Four or five boys also were sent running about the settlement, announcing a meeting at nine o'clock. The settlers listened with good spirit to the word from Brigham.

After meeting, Loveland unloaded his buggy, hitched his mules to the wagon, and started with Conover for Eagle Valley, some twenty-five miles away; Oliver Huntington rode on to Carson Valley, to carry the word to the brethren there and to send off the California mail. At two in the afternoon the Eagle Valley settlers gathered to listen to Conover and their president. They must return to Salt Lake; they must furnish all the guns and ammunition they could; they must donate what they could to buy powder. This was not a large branch, but it made a generous donation.

Their job still not done, Conover and Loveland set out for Genoa. The Saints here were not behind their fellow missionaries. Conover now had a substantial sum for Israel.

Next morning one of the Saints living in Genoa was dispatched to San Francisco to buy the ammunition. He was to deliver it to Stockton by steamboat along with 12,000 pounds of his own goods. The Carson Valley Saints would freight it from Stockton.

But, Conover discovered, the people concluded that if they had to move to the Valley, they had no more teams than they needed themselves. After four days, Peter consulted with the authorities. It was agreed that horses, saddles, blankets, and other necessities should be furnished and that Conover with Oliver Huntington should cross the Sierras for the ammunition.

Nelson Hollingshead and another young Saint went with them, as the Indians lately had been bad in the Sierra. In two days they reached Angels' Camp on the west slope of the Sierra. The tavernkeeper received the company kindly, after they produced a letter of introduction from a mutual friend, and of him, next morning, Conover made inquiry about Robert Walker, who had undertaken the mission to San Francisco. "I'd give almost anything to hear from him," Conover fretted.

The tavernkeeper grinned largely. "Would you give

two dollars and a half? I can get ahold of him for you in an hour."

The telegraph, it developed, had reached Angels' Camp. In ten minutes there was word from San Francisco: GOT ALL I WENT FOR HAVE IT ALL READY TO BE SHIPPED ON STEAM-BOAT WALKER.

Peter decided they would do well to wait here. Two days later he picked up a late copy of a Sacramento paper and read that General Harney, who had started on July 22nd with an enormous force to subdue the Mormons, had had a fight with Mormons, had lost 600 men, and had gone back for reinforcements. Further, the Mormons had sent to California for $2,000 worth of ammunition, and as many pistols and guns. The governor of California had issued orders to stop them at Angels' Camp.

"What's up now?" demanded Travers, the tavernkeeper, at the sound of Peter's guffaws.

"This damned lie in the paper."

Travers came over to read the news. "How do you know it's a lie?"

"Because," said Peter, "I started out on the 17th, and the Mormons were all at home, minding their own business." At a venture he gave a Masonic sign. Travers returned it.

"John," said Peter Conover, "two heads are better than one—"

They went into a back room and Peter told him all about it, how he had come, what he had come for.

Slowly Travers said, "You have paid for it and you shall have it. It's a shame you should have such a time after buying anything from the government, to have it taken away by the government. If I have influence enough to get it for you, you shall have what you have bought."

In the morning Travers gave Conover the key to his warehouse. Peter went in to breakfast, and the newly arrived newspapers bore headlines even more excited than yesterday's. Behind his back the miners talked with glances in his direction. Peter realized that they were planning to take the ammunition away from him.

Two nights later, in a rainstorm, the wagons rumbled up with the ammunition. As Peter's men roused, he opened the gate and let the wagons in. The trail wagon was run into the warehouse immediately and locked inside. Then, dexterously, Conover took the hind endgate out of one of the big wagons loaded with Walker's goods.

A door slammed, and some fifty men thronged out into the rain. "Gentlemen," Conover said, "thank you for coming out to help me; you're just in time. I want to get away as soon as I can."

A burly miner growled. "What we come out here for is the ammunition." Nevertheless, he lent a hand at lifting down a big barrel of whisky. After weighing it, Conover directed that it be set on a platform. Taking a big auger, he bored a hole and drew out a bucketful. "All hands," he roared.

Everybody had a drink, then the miner and Conover climbed into the wagon and commenced handing out the goods; Walker directed the loading into the other wagons. "The Captain," Conover says of the miner, "did not know anything about carrying powder in boxes, so we handed out the cases of canister the same as the other goods, and kept on until we had it all unloaded and loaded into the other wagons. It was now about 11 o'clock at night. The Captain was very much disappointed at not finding a keg of powder in the wagon and got very mad over it and swore that if he had the man who printed that newspaper he would hang him in a minute, for there was not a pound of ammunition, nor a gun, nor a pistol."

The miners began to move off by twos and threes. Finally only Conover's men remained. He rolled out the trail wagon. Two small wagons had been reserved for the ammunition, and quickly they were loaded. The skies had cleared now, and the moon had turned the world to silver. The teams were hitched up and the wagons started east. Huntington, Conover, and Walker, however, turned in for the night, to settle with Travers and get some breakfast.

Next morning the miner came up to Conover. "What," he demanded, "are you going to do with the guns and ammunition you bought?"

"What I've bought is mine, and it's none of your damned business what I've done with it," Conover grunted.

"Well, I'll see you before you get to Carson."

"If you follow me," Conover promised, "I'll bury you without a sheet."

He set off. It took three days to double-team the wagons to the summit, but there was no trouble with the descent to Carson, and the explosive cargo came safe to Washoe Valley.

The whole population was on the move. Over four hundred had sacrificed their property for anything they could get and now were ready to abandon to the unrighteous this land at the far end of the Humboldt trail. In all, Oliver Huntington says, 130 wagons rolled out from Eagle Valley on September 22, 1857, "embracing every good Mormon within our reach and time, either in the valleys about Carson or California."

"The camp had moved out about four miles on the road," Peter Conover relates; "we went on and overtook them that night. I went to the President to know about getting wagons to haul the ammunition in the rest of the way. He said they had not a spare wagon. Every one was loaded to the bows." But Peter was persistent and finally ironed out his transportation problem, with the aid of a few faithful Saints.

So they started for home. On the third day they reached Ragtown. Taking all the water they could carry, they set out on the desert at four in the afternoon. They drove hard, and at noon next day reached the Sink of the Humboldt. And it was here that they were overtaken by Gentiles who had determined that arms and ammunition should not be carried to the Mormon fastnesses in the mountains.

"Before we got supper ready," Conover tells the tale, "the men that had been sent to take our ammunition away from us came to camp. They tried to stampede our horses, but we were on our guard. I told the guard to hollow every hour or half-hour. This they did lustily. They could have been heard half over the world it seemed to me.

"When I went to relieve the guard at midnight, three of the men came and wanted to get their horses, as they would rather travel in the night. I told them they could not get their horses, for if they tried to catch them, it would stampede all the horses, that was what they wanted to do. John Murdock said, the first man that swung a lasso in that band of horses was a dead man, and he meant it too. I told the men to come back to camp and stay till morning, then we would get them all right. I put them under guard until morning, then I went to Nickerson and told him I wanted some liquor to treat the men with. I got a quart and held it up and called the six men to come up and we would settle the scrap about the horses.

"They left their breakfast and came up to get their bitters. I handed the bottle to the Captain, and told them to drink heartily as there was plenty. The six men emptied the quart bottle, then they asked me if I would sell them some. I said yes, I would sell them all they could find dishes for. The Captain sent for all the canteens and flasks they had. They each had a canteen and there were five flasks among them. The first thing they handed me was a pint flask. I filled it and they emptied that. I kept on until I had filled all they had. I then asked them if they would sell me some of their guns, as they were going back, as they had told

us they would never follow a Mormon again. They said yes,
they would sell them. We bought all but one pair of re-
volvers, that one young man said were his fathers. They
acknowledged that they had orders from the Missouri Captain to stampede our horses and run them back, but they
were sick of their trip, they then took their horses and
left us."

So the caravan for Zion pulled up the long trail of the
Humboldt, through the dust and the dryness, between the
black basalt hills, the barrenness ever about them. The sun
burst in the morning upon this enchanted world of jagged
mountains, of plains caked white with alkali, of greasewood
stubbornly green in any season, and tall sagebrush that filled
the air with its strangely fragrant stench. The shadows
marched across the earth and were lost in night; the stars
came out, and there was singing about the fires, the clear
soprano of women's voices joined to men's dark bass. In the
hills the coyotes were roused, a lonely, chilling music that
sounded in the night long after the children of Israel lay
close in their wagons and slept.

East of Haws' abandoned ranch, Conover, Huntington,
and four others left the company to strike out as an express
by the Desert Route. It took them seven days; they rode into
town on October 25th, and next morning reported to Brigham. The wagon train began to arrive November 1st, and
by the 3rd all had reported in. Three children had died en
route and six had been born: it might almost have been an
augury, Israel always stronger, triumphant forever in ad-
versity.

The *Deseret News* provided a valedictory: "It is reported
that the gentiles were mad when the 'Mormons' settled in
Carson, and madder still when they left, proving the truth
of the saying that 'the wicked are like a troubled sea, casting
up mire and dirt.' But as they are not pleased with themselves,
how can it be expected that they should be with anybody

else? With them it is, 'life and salvation to do everything to
serve the devil, but death and destruction for the Latter Day
Saints to serve the Lord.' "

The Olive Branch of Israel could not quite let it go at
that. It graveled an apostle of the Lord to yield up his riches
to apostates, blacklegs, and the iniquitous. Some five years
later, out of his firm conviction that the hand of the Lord
had been set, since the breaking out of civil war in South
Carolina in April last (Joseph Smith had prophesied it, and
the woes to be loosed on this generation), Orson Hyde lifted
his voice in solemn warning to the people of Carson and
Washoe valleys. For his sawmill he had received in payment
nothing but promises:

"We have been patient and not murmured. We have
made little or no effort to sell our property there, because
we considered that those who had it thought they were doing
God and themselves a service by wronging the Mormons;
and for me, I felt backward to do anything in the premises
until the Lord should tell me what to do. . . . That time
has now come, and the Lord has signified to me, his unworthy
servant, that as we have been under the circumstances that
compelled us to submit to your terms, that He will place you
under circumstances that will compel you to submit to ours,
or do worse."

If he were paid $20,000 for his mill, all might yet be
well in the western valleys. But lo, this demand, remaining
uncanceled, should be to the people of Carson and Washoe
valleys as the ark of God among the Philistines:

"You shall be visited of the Lord of Hosts with thunder
and with earthquakes and with floods, with pestilence and
with famine until your names are not known amongst men,
for you have rejected the authority of God, trampled upon
his laws and his ordinances, and given yourselves up to serve
the god of this world; to rioting in debauchery, in abominations, drunkenness and corruption. . . .

" 'Behold ye despisers, and wonder and perish! I will work a work in your day—a work which ye shall in no wise believe though a man declare it unto you.' God is now beginning to deal with the inhabitants of the earth for the wrongs which they have done unto his people, and for rejecting his authority and counsel, given forth from Heaven through the Mormons. His dealings with them will be neither light nor on a limited scale. But those who do repent, and make right their wrongs, acknowledge the authority of God in the channel through which he hath sent it, may find mercy and protection in that channel and nowhere else."

So spake God, through his servant Orson, to the people of Washoe in the year 1862. And, indeed, the wrath and the power of God were already manifest.

XVII

The Sulphurets of Silver

THE heights of the Sierra Nevada frown easterly upon a world of jumbled brown and gray desolation. A string of valleys hugs close to the shelter of the Sierran foothills, ribbons of green demarking their brief rivers. The land lifts again eastward of these valleys, as though God, not shirking his duty absolutely, had raised low mountains to provide for the valleys some sort of bulwark against the consuming white and olive desert. A brown bald peak cresting this low range is first to rear itself into the sunrise; a crown of gold is set upon the world and the day is heralded by Sun Peak.

Atop its world, Sun Peak turns its back upon the great California range to brood upon the desert. Eastward the land twists and spills, wide low flats convulsing into mountains that lift at all angles to the sun in tones of blue, brown, purple, gray, green, and ocher. South and southeast the Carson River flows reluctantly toward its sink; a canyon heading on the lower slopes of Sun Peak winds to join with it. North and northeast the sun glares and smokes upon the Forty Mile Desert; the Humboldt is lost in the blue haze of the mountain-wrapped horizon.

Though burnt and dark and inhospitable, the ravine that plunges from Sun Peak toward the Carson had attracted Abner Blackburn and others. In the year that the Saints climbed into their wagons and set out for Zion there was already a scattering of settlement there. At its mouth huddled Chinatown—the rickety dwellings of Chinese who had come over the Sierra to work at a canal for Reese; some four miles up the canyon was another precarious cluster of shacks named Johntown, also in honor of the coolies.

During the Mormon years Gold Canyon had been almost a refuge against rectitude. In winter there was water in the canyon for the hangers-on of El Dorado. Gold could be panned here, though of inferior quality. The day wages, to be had from Gold Canyon, would buy rotgut, an hour at poker or monte, or the favors of a Digger squaw in the brush.

Old Virginny had come to Gold Canyon early in the fifties, at first calling himself Finney. Later, he acknowledged the name of James Fennimore and had something to say about a man knifed in California. Equally ragged, equally dirty, equally shiftless was the sheepherder, Henry Tompkins Paige Comstock. Self-important, lazy and licentious, Comstock found Gold Canyon a congenial climate. There were others of the riffraff, offscourings of the California mining camps, but also there were men of more substance, like the mule skinner, Lemuel Sanford (Sandy) Bowers. And there were men of quite different stamp, like the Grosch boys; they had drifted over the mountains, returning again and again to Gold Canyon and something in the earth here. . . .

Eilley Cowan knew them all. With her husband Eilley had come to this blistering country in '55 with Apostle Hyde. They took up a land claim on which they lived in summer; but more satisfying was her boardinghouse in Gold Canyon and the gabble of the placer miners. They hated to bathe and guzzled in quantity the tarantula juice freighted over the Sierras, but there was a fever in their language that warmed her blood as Alex never had. If this country, as the elders swore, was too close to hell, she liked the smell of the brimstone.

In the summer of 1857 Allen and Hosea Grosch realized at last the immensity of the thing they had been trailing. They had found a vein that was inconceivably rich. Not gold. They could feel a contempt for the placer miners who worshiped the clay-footed image. Theirs was a hard-rock knowledge. Silver! Quartz that was rotten with it.

But as millionaires they bade fair to starve. A partner who was to have sent them money or supplies was somewhere on the Humboldt, God knew where; for a while they cursed him. But word later came along that he had been killed by thieves at Gravelly Ford. Reluctant to abandon their claims even for the usual winter's work in California, they turned during August to placer mining. Pickings were slim; and Hosea drove his pick into his foot. The wound seemed to heal, but he presently died of lockjaw. Allen buried his brother and prepared to abandon his claim for the winter.

It was mid-November, and the Mormons were gone, save for those few of little faith, before Allen got away from Gold Canyon. He was caught in a Sierran storm. He fought off the miners who would have amputated both of his legs, and he did not live two weeks. Nothing survived of the Grosch brothers' discovery except the burning lines they had written to their father.

Yet someone had guessed. All through 1858 Comstock wandered up and down Gold Canyon, searching for the Grosch locations. At times, he dropped down the canyon and intimated to the placer miners that he had found something big. Nobody believed a word of it. But sometimes they looked at him and wondered. Once in a while one of them stumbled on him out in the hills restless and preoccupied, and they had a new name for him, "Old Pancake," because he couldn't take time to mix up sourdough bread.

One day in January, 1859, Old Virginny, high up Gold Canyon, fell over a mound of red earth. As he picked himself up, he saw something in that earth. . . . With his three companions he began to dance in frenzy. He had found a pocket of gold. He had found, indeed, the Gold Hill outcroppings of the Comstock.

By chance, Old Pancake was riding up the canyon; from afar the rejoicing sounded upon his ears. He galloped up to howl his ownership at them. They paid no attention, busy at staking out 50-foot claims. Comstock presently exhibited enough good sense to go and do likewise.

By nightfall the settlements down the canyon were moving bag and baggage up toward the new diggings. Eilley Cowan, who in 1857 had flatly refused to go back to Zion with that sheep Alex, pressed into service three of her boarders, and on the backs of mules her boardinghouse climbed the rocky canyon to the new Ophir. Sandy Bowers got there early enough to stake out a claim, and so did Jim Rogers. Jim, who was broke, presently made over his claim to Eilley in settlement of his board bill. The claim adjoined Sandy's . . . and Eilley, newly divorced, had already settled Sandy's future in her mind.

Frenzy settled on the barren slopes of Sun Peak as the weeks passed. Three hundred dollars a day! Five hundred! Even the damned black rock that filled the rockers and was hurled down the canyon could not flaw such opulence. One day in June Comstock heard that Pete O'Riley and Pat McLaughlin were mining in Spanish Ravine, near a spring where he had staked off a ranch. Climbing on his half-blind nag, he galloped over the Divide. "Manny Penrod and me located this claim last winter and sold a tenth to Old Virginny. You gotta let Manny and me in!"

He browbeat them into acquiescence. Next he demanded that his name be added to their notice of location, and finally he gouged another hundred feet out of them for his water rights in the spring. Then he rode furiously in search of Old Virginny. For a bottle of whisky, a couple of blankets, and his nag he bought Old Virginny's share in the claim. Often, later, Old Virginny told the tale, riding sadly about on the $60,000 plug.

Knowing nothing, claiming everything, Comstock got into everything, a blowfly buzzing up and down and across and around the new diggings. He emblazoned his name on this kingdom by largess to passers-by, by lordly suzerainty of the bars and gambling hells, by interminable haranguing of newcomers in search of information. It is one of the pleasant ironies to which the West is heir that the greatest treasure hill ever known should bear the name of a loud-mouthed sheepherder.

Two years now had passed since the Grosch brothers realized that Gold Canyon held a treasure in silver such as the world had hardly dreamed of; the rock they had pounded for their assays was daily hurled from the rockers of miners who knew only the color of placer gold.

One night Old Virginny had the ill-fortune to stumble and smash a bottle of whisky. Sprinkling upon the sage the few drops that clung to the shattered glass, he hiccoughed, "I baptize this spot Virginia Town." His comrades adjourned to the bars of the newly dignified town. The word spread up and down the streets, in and out of the bars and gambling hells. Queen City of the West, Virginia Town!

The Queen City at first could not quite make up its mind where to take up residence, and indeed, the "Washoe Zephyr" that whooped around the shoulder of Sun Peak sometimes bade fair to blow it off into interstellar space. Gradually, however, a measure of substance came to the town. Perched precariously under the brown, bald knob of Sun Peak, climbing hillsides so steep that roofs were flush with the doorsteps of houses on the next level, Virginia City began to take shape, a rickety city, an inflammable city, a gaudy, hell-for-leather kind of city which now found, cropping out almost in its cellars, a dumfounding treasure.

In the summer of '59 a visitor picked up some of the dark rock despised by the miners who worked and brawled under the shadow of Sun Peak. Suspicious of its weight and color, he had it assayed. The report was flabbergasting. The stuff ran $4,791 to the ton, $3,196 in silver, the rest in gold. The news crashed down into California, wrenching and tearing at the hearts of men who for ten years had searched and dug and killed for yellow metal. The miners flooded over the Sierra to Sun Peak.

Washoe swallowed them all. The adventurers who had ranged the West like kings marched into the broiling caverns of Washoe. The silver bonanzas of the Comstock were not amenable to the easy looting of washpan and rocker; the ores bore the mark of a strange and refractory chemistry of the earth. For $4 a day, the forty-niners descended into other men's mines and shoveled ore that was brought to the surface to be milled and smelted until it reluctantly yielded forth its riches.

They were hard, able men who came to Washoe, a magnificent breed that has left its stamp on all the West.

Here is Bill Stewart, six feet two in his stocking feet, hair and beard a red-gold flame burning around his face, eyes that could grow colder than Washoe's winter skies: Bill had a Yale law degree, and took up lawyering in preference to mining. One day in Genoa he was prosecuting a man for murder. In swaggered Sam Brown, most notorious of the killers who had come to the Comstock lode; a hulk of a man, enormous and mean, he tied his whiskers in a knot under his chin. It was not long since he carved the heart from a man. This trial of his friend, he had already advised the town, distinctly displeased him. Bill Stewart closed his hands about a pair of derringers and trained them on Sam Brown's heart. "This gentleman," he said suavely, "has some testimony for us." The derringers in his hands, he proceeded to cross-question the witness. It developed that Sam knew nothing about the case. It developed that Sam thought the defendant had a bad reputation.

The attorney for the defense objected that the witness was being intimidated.

"Are you," Bill demanded of the witness, "being intimidated?"

Badman Sam Brown was shocked by the idea. No badman could admit being intimidated. He was under indictment in Plumas County, California, he said, for assault with a deadly weapon. Stewart struck him as the kind of man he'd like to defend him, and he'd come into court to retain him. He arose from the witness chair with a $500 retainer in his hand. Blandly Stewart accepted the money. On Brown's motion, court adjourned to the nearest bar, where Brown set up the drinks.

It had been a lacerating deflation for the hardest man known to the Comstock. Sam Brown rode up to Henry Van Sickles' tavern, and when Van Sickles came out to put up his horse, Brown started shooting.

The mild-mannered innkeeper dived back into the house and came up with a double-barreled shotgun. Jumping on his horse, he set out after the badman. The badman's shot went wild, and Van Sickles blew him off his horse. Sam scrambled back on his horse to get the hell away. Van Sickles leveled on

him again, and shot his hat off. Sam clung to his horse and
flew. In the gathering darkness he evaded this nemesis.

It was kill or be killed. Van Sickles posted himself along
the road to Sun Peak and waited in the darkness. Sam came
along at last, and Van Sickles blew him into eternity. The
verdict of the coroner's jury undoubtedly met with Bill
Stewart's entire approval. Samuel Brown had come to his
death "from a just dispensation of an all-wise Providence."

This was Bill Stewart and his world. It was Bill Stewart
whom Washoe dispatched east when the time arrived for
representation in the United States Senate, and Bill Stewart
is no more forgotten by Washington than by Washoe.

Here is Uncle Billy Lent, soft-voiced, kindly, every man's
friend, his word better anywhere than a certified check. He
might meet a friend on the street, and say, "Ophir is looking
pretty well; I put aside fifty shares at thirty dollars for you
this morning. When it touches forty I believe you had better
sell." On his deathbed he delivered his own epitaph: "I think
I has bested as many as has bested me." Here is John Mackay,
who came to the mines as a mucker, took his wages in feet,
and at last gripped all the Comstock in his two hands. Here
is Colonel David T. Buel, who could force his way through
a crowd of vigilantes, cut the rope from around the neck of
a man about to be hanged, face down the angry crowd, and
see the man free.

They were of the great blood of the land, hard with a
man's hardness in a male world.

The frowsy firstcomers to the Comstock were quickly
dispossessed. Old Virginny had traded off his claims to the
Ophir for a bottle or two of rotgut and a half-blind nag, but
Henry Tompkins Paige Comstock sold out his own claims
for $11,000, and wandered out of history. One and all, they
made haste to unload on the gullible Californians, and they
went to sheepherding, to sweeping out saloons, to prospecting
in the desert ranges, while the Comstock blazed in the eyes

of the world. Only Eilley Orrum Cowan, who married Sandy Bowers and united her ten-foot claim to his, clung to the Comstock as it reared in its magnificence.

Wealth poured in on Eilley. She had always known it would. Now she dreamed of a regal mansion, of herself as the Queen of Washoe. She went with Sandy to Europe, and bought everything in sight; she came back to the Bowers Mansion in Washoe Valley, and here she lived with Sandy in a tight, formal world quite out of key with the Comstock except in its extravagant mingling of absurdity and magnificence. Sandy died, and Eilley's money fell to the wolves. In old age she earned a living by crystal-gazing; she was buried in 1903 with legends for her shroud.

While Virginia City and Gold Hill crazily overspread the hill slopes, shafts tore at the vitals of the lode. First-grade ore was sacked for shipment to England, so rich that it paid to ship that distance for superior milling. Second- and third-grade ores were piled up for future attention. Lower grade stuff, fifty dollars a ton or less, was used to grade the streets.

The deepening shafts multiplied the problems of mining the ore. Water was the particular bane; pumping and drainage expedients were only makeshift solutions. Adolph Sutro began to preach his vision of a six-mile tunnel from the Carson River, which would drain all the Comstock and permit looting the lode from below, but he was slow in winning converts.

As the Ophir got down below the 50-foot level the vein began to widen out. It had been thought wonderfully rich when three or four feet wide, but at the 175-foot level the vein was 65 feet wide! The ore could be shoveled up almost without the use of a pick. Madness seized upon Washoe. Millionaires! The mind filled with the certainty of riches. Even the miners of Washoe, whom hard rock had forced into the servitude of day wages, could feel themselves sharers in this wealth. The stock market offered an avenue to riches even though they knew that the Comstock was being mined also "from the other end"—from the richly appointed offices of San Francisco's financial barons.

The very richness of the first bonanza almost ruined the Ophir. It was impossible to get the ore out. The mines could not be timbered securely, and the drifts caved in upon the muckers. When other expedients had failed, the Comstock was saved by a German mining engineer. Philip Deidesheimer evolved a system of timbering analogous to the walls in the cell of a honeycomb. Deidesheimer's method of stoping out the ore made it possible to mine at any height, width, length, or depth. The only enemy was fire in the shafts. Or water. (Sometimes Washoe thought seriously that Tahoe had an underground outlet in the Comstock.)

The ingenuity of the Comstock was equal, also, to the evolution of new milling processes. The mills that rose in Gold Canyon, in Carson and Washoe valleys, added an essential characteristic to life in Washoe—the periodic shuddering of the earth under the impact of the stamps, and the almost imperial magnificence of many of the mills.

The Ophir was the first of the bonanzas, and gave that Spanish term its royal significance in English. But there were others, as the numerous shafts cut into the bowels of Sun Peak—the Gould & Curry, the Mexican, the Belcher, the Yellow Jacket, the Crown Point.

It had not required bonanzas to arouse in Washoe what Orson Hyde might have termed a stubborn, stiff-necked spirit. The Mormons who trekked east from Carson in 1857 carried with them their exasperation that Gentiles in the valleys had met in convention to petition Congress for a separate territorial government. Washoe's delegate reached Washington at the height of the government's exasperation with the Mormons, but the war with Brigham fizzled out in oratory, and the bill for the Territory of Nevada (it had been Columbus at first) got lost in the shuffle.

While their delegate was in Washington, and after he returned, the citizens of Washoe experimented with provisional governments of one kind and another. In the summer of 1859, at the new town of Carson City a few miles north of Genoa, a state constitution modeled after that of California was adopted, and Isaac Roop named governor. The silver rush to Washoe ruined the brave new state, but the shack towns that swayed dizzily around the periphery of the Comstock made it certain that something definite would be done about getting an authorized government.

Congress finally got around to creating a government for Washoe. As Buchanan's administration ended, a bill created the Territory of Nevada. All that remained was for the new president to nominate territorial officers. Abraham Lincoln did so with dispatch. James W. Nye of New York was named governor. The secretary was a fellow named Orion Clemens, from Hannibal, Missouri. Nye came in style by way of Panama and California, a fire and smoke of oratory marking his passage. Orion Clemens, considerably later, arrived by the Overland Stage, accompanied by his young brother, Sam.

Carson City Sam found a "wooden" town. "The main street consisted of four or five blocks of little frame stores which were too high to sit down on, but not too high for various other purposes; in fact, hardly high enough. They were packed close together, side by side, as if room were scarce in that mighty plain. The sidewalk was of boards that were more or less loose and inclined to rattle when walked upon. In the middle of the town, opposite the stores, was the 'plaza' which is native to all towns beyond the Rocky Mountains—a large, unfenced, level vacancy, with a liberty pole in it, and very useful as a place for public auctions, horse trades, and mass meetings, and likewise for teamsters to camp in. Two other sides of the plaza were faced by stores, offices, and stables. The rest of Carson City was pretty scattering."

During the afternoon the Clemens brothers were initiated into the wonders of the Washoe Zephyr. It appeared promptly at 2 P.M.: a "soaring dust-drift about the size of the United States set up edgewise came with it, and the capital of Nevada Territory disappeared from view."

Even so, Sam thought, there were sights to be seen not wholly uninteresting to newcomers, for the vast dust cloud "was thickly freckled with things strange to the upper air—things living and dead, that flitted hither and thither, going and coming, appearing and disappearing among the rolling billows of dust—hats, chickens, and parasols sailing in the remote heavens; blankets, tin signs, sage-brush, and shingles a shade lower; door-mats and buffalo robes lower still; shovels and coal scuttles on the next grade; glass doors, cats, and little children on the next; disrupted lumber yards, light buggies, and wheelbarrows on the next; and down only thirty or forty feet above ground was a scurrying storm of emigrating roofs and vacant lots."

Sam had come west as private secretary to the secretary. He now discovered that he had little to do. This was agreeable, but the lack of any salary for doing it was not. He climbed to Tahoe, amazed at its blue magnificence, and then returned to Carson and attended the first session of the legislature, which was granting steamboat charters for the Carson and Humboldt sinks and the Humboldt River, and passing toll road franchises. Sam remembered later, with some artistic license, that the legislature passed these toll road franchises "all the time." Freighting in fact had become big business; there was nearly as much excitement over it, Sam remarked with suddenly expanding awareness, as over the wonderful silver mines.

It was, after all, the silver mines that were responsible for the presence here of Orion and Sam Clemens. The Comstock was booming now. The earth might hold greater bonanzas. Prospectors wandered the Nevada hills. Now and again frenzy shook some far corner of the land—south in Esmeralda County or north in Humboldt County. Sam Clemens, in the late winter of 1861, was lured by Esmeralda, but Humboldt exerted a more powerful spell. ("A week or two ago an assay . . . made returns of *seven thousand* dollars to the ton," the *Territorial Enterprise* babbled.) So Sam with three companions set out for Unionville on the lower Humboldt, riding in style to begin with but soon climbing out of the wagon—first to walk and then to push. "We could really have accomplished the journey in ten days if we had towed the horses behind the wagon, but we did not think of that until it was too late, and so went on shoving the horses and the wagon too when we might have saved half the labor." Picturing the Humboldt as offering a pleasant and invigorating exercise—a man might run and jump across the river till overheated, then drink it dry—he arrived at Unionville.

There had been some expectation that masses of silver would be found lying on the ground, or at the very least that it should glitter in the sun on the mountain summits. Sam found, instead, that digging a hole in the ground was terrifically hard work, and that the *real* secret of success in mining was "*not* to mine the silver ourselves by the sweat of our brows and labor of our hands, but to *sell* the ledges to the dull slaves of toil and let them do the mining!"

Sam Clemens now found that he had business in Esmeralda County, and his sojourn in the lower Humboldt country ended within a few weeks; but from afar he may have enjoyed William Forbes' caustic pictures of affairs in Buena Vista Canyon. In summer issues of 1863 this editor had sardonic remarks to make in his *Humboldt Register* about the prevailing lack of industry among the miners—in case sudden rains should set in, they would be truly in desperate case— "Most of the miners have not been here more than two years and haven't got their tunnels in far enough to protect themselves from the rain." Forbes was solicitous for the miners' health, and thought a gymnasium in which they could exercise would be a worth-while institution for the town.

Although abandoned by Sam Clemens, Unionville had its boom years. For a time it maintained its distinction as Humboldt County seat, regardless of Winnemucca's "morbid hankering" for that honor, but past glories proved, finally, inadequate against live voters and political shenanigans.

It had been an unlucky venture into the Humboldt, and Sam moved to the Esmeralda country. A feverish half year followed. Some mines might not begin to produce for another year or two, but others of his properties must make him and Orion millionaires within months; money could not buy a foot in one holding, he assured Orion, whose stuffy job in Carson City was having to finance this, for "I know it to contain our fortune." Claim jumpers appeared, and Sam bleakly informed Orion that the Clemens Company was about to drive them out by force. But soon Sam had to wonder how in hell he could live three months on a hundred dollars; and he went to day-labor at one of the mills. In odd moments he solaced himself by writing humorous sketches which he sent to the *Enterprise* at Virginia City. Signed "Josh," they aroused laughter and the interest of Joe Goodman. An offer of a job followed, and one hot August afternoon in 1862 a tousle-haired, sharp-faced, irritably energetic young man walked into the *Enterprise* office slapping the dust from his clothes. It was a consummation in Sam Clemens' life, and from it issued Mark Twain.

Life on the *Enterprise* was central to the whole life of the Comstock. Joe Goodman gave his reporters full rein. Rollin M. Daggett was Goodman's associate editor; small, swarthy, heavy-set, "but savage as a trapped bear when he was angry." One night a dairyman walked in to complain about an article derogatory of his dairy. "You're a pretty fellow to come to me," Daggett exploded. "I was down by your corral night before last [he had not been there in three years, Judge Goodwin says]—as I walked along the high-board fence I heard your cows gnawing bones, and when I turned the corner they looked up at me and growled like dogs." The dairyman threw up his hands: "Well, by God!" Daggett went back to work. "That son of a gun will not bother us again for eighteen months."

William Wright, much better known as Dan DeQuille, was master of a gentle humor. Judge Goodwin remembered: "Daggett, with his intellectual cleaver, would chop a man to pieces. Mark Twain, with his droll humor, would lead his victim up to the shambles he had in waiting for him, and the unconscious creature would never suspect what was going to happen until the ax fell. But Dan had a softer way. The intended victim would know all the time after the first ten lines that he was going to be sacrificed, but he was under a spell, enjoyed the process, and laughed after he was downed." Some of his stories have a still-exquisite flavor, violent with the headstrong humor of the frontier. There is the tale of the traveling stones of Pahranagat Valley. By some mysterious power these stones were drawn together and scattered apart again. "A single stone removed to a distance of a yard, upon being released at once started off with wonderful and somewhat comical celerity to rejoin its fellows." German scientists wrote to demand details. A circus man offered $10,000 if Dan could make these magnetized stones behave under canvas. . . . And the tale of the solar armor. A genius had invented rubber armor to counteract the terrific western heat; by means of a compact air compressor equipped with a pocket battery to run it, the wearer was enabled to cool off when the heat became oppressive. However, testing it in Death Valley one day when the temperature was 117° in the shade, the genius failed to return. Next morning a search party found him dead. He had started the compressor but had been unable to stop it, and had frozen to death. When he was found, the machine was still running, and there was an icicle eighteen inches long hanging from his nose. A writer for the London *Times,* to the delight of Washoe, recommended that the British government investigate this armor. Sam Clemens was hired, initially, to fill in for Dan DeQuille while the latter took an extended vacation. When Dan returned, Mark Twain had established himself, and the *Enterprise* published the humor of both until Mark departed the Comstock for world fame. Dan, whom the Comstock would have granted a higher talent than Mark's, lacked the spark that took Mark to greatness, but he remains a warm humanity: "the most winsome of men . . . gifted in a hundred ways: he was one of the most efficient and valuable men that ever wore out his life in a newspaper office, and no one who knew him well has ever ceased grieving for him. He was above both bribes or bluffs; no man could ever corrupt him; no man could scare him."

Bernard DeVoto, energetically redrafting Van Wyck Brook's dour conception of Mark Twain as a frustrated artist who, on the Comstock, sold his birthright for pottage, has written of Washoe's vastly exciting male life and of how Mark ripened during his years at the heart of this spectacle. *Mark Twain's America* resummons the era.

Sam's months of apprenticeship coincided with the onset of the "flush times." All the major shafts were deep now, and there was one bonanza after another. A heady madness flowed from the Comstock into the nerves of the Pacific slope. The loot built San Francisco's marbled public buildings and the palaces of the nabobs on Nob Hill.

Wilderness adventurers looting the fur of the beaver had begun the epic of the Humboldt; the lure of piracies on the land had made of it a thoroughfare for the nation. It is fitting that at the far end of the Humboldt trail the desolate hills, blasted and burnt by the suns of a thousand thousand years, add a climax to rapine without parallel in the American wandering.

Into the bowels of the earth, into the teeth of flood and flame, brawny miners followed the wealth of this land, to strip it out ruthlessly, wastefully. Aboveground, in the great buccaneering tradition of the land, the caliphs of the Comstock warred in the courts and the stock exchange. The mines were instrumentalities only; it was power they wanted. In the mines their warfare was violent. The miners ran drifts into each other's shafts, fighting with fire and stinking smudge, sabotaging timbers and cables, opening gangfights in which a man was lucky if he lost no more than an eye, an ear, or his nose. It was a brutal, ugly business, normal to the place and the time.

As bitterly fought was the struggle in the courts for control of the Comstock empire. The courts were unutterably corrupt. It is told that Chief Justice George Turner, who sold decisions to the highest bidder, on one occasion notified a litigant that a favorable decision was contingent upon the delivery of $10,000 before morning. Though it was already dark, the man was resourceful and obtained the sum in gold coin from gambling houses. With the forty or fifty pounds of gold in a burlap sack, at about one in the morning he rang the doorbell. The judge's wife finally answered the door. The judge was asleep, but she agreed to receive the money. The earnest litigant tugged at the sack, and Mrs. Turner, wearing only a fragile nightgown, gathered it up as though it were an apron. Into the improvised receptacle the man poured the heavy gold. It ripped the nightgown completely off her, and the man ran from the spectacle of the judge's wife naked in the half-light from the door, golden coins rolling about her feet. . . . Era of venality, it produced from Zinc Barnes an unembittered, hardmouthed wisdom: "An honest man is a son of a bitch who'll stay bought."

Corruption in the courts was a powerful incentive toward statehood, though Washoe had only a fifth of the requisite population. The drive for statehood was aided by the political situation in Washington. Since April, 1861, Lincoln had been pursuing his fight to reconstitute the Union; as a tool of warfare he conceived the Thirteenth Amendment, by which the slaves were to be freed. To obtain the required two-thirds majority in Congress, the voting weight of an additional state was necessary. Driving some patronage bargains with the New York and New Jersey delegations, he got an enabling act for Nevada through Congress. A constitutional convention in Carson City, in July, 1864, framed a constitution acceptable to the people of Nevada and on October 31, 1864, the new state was admitted to the Union.

Political exigencies were the immediate agent, but it was the silver mines, roaring along the continent's western sky line, that wrought statehood for Nevada years ahead of the other western territories. There had been some secessionist sentiment on Washoe; an abortive warfare, even. But the Unionists had prevailed; and the wealth from Washoe was profoundly important in the financing of the whole war— solid metal money in a time when the government's "Lincolnskins" were discounted at 50 per cent. The certainty of more wealth did much to underwrite the nation's credit.

The close of the Civil War launched Washoe into "borrasca" (meaning squall or bad weather, synonymous with unproductivity). There had been twelve great bonanzas, the looting of them, indeed, not yet finished, but public belief in the Comstock wavered; in the stock markets Comstock shares sank week by week. The first violent period of rapine was over.

Drama attaching to the treasure hill though the late sixties centers about the obstinate struggles of Adolph Sutro. This German Jew projected a four-mile tunnel from the floor of the Carson Valley into the heart of the Comstock, to drain and ventilate the shafts and provide a means for transporting ores to the mills along the river. The Nevada legislature incorporated the Sutro Tunnel Corporation in

1865, and next year twenty-three of the principal Comstock companies agreed to pay $2 per ton on all ores extracted above the level of the tunnel, when it should have been driven to points within their property claims. Sutro effected the passage of an act of Congress authenticating the rights granted him by the Nevada legislature, but at the last moment the mine-owners made an about-face and flatly refused to join in the undertaking. A lion of a man, Sutro carried his battle to the miners, and public subscriptions enabled him to start drilling his tunnel from a point near Dayton on the Carson River in October, 1869.

For eight years this valiant little man warred single-handed against all the power of the mining corporations which, in this matter at least, arrayed themselves solidly. Surmounting all difficulties, he holed through into the Savage mine in July, 1878. By the terms of the old contract, he had put the companies under tribute of $2 per ton on all ores taken from their mines, but to collect this sum was another matter. The other companies, moreover, attempted to drain their mines into Sutro's tunnel through the Savage shaft. Sutro commenced a drainway to conduct this incoming water back into the lower levels of the Savage mine; when halted by legal process, he built two watertight doors of solid oak, bulkheads which would shut off all drainage through his tunnel, and flood the Comstock shafts. The mine companies were brought to terms, and ultimately a compromise was signed. Though Sutro's tunnel never made him the fortune he had dreamed, it brought him money and influence; he became mayor of San Francisco and a power in California politics; his stamp remains on the city of the Golden Gate.

The last of the Comstock's bonanzas, the richest and most brilliant of them all, was located during the long period of Sutro's fight for his tunnel. "The Big Bonanza" was found in 1872; the enduring international fame of the Comstock owes to this lode more than to any other. Some $19,000,000 came out of the Big Bonanza, and the warfare over its riches overthrew financial empires and founded new dynasties. It was the last splendor of the Comstock, the bright flame of an era unmatched in American history. When the Comstock guttered out, the shadows of great men fell more dimly upon the American earth. Against this blaze they had stood in boldest relief. America would hardly know again the power, the joy, the exaltation, the drunkenness of sheer living, or the young flaming spirit that dwelt here under Sun Peak.

XVIII

The Traveling Men

THROUGH this fourth day of April it had been snowing in the Sierras. The stage lines for the first time in three years were snowed in both ways from the summit. Hunched low upon his pony, a rider in buckskin forced his way eastward before the blizzard, from station to snowbound station. Now and then he had to dismount and break a trail for his pony, but as the afternoon waned he got down out of the drifts to firmer going. As night fell the pony stretched out against the trail down through the forested canyon. Chilled and stiff, the rider saw at last a cluster of lights ahead. He was into the town and off the pony, station tenders swift to aid, and he was almost instantly out of town again, the fresh mustang settling to its work, fourteen miles of it. Again lights arose out of the darkness. They thundered into town; another pony was standing in the street, rider at its head and stationkeepers standing about. Swift hands stripped the mochila from his pony and to an exultant hurrahing the other rider was off.

The first Pony Express from the west had gone through Carson City. It had left Sacramento at 2 A.M. this morning. It would be in Great Salt Lake City just before midnight on the 7th, and at 3:55 P.M. on the 13th it would be in St. Joseph, Missouri. Four days later the first mail by Pony Express would be delivered in New York City. It was an accomplishment to make the country gasp, the nation bridged from ocean to ocean in fourteen days, and the "Great American Desert" in ten.

The Pony Express, in 1860, was the climax to many years of struggle with time and distance. Those who had gone to California in the days before the war with Mexico had gone with a simple finality. Those who returned east were not many. Home and the heart journeyed with them. By contrast, the Golden Army marched to wrest from the Golden Shore the means of fortune and power. Most wanted only to loot and to return from whence they had come.

Mail was the event of any week or month; men who worked along streambanks all day and drank and whored all night cried unashamedly over a letter from home. It was these who shouted for an overland mail. Congress presently established an ocean mail, but it was 1851 before California got an overland mail service.

In April of that year the government contracted with George Chorpenning and Absalom Woodward to carry a monthly mail between California and Great Salt Lake City; the route by way of the Humboldt—"the then traveled trail, considered about 910 miles long." The first "jackass mail" left Sacramento on May 1st. It took sixteen days to get

through the Sierras, Chorpenning and his men having sometimes to go ahead of their mules, beating down the snow with
wooden mauls. Chorpenning made good time up the Humboldt, and though delayed by snow in the Goose Creek
Mountains, got into Great Salt Lake City with the mail on
June 5th.

Less difficulty was experienced through the summer,
though Indians made the passage of the Humboldt extremely
hazardous, but Woodward, with the November mail, was
ambushed with his four men beyond the Humboldt's Palisade Canyon and none got into the Mormon settlements
alive. Snow in the Sierras closed all the passes, and Chorpenning had to return the December and January mails to
Sacramento. The February mail got over the Sierras, but
halfway up the Humboldt a blizzard struck, so fierce they
lost all their animals by the time they reached the head of
the river. Living on the frozen flesh of their mules, they got
through to the Mormon settlements on foot, packing the
mail on their backs.

The March mail Chorpenning sent to Los Angeles and
thence to Great Salt Lake City by the Southern Route, but
the April mail was brought across the Sierras again and, like
all the mails until winter, came east through the valley of
the Humboldt.

When storms howled in the Sierras, there was no passage
for the mails, save those local mails for Carson Valley carried
on skis by such frontiersmen as "Snowshoe" Thompson.
Until July, 1854, by stipulation with the Post Office, Chorpenning's men carried the mails through the Humboldt Valley in summer and by the Southern Route in winter. Then,
for four years, the northern route was abandoned. It was not
until 1858 that the Humboldt Route was re-established, in
answer to furious denunciation of the circuitous Butterfield
Overland Mail Route through Texas and New Mexico.

Chorpenning again was given the contract west from

Great Salt Lake City, a rather better contract than he had had before. Chorpenning was asked to establish a semimonthly service through in twenty days, for $34,400 a year; and a provision in the contract soon enabled him to establish the mail on a weekly basis with a 16-day schedule, for $130,000 a year.

Although occasionally lambasted by the newspapers ("Chorpenning intends to run over the route at a snail's speed until the Department will make him another allowance for shortening the time, when the four hundred miles section now being run with one jaded train, will perhaps, be properly stocked"), Chorpenning managed usually to keep within schedule time. In the fall of 1858 he dispatched Howard Egan to have a look at Simpson's new trail west from Camp Floyd; a likely route was found west to Ruby Valley, and when Captain Simpson embarked upon further western explorations in May, 1859, the mail contractor already had worked a wagon road as far as Ruby Valley. Although pack trains had to carry the mail by Hastings' old route between Ruby Valley and the Humboldt, it was plain that Chorpenning would soon have mail coaches running all the way to the desert river.

The contractor of the Central Route refused to be balked even by the Sierran snows. Through the winter of 1858-59, and again next year, he got his mails across the Sierras almost on schedule time, though sometimes he had to utilize pack animals or even men on snowshoes. Simpson's new route to Carson Valley was soon proved entirely practicable by Chorpenning; he abandoned the detour from Ruby Valley to the Humboldt down through the valley of the South Fork, and erected his lonely stations along the Simpson trail. With an improved road, more equipment, more and better stock, and increasing passenger business, Chorpenning's Central Route was vindicated as an entirely worthy rival to John Butterfield's efficient Southern Overland Mail. But now he was ruined by a change of postmaster general. The new official hewed about with a sharp ax soon after taking office, and in May, 1860, Chorpenning's contract was annulled for alleged failure in his service. Protests availed Chorpenning nothing, and he never regained his investment. His name soon was all but forgotten through the Humboldt Valley; mail and passenger traffic was withdrawn to the south, and the desert river was abandoned to the Indians, to trail herds of sheep and cattle, and to emigrants who still were drawn by the western dream.

For ten years the river had been the nation's thoroughfare. And in those ten years the river had yielded nothing of itself to the persuasions of civilization. In 1859 as in 1849 it was barren and dangerous, a strange brightness ribboning the desert West. Thomas Ambrose Cramer in 1859 wrote into his journal the unalterable hostility of the river. In mid-August, he at first was "agreeably disappointed in the character of its grasses and waters, for a bad quality of both of which, its fame had reached us a long way east." But though he foresaw that grass and water should worsen as they descended toward the Sink, he was hardly prepared for reality. Stock began to die of the alkaline waters; the land was perpetual sand and sagebrush, the mountains barren and brown. "Traveled on down the Humboldt River and find that it is rapidly assuming the character which it bears abroad, and that it is a miserable waste only fit to be inhabited by Digger Indians and rattlesnakes."

By forced marches his company moved down the Humboldt, "and no change except for the worse," an "inhospitable and poisoned waste." The region below the Big Bend seemed clothed with the terror of desolation; he had no words for the gloom and despondency with which it bore upon his mind. It was a relief even to march out upon the dreaded Forty Mile Desert, with its gleaming bones. "The losses in cattle continue and even increase beyond this, as is supposed, from the effects of the poisons taken in with their food and drink during their travels over the region. And, indeed, when I look around me, I am surprised that any get through and not that some die."

Valedictory for an American era!

The Pony Express was not a novel idea. A relay system of mounted couriers was known in ancient Persia, and in the great empire of Genghis Khan. California, after the arrival of the Golden Army, received much of its mail from horsemen who made a business of riding the length and breadth of the diggings; and as early as 1855 a fast mail "express" had been suggested to Congress. Not for its novelty but for its brilliant execution of an idea the Pony Express is fabulous in American history.

Russell, Majors, and Waddell were contractors who reaped a fortune from the government's "war" with the Mormons in 1857-58, and their position was fortified by the Pikes Peak gold excitement next year. They had the organization and the resources, and when by the back door they got into the overland mail and express business, they presently embarked on an enterprise that would dramatize their capabilities, the flamboyant Pony Express.

During the winter of 1859-60 the firm established its series of relay stations from Sacramento to St. Joseph. West of Great Salt Lake City they had to build and equip their own stations. Before the first Pony Express riders galloped out of St. Joseph and Sacramento, the firm had sunk something like a hundred thousand dollars into the enterprise. They bought five hundred of the best horses they could lay hands on—blooded American stock in the east, California half-mustangs in the west—and manned 190 stock stations. Two hundred station tenders were hired to care for the horses, and eighty rigorously tested riders were hired, for runs varying from seventy-five to a hundred miles a day.

Maintenance of the Pony Express was possible only by reason of the enormous resources of the company, as supplies for men and livestock had to be carried long distances to the stations. It was obvious that the Pony Express could not expect to pay its own way, even with charges of $5 per half ounce, for letters and telegraphic dispatches. But, in the western manner, Russell, Majors, and Waddell were gambling for big stakes. If they could dramatically establish the feasibility of courier mail by the Central Route, day in and day out, winter and summer, Congress might subsidize a daily Pony mail.

A great proportion of that initial hundred thousand dollars for the Pony Express was sunk in establishing the express line along Simpson's Short Route. It is said that the alkali burned the skin from the hands of the men who erected the adobe walls of stations east of the Carson River. Hay and grain had to be hauled out into the desert, and hay and grain were costly west of the Mormon frontier.

That first eastern mail of April, 1860, blazed into the mind of the country the whirlwind linkage of West with East, and Americans exclaimed their pride and pleasure, though Easterners were preoccupied with the preliminaries of a presidential campaign that would precipitate the Civil War, and in the West the cry, "Ho for Washoe!" was sounding up and down the Pacific slope. The Pony Express owes much of its desperate glamour to the Indian hazard, even more than to the split-second schedule riding. Collis P. Huntington, later of the Central Pacific, felt the whole enterprise of sending out lone horsemen nothing short of "constructive murder," for not one in five could escape the Indians. And, in fact, during these first weeks of the Pony Express a grim Indian drama began to be enacted along the Nevada trails.

The tradition of murder in the Humboldt Valley by 1860 had become almost commonplace. Regularly there was word of burned wagons, of mutilated bodies; and sometimes

THE TRAVELING MEN 275

there were tales almost of pitched battles. Battle Mountain, where Reese River joins with the Humboldt, took its name in 1857 from such a fight between an emigrant company and a war party of Paiutes. During 1859 the Paiutes, Washoes, Shoshoni, and Bannocks were in ugly temper. The whites were pressing upon their domain, not only in the Humboldt and Carson valleys, but in the desert valleys north and south. There had been gloomy anticipations of a war. Yet nobody was really alarmed, and nobody foresaw the result when miners poured across the Sierras to Washoe, staking out claims through the mountain ranges, killing and driving away the scanty game, laying waste the piñon forests which had yielded annual harvests of pine nuts. There had been reports through the winter of 1859-60 that the Indians accounted the whites to blame for the extreme cold, but this also had made no impression. Whites carelessly raped the squaws or stole from the bucks.

During April, 1860, as the Pony Express began to ride, the Indians gathered in conclave at Pyramid Lake. There were leaders fiery for war, and others more doubtful. The issue was decided for them by a happening at Williams' Station on the Carson River.

Tradition would have it that during James Williams' absence several young men around his place abducted two Paiute squaws. Their Bannock husbands traced them to the station, but the whites chased the men into the brush when the Indians demanded their women. The Bannocks rounded up thirty tribesmen, and in a sudden, ferocious onslaught burned the station and killed the five men there.

The news reached the settlements on the upper Carson early in May, and set Virginia City, Dayton, Carson City, and Genoa by the ears. Couriers rode to warn prospectors and outlying settlements, and the men of Washoe gathered at Buckland's Ranch. In all, about 105 men, divided into four companies, set out from Buckland's for Williams' Station on the morning of May 9th. In the vainglorious tradition of the American militia, they declined to name a commander in chief.

At Williams' Station the troops buried the slain and resolved to go on to Pyramid Lake. On reaching the Truckee near its bend they encountered five men, remnant of eight, who for several days past had fought a running battle with Paiutes. From this they might have taken warning, but recklessly, on the morning of the 12th, they set out toward Pyramid Lake. The whites rode fourteen miles along a dangerous trail, and had almost reached the Indian camp when they saw a score of Paiute men and boys atop a low, flat mound. They halted and opened fire.

Craftily the Paiutes had waited in ambush. Now they loosed upon the whites a cloud of poisoned arrows. Though Major William M. Ormsby and a few others tried to rally the men, the whites fled in panic. Ormsby himself fell. The Truckee was too deep and swift to cross, and the whites had to run the gantlet of the back trail. Forty-six, it is estimated, died along the Truckee, and those who finally escaped fled in terror of their lives.

The first refugees got back to Buckland's Ranch on the morning of May 15th. A thrill of fear went through Washoe. Virginia City gathered its women and children into an unfinished stone house, in Carson City a hotel was barricaded as a fort; Silver City erected a fortification above the town, with a wooden cannon to overawe attackers. Genoa piled into Warren Wasson's small stone house while Wasson himself set out alone through the Paiute country to summon troops from Honey Lake Valley.

The news was telegraphed across the Sierras, and regular troops and volunteers were raised. More than 800 men rendezvoused at the Bend of the Truckee on the last day of May and, well organized and disciplined, marched for Pyramid Lake. On June 2nd the second battle of the Truckee was fought, and after a sharp skirmish with losses on both sides, the Paiutes fled north into the mountains. Left in possession of the field, the whites erected fortifications that were manned until midsummer.

Organized warfare ended with the second conflict of the Truckee. But now murder broke out along all the trails. Raiders fell upon the stations of the Pony Express, killing tenders, burning the stations, and driving off the livestock. A young Mexican rode into the station at Dry Creek, twenty-seven miles east of Reese River; mortally wounded, he died within a few hours.

No other Pony rider was slain running the mails, though more than once a rider blazed his way through an ambush by sheer speed and courage. Riding proved less dangerous than manning the stations. All too frequently a rider arrived at a station to find it in flames.

Four successive expresses from the east were held at Great Salt Lake City, and no express went out of San Francisco on May 31st. With the express of June 9th, twenty picked men rode as far as Great Salt Lake City. It was fruitless to appeal for troops, as the government had commenced marching back to the States the army that had set out with such éclat three years before to settle the Mormon question. The company therefore took steps on its own initiative to protect the central trail across Nevada. Stations were rebuilt almost as stone or adobe forts, more men were placed at each station, as virtual garrisons, and stock replaced as expeditiously as possible.

The Pony Express was re-established, to the admiration of everyone. Riders passed through these sharp dangers almost on schedule time. Willingness to spend money, and the loyalty of the men, enabled the Pony Express to keep going, and even, presently, to ride semiweekly. But it is estimated that the Indian warfare along the trail through Nevada during 1860-61 cost the company $75,000, and already the enterprise was being run at a loss. Eastbound mail there was in plenty, but Easterners seemed more inclined to count their pennies, and westbound mails rarely approached the 20-pound maximum a rider could carry.

Things promised to get worse before they got better. The whole West had a lively expectation of a general Indian war breaking out in the deserts west of the Mormon settlements. It was not much comfort to the company that the government, in July, 1860, established Fort Churchill on the lower Carson near Buckland's Ranch, for the military post had only a limited utility in policing the trails to the east. Later, in September, 1862, another post was established in Ruby Valley to provide greater protection for the Overland Trail, but by then the Pony Express was finished.

Most memorable of the rides of the Pony Express was the carrying of Lincoln's inaugural message. All along the line, division superintendents had been ordered to see that the message went through at whatever cost. Riders picked out the horses they wanted to ride, and these were groomed for the occasion.

The new magnetic telegraph, gradually extending its wires west from the Missouri River and east from San Francisco, had now got as far west as Fort Kearney and as far east as Fort Churchill. This simplified the job in this worst weather-month of the year, but sixteen hundred miles of winterbound land had to be bridged by the Pony Express. It took seven days of desperately hard riding to bring the dispatches from Fort Kearney into Great Salt Lake City, and another five to reach Fort Churchill. San Francisco's morning newspapers on March 18th published in full the message, telegraphed from Fort Churchill. The riders had cut perhaps five days from the normal winter schedule and brought to the West a momentous excerpt of the future.

The Pony Express is of the very pattern of the West— dramatic, colorful, indomitable, impracticable, a magnificent gesture on a magnificent scale. No subsidy could have repaid Russell, Majors, and Waddell what they sank into the venture, for expenses ran perhaps half a million dollars above receipts. But the men who established the Pony Express and the riders who maintained it contributed to the American heritage something beyond price, a proud, free, adventurous symbolism of the American spirit. It is appropriate that its end came by the attack of American technology upon the wastelands of the West. It was not war, financial debacle or human inadequacy but the humming wires of the Overland Telegraph that ended the gallant Pony Express.

Samuel Morse put the first American telegraph line into operation in the spring of 1844, and by December, 1847, the wires had reached St. Louis, but a cable had been laid across the Atlantic before the telegraph was ready to tackle the West.

As early as 1853 James Eddy proposed to Congress a subterranean telegraph to California—subterranean because, he thought, only thus could communications be rendered secure from storms, Indians, and the simplehearted American folk who gratefully cut lengths of telegraph line whenever pressed for baling wire—but Eddy, taking a leaf from the book of railroad promotion, asked 1,500,000 acres of land in recompense, and underground wires were not proving very successful in Europe. California in this year put up its first telegraph wire and began to string lines to the mining camps. Five years later the Placerville, Humboldt and Salt Lake Telegraph Company was organized to build across the Sierras and up the Humboldt Valley to Great Salt Lake City. When Captain Simpson came out of the deserts east of the Sink of the Carson in June, 1859, the line was in operation as far as Genoa. Not least among the advantages Simpson saw for his new road was its superiority for a telegraph. John Reese had told him that for some three hundred miles along the Humboldt there was no timber except small willows, nor was there any in Thousand Springs Valley or on Goose Creek. "Poor prospect this for the magnetic telegraph." By contrast, on his route the mountain ranges were covered with timber, the maximum haul of the poles, except at a few points, being only about ten miles. Simpson was congratulated for his trail-finding by Colonel Frederick A. Bee, who announced that the captain might consider his route adopted for the telegraph line.

"Bee's grapevine," so called because strung when possible to trees rather than to poles, got only to Fort Churchill, and when the Pony Express began to ride there was no prospect in the foreseeable future of an overland telegraph. Hiram Sibley, however, firmly believed in such a telegraph. When the Western Union and the North American Telegraph Association shrank from the undertaking, he went to Congress and was instrumental in the passage of an act "to facilitate communication between the Atlantic and the Pacific States by electric telegraph." Sibley and his associates incorporated on June 11, 1861, as the Pacific Telegraph Company and proposed to the four existing California companies that they consolidate as the Overland Telegraph Company and build that portion of the line to Great Salt Lake City. The reorganization was made in the West, and in May, 1861, the Overland Telegraph Company began rebuilding its line from Placerville to Fort Churchill. Although the Pacific Telegraph Company did not formally begin construction until July 4th, they already had a line from Omaha to Fort Kearney.

The telegraph companies began construction both ways from the ends of the line. The Pony Express riders gasped at the way the poles went up. The western crews moved along a hundred miles or more a month, and the eastern crews even faster. On October 24, 1861, the Pacific Telegraph Company placed Great Salt Lake City in telegraphic communication with the eastern states, and two days later the

Overland Company linked the Mormon capital with San Francisco. It was an amazing accomplishment, the entire line built in four months and eleven days. This overland telegraph ruled western communications until, seven and a half years later, lines were completed along the right-of-way of the Pacific Railroad.

The gap bridged by the Pony Express had grown smaller as the poles of the Overland Telegraph were strung with humming wires, and news dispatches were carried only between telegraph terminals. But the Pony Express continued its operations all the way from St. Joseph to Sacramento, until four weeks after the telegraph was completed. In the last days of November the brilliant organization began to break up. The riders left for other jobs, some riding local runs and others turning to freighting or to scouting for the army. The horses, many of them, were broken to harness. The stage lines took over the stations and the maintenance forces strung out along the Overland Trail.

On Christmas Day, 1860, news broke in Washington of a defalcation in the Indian Trust Bonds, to the sum of about $870,000. Unwittingly or otherwise, William Russell was involved. He may have been guiltless but the story broke at a peculiarly inopportune time. Two years of constant effort to effect the passage of an act authorizing a daily overland mail by the Central Route was just now coming to fruition; and at the end of February Congress was to make provision for such mail. In these last months before outbreak of the Civil War, spreading violence in the South was making it clear that Butterfield's Overland Mail line, long objected to for its circuitousness, could not much longer be maintained. Proposals were made in Congress that Butterfield be moved, bag and baggage, to the Central Route; and when objection was made that Russell, Majors, and Waddell, whose imagination and daring had demonstrated the practicability of the Central Route, should be asked to give way to Butterfield, it seemed sufficient explanation to Congress that Butterfield was reported willing to purchase their properties at an appraised value. The act itself required the contractors for the Central Route to run a semiweekly Pony Express until completion of the Overland Telegraph.

Nothing but ruin was to be anticipated. They had the option of selling out at an "appraised value" which obviously could take into account only the current operating equipment of the company, without regard for the money that had gone into development, or of competing with a government-backed contractor required by law to meet them on their own ground.

The passing months dragged Russell, Majors, and Waddell toward insolvency. A subcontract with Butterfield for the daily mail and Pony Express east of Great Salt Lake City did not help much. They had been able to borrow some money from Ben Holladay, a Kentucky-born Missourian who had made money merchandising and freighting in Utah and California; but Holladay refused to advance more funds without security, and a mortgage was drafted in July, 1861. The company was able to operate another nine months, and then had to turn over its properties to the auctioneer. Forced, he said, to bid in the property to protect his $208,000 loan, Ben Holladay bought it for $100,000. Although he offered to sell to anyone who could raise in ten days enough money to cover his investment, on this March day in Atchison the "Stagecoach King" climbed upon his throne.

The "King" swiftly set up a regime that commanded the admiration of the West. The name which, after taking over the Butterfield interests, Ben Holladay gave to his company is still lordly: "The Overland Stage." Holladay's thorough efficiency is reflected in Mark Twain's account of a panegyric to Moses, delivered in Palestine to a youth who had traveled in the Overland Stage:

"Jack, from this spot where we stand, to Egypt, stretches

a fearful desert three hundred miles in extent—and across that desert that wonderful man brought the children of Israel!—guiding them with unfailing sagacity for forty years over the sandy desolation and among the obstructing rocks and hills, and landed them at last, safe and sound, within sight of this very spot; and where we now stand they entered the Promised Land with anthems of rejoicing! It was a wonderful, wonderful thing to do, Jack. Think of it!"

"*Forty years?*" said the youth. "*Only three hundred miles?* Ben Holladay would have fetched them through in thirty-six hours!"

The stage lines of the West produced a lordly caste of drivers. The tale of Hank Monk, who, legend says, bounced Horace Greeley hair-raisingly across the Sierras to the crooned reassurance, "Don't worry, Mr. Greeley, I'll get you there in time," has been told in a thousand shapes and forms, and damned in a riotous anecdote by Mark Twain. There were others of the nobility, men in whom it was a matter of pride to roar with their six-horse teams along precipitous mountain roads, sometimes driving off into the abysses, but more characteristically bringing stage and passengers safe, if shaken, to their destination. Sometimes they condescended to reassure nervous passengers: "Now, don't you worry, the stagecoach company is rich and responsible, and if anything happens, they'll pay yore heirs without buckin' or sweatin' a ha'r." But also they announced their willingness, in the event of an accident, to knock in the skulls of injured survivors, as it always cost more to pay off on live men than dead ones.

Stagecoach driving west from Washoe had its own peculiar flavor, for, as Sam P. Davis has observed in his delightful history of Nevada's lawless element, stagecoach robbing early became a recognized industry of the country. The Wells, Fargo stages were held up for the bullion they carried; the passengers were seldom molested, and indeed might even be invited to participate in extemporized fêtes champêtres, buffalo robes spread on the ground for the ladies, and the whole affair conducted with faultlessly elegant courtesy. Most notorious of these gentry was Jack Davis; he "might have been mistaken for a studious professor or a clergyman of remarkable placidity and meekness; and the judges, lawyers and bankers of the Comstock, when sitting down to a stiff game of poker, welcomed no one more warmly to a seat with them." Davis was fabulously successful while he stuck to stagecoach robbing; his downfall came when he branched out to train robbing.

By and large, the stagecoach drivers considered the fighting of robbers no part of their business, and made no bones about "throwing down the box" when a masked gentleman stepped out from some likely boulder or clump of sage, although there were a few drivers who maintained reputations for shooting holes through the banditti. By the community at large, stagecoach robbing was by no means regarded as without the pale; in the light of the extortions of Wells, Fargo, it was viewed as "a mere wrangle among robbers over the division of a common spoil. . . . The week that went by without one or more coaches being held up produced a feeling of dull times generally, and was sure to be followed by a depression in the tenderloin district."

West of Washoe, then, the shining hero was a little tarnished; and the express companies had even to accompany him with armed "messengers." But the drivers are remembered for the skill, the competence and the devotion they brought to their profession.

"Happy Harry" Harper, eastbound with the Overland Stage in March, 1863, drove his coach up to Eight Mile Station immediately after the murder of the stationkeeper. Gosiute raiders from ambush unloosed a volley that mortally wounded the driver. The frightened horses dashed off along the trail, still guided by the inflexible hand of Happy Harry. There were four passengers, an old man and his two sons, and

Nevada's delegate to Congress, Judge Gordon N. Mott. The old man, wounded, rolled about on the floor of the coach unconscious, but at Happy Harry's call, as the trail darkened before his eyes, the judge climbed out of the rocketing stage and, clinging to the sides of the coach, reached the driver's seat in time to grasp the lines as Happy Harry pitched dying under the seat. Washoe remembered chiefly the acrobatics of the judge, who brought the stage into Deep Creek Station, but by the fraternity Happy Harry's name was not forgotten.

Ben Holladay's Overland Stage was the foundation of the kingdom he ruled four years, a kingdom coextensive with the West. He conceded nothing to the Indians who plundered and killed along the trails south of the Humboldt; though he lost 150 horses, seven stations, and sixteen men, he drove his stages through, and when soldiers at length marched east toward the Mormon settlements, it was not toward the protection of the Overland stations that they had, finally, to direct their military energies.

Highwaymen, Indians, the weather, and business competition all were inadequate antagonists for King Ben Holladay. Abdication came at the summit of his power, in 1866, just after he had bought out the only opposition that threatened his reign. To Wells, Fargo for $1,500,000 in cash and $300,000 in stock, he sold the property he had created in four years from his $308,000 investment. Wells, Fargo gambled that the Pacific Railroad could not be completed in less than six years; its completion in three was catastrophic for their investment. Ben himself went into business in Oregon; perhaps it is appropriate that when the panic of '73 stripped him of most of his money, the most costly of his investments was a projected railroad to California. He died in 1887. Let his epitaph come out of his royal years: "Nothing was too big for him."

A final splash of color for the turbulent pageantry of the sixties in the country south of the Humboldt! A railroad in the valley of the desert river at the end of this decade enforced a new pattern upon the West. But let us listen to the drums and the clear voices of the bugle. . . .

Colonel Patrick Edward Connor marched his regiment of California Volunteers east out of Fort Churchill in August, 1862, to establish a military post in Ruby Valley to safeguard communications along the Overland Trail. He was also to establish a post in the vicinity of Great Salt Lake City— ostensibly to extend government protection against Indians, but actually to keep an eye on the Mormons.

Connor and his men wanted action against Johnny Reb, not inglorious garrison duty. But they began the eastward trek, brightening at the prospect that the Mormons, that cross-grained people so alien to the tradition of the West, might prove bellicose.

So the California Volunteers marched eastward through dust and sun, an anachronistic infantry traversing this horse-man's world, the blue of their uniforms and the bright flash of their buttons a defiance to the smoking grays and blues and browns of the desert plains and ranges. Ruby Valley was reached the first day of September, and while the troops built quarters there, Connor got into civilian clothes and departed by stage for Great Salt Lake City. On arrival in the Mormon settlements, he decided to establish his force on the bench above the Mormon capital, not out in the desolate valley thirty-five miles southwest, where Johnston had quar-tered his troops; he did not like the look or the sound of the Mormons. Two companies were left to garrison Fort Ruby, and with the rest of his force, on October 2nd, Connor marched for the City of the Saints.

Approaching Great Salt Lake City, it was rumored in camp that they would have to fight their way in. Connor, who had won his spurs in the war with Mexico, vowed to cross the river Jordan if hell yawned below, but the farther bank of the Western Jordan was barren of Mormon soldiery, and they marched up the State Road and north into the city, turning up First South Street to salute the governor. From the rooftops the Mormons watched their passage, without a cheer, without a jeer. Connor's six hundred marched up to their Camp 49, soon called Camp Douglas. Gentile civilization had come east out of the Humboldt country, and life for the Mormons could never again be quite the same. Aside from fighting Indians on Bear River and in Montana—and, less frequently and on no impressive scale, in Nevada—Connor would set his men to prospecting, open up Utah's long-neglected mines, and establish a basis for the rapprochement of Mormon and Gentile as twentieth century Americans.

In the country of the Humboldt, in the desert valleys and amid the desert mountains, the inevitable warfare of Indian and white would continue for another decade with stroke and counterstroke of murder and murderous reprisal, emigrants a prey to Indians and Indians to soldiery. Even before the departure from Ruby Valley, Connor had dispatched Company H of the Second California Cavalry to hang in the Humboldt Valley whatever Indians they could lay hands on, whose guilt in late depredations might be established. Three times this detachment captured Indians who, "attempting to escape," were fired upon and killed. The Indians might have made other report of this and later encounters; but it was the whites who wrote the records and the whites who, by the inescapable pressure of American life, must come into possession of this land. At the end of the decade came the railroad, brand of irrevocable purpose set upon this country. The free years of ranging the Unknown Land were finished, and the red domain was made the white.

XIX

The Trail of Shining Steel

I N THE spring of 1859 Horace Greeley embarked upon an overland journey to get some firsthand information on this turbulent West which he was commending to the attention of young men. The mail stage brought him into the valley of the Humboldt in August.

The Humboldt trail had become normal to the existence of the West, but the Easterner winced to a condition of national being: "All things considered, [the Humboldt] is the meanest river of its length on earth . . . its water, for at least the lower half of its course, is about the most detestable I ever tasted. I mainly chose to suffer thirst rather than drink it. Though three hundred and fifty miles in length, it is never more than a decent mill-stream; I presume it is the only river of equal length that never had even a canoe launched upon its bosom. . . . It certainly is not a pleasure to ride, night and day, along such a stream, with the heat intense, the dust a constant cloud and the roads all gullied, and ground into chuck-holes; but then, who would stay in such a region one moment longer than he must?

"I thought I had seen barrenness before—on the upper course of the Republican—on the North Platte, Green River, etc.—but I was green, if the regions washed by those streams were not. Here, on the Humboldt, famine sits enthroned, and waves his scepter over a dominion expressly made for him. On the above-named rivers, I regarded cotton-wood with contempt; here, a belt, even the narrowest fringe of cotton-wood would make a comparative Eden. The sage-bush and grease-wood, which cover the high, parched plain on either side of the river's bottom, seems thinly set, with broad spaces of naked, shining, glaring, blinding clay between them; the hills beyond, which bound the prospect, seem even more naked. Not a tree, and hardly a shrub, anywhere relieves their sterility. . . . As the only considerable stream in the Great Basin that pursues a general east and west direction, the Humboldt may continue for years to be traveled, but I am sure no one ever left it without a sense of relief and thankfulness. There can never be any considerable settlement here."

Yet the exhortation with which he closed the record of his *Overland Journey,* answer to the vigor and exultation that swelled in the life of the Pacific slope, was exhortation that must bring inevitable change, even fruitfulness, to the desolation that had chilled his nerve ends: "Men and brethren! let us resolve to have a railroad to the Pacific—to have it soon."

It had been dreamed about, talked about, demanded and explored for. There were no illusions about its cost. A Pacific railroad must cross both the Rockies and the Sierra Nevada. The West was waterless and treeless, roved by haughty red men, uninhabited and possibly uninhabitable. The cost of bridging two thousand miles of wilderness was staggering.

But it has been the way of America to dream greatly and cast about for means of realization. Only twelve years after a horse-drawn railroad was completed at Quincy, Massachusetts, in 1826, Congress was actually receiving petitions for the building of a Pacific railroad. In 1844 Asa Whitney began to agitate his idea for this railroad and for seven years, while Americans assaulted the farther West, he besieged Congress. His ideas were impractical enough, but they appear almost hardheaded compared to others. None of the dreamers wanted the railroad built by the government. "If the railroad to San Francisco is undertaken as a public work, we are warned by the fate of our system of permanent fortifications that the great resurrection gun may fire before its completion." In general, they asked special land grants and the right to take from the public lands natural resources requisite to the building. Plans for financing the railroad were vague.

Whitney finally abandoned empire building for running a dairy in Washington, D. C., but eventually five exploring expeditions of United States topographical engineers were sent out. The reports of those expeditions are among the most valuable documents in the literature of western exploration, but they were primarily reconnaissances of the country.

Now the Pacific railroad got tangled up in sectional jealousies. Conflicting feelings about the spread of slavery, and the more sharply immediate conviction that the value of land traversed by the railroad would be greatly increased, and settlement stimulated, with a powerful new force operating in the struggle for sectional power, invariably mired down the railroad in Congressional rhetoric. Compromise availed nothing. When two railroads were suggested, a third was wanted. In all the years until the outbreak of the Civil War, while the West argued for a Pacific railroad, the East quarreled over the West as an instrumentality of its imperial destiny.

In 1854, while the exploring expeditions were still in the field, a young man sailed for California. Theodore Dehone Judah at the age of twenty-eight already was a railroad engineer of note. California promoters sought him out to plan and build a railroad from Sacramento to Sierran placer mines. Even before his ship steamed through the Golden Gate, he had the vision for his life, the Pacific railroad: "It will be built," he said again and again to his wife, pacing nervously about, stopping now and then to glare in exultation. "It *will* be built, and I'm going to have something to do with it!"

The completion of California's first railroad was triumphantly celebrated in February, 1856. Judah now preached his vision almost from street corners. Men warmed to the fire in him; and indeed none in California had ever required to be convinced that the Pacific railroad must, and someday should, be built. But in the stagnation of California's mid-fifties nobody had the money or the will to embark upon railroad building. Judah went to surveying wagon roads into the Sierras. He returned, however, to talk of his Dutch Flat route for the Pacific railroad. Other men could build roads or turnpikes.

Four years of talking, talking, talking had its effect. In September, 1859, Californians organized a Pacific Railroad Convention whose recommendations Judah took east. "On every conceivable point," said Congressman John C. Burch, who became his friend en route, "he was armed with arguments, facts and figures." He had ideas as to routes, ideas as to finance, ideas as to legislative expedients. Arriving in Washington, he preached to all whom his evangelism could reach. A friendly congressman obtained the use of a room in

the Capitol, where he organized a brilliant lobby, with reports, diagrams, maps, and graphic illustrations of all kinds.
Congressmen drifted into his room to look over his exhibits
and talk with him. But Congress in 1860 was wrestling with
slavery under the shadow of secession; it was, besides, a year
of presidential election.

Undiscouraged, Judah returned to San Francisco. When
Congress again convened, he would have not only his flaming
conviction in the Pacific railroad; but actual maps, profiles,
and estimates of a route across the Sierras. East of the Sierras
there was no question that a railroad was practicable. The
valleys of the Humboldt and the Platte long since had announced their feasibility.

Judah labored in the mountains until frozen out. The
papers he spread on store counters in Dutch Flat were the
vindication of the summer's work. These field notes and
profiles proved once and for all that a railroad could be built
through the Sierras. Judah scratched out on a stray piece of
paper the Articles of Association of the Central Pacific Railroad of California.

To begin with, he proposed to run his railroad to the
state line. That was 115 miles from Sacramento, so by state
law he had to secure subscriptions of $115,000 in capital
stock before he could incorporate. Within three days he
raised $46,500 from the Dutch Flat vicinity, and he set out
for San Francisco to raise the balance. But the San Francisco
capitalists were wary. Angrily Judah set out for Sacramento.
And to a jeweler, a lawyer, a druggist, a wholesale grocer, the
owner of a dry goods store, and two hardware merchants, one
night he sold his idea. He painted no wild pictures of a transcontinental railroad. He sold them the proposition that they
could control the traffic to the Comstock. The Comstock's
supply business was something they could reach out and put
their hands on.

Of the men he talked to in the room above Hopkins &

Huntington's hardware store, four were to be exalted to places of power by his vision. Leland Stanford, Collis P. Huntington, Charles Crocker, Mark Hopkins. The light splinters a little on these names today, but in the spring of 1861 they were the names merely of four middlingly successful Sacramento storekeepers.

Money was put up for detailed surveys, and while insurgent South Carolinians opened the inevitable conflict, Judah pursued his investigations in the Sierras. The problems were serious: the western slope rose with forbidding abruptness and was slashed by canyons and ravines; cuts and tunnels would have to be blasted from almost solid granite, and there was always the fear that in winter the rails might be buried in twenty or thirty feet of snow. But Judah's report was even optimistic; the difficulties were fewer than might have been anticipated, and the road, he insisted, "commands, and will perform, the entire business of Nevada Territory, Washoe, and the silver mineral region." He added, "The line over the mountains completes the first Western link of the Pacific Railroad, overcoming its greatest difficulties."

It now remained to be seen what could be done with Congress.

In October Judah set off for Washington. He found a greatly changed Washington, an even more greatly changed Congress. It was swamped with emergency war measures but at least there was no longer any argument about the route. Every reason of national security and national interest ever advanced for the construction of the railroad now had quadrupled force. Washington had to worry whether secessionist sentiment in California and Nevada might not result in sundering the Pacific area as a separate republic if not as an associate of the Confederacy. A Pacific railroad was an essential instrument of national policy, evidence to the people of the Pacific states that their welfare counted for something to

the nation, and a means of getting troops west and the produce of the country east.

The mills of Congress began grinding. The authentica-
tion by "A. Lincoln" on July 1, 1862, created as a reality in
law the dream of which Judah had become the finally effective
voice.

The expressed intention of the Pacific Railroad Act was
"to aid in the construction of a railroad and telegraph line
from the Missouri River to the Pacific Ocean and to secure to
the Government the use of the same for Postal, Military and
other purposes." The builders were to be given a right-of-way
through the public domain, cash subsidies and, among other
things, every alternate, odd-numbered section of land, checkerboard fashion, for ten miles back on each side of the tracks.
Construction was to be carried on from both the east and
the west.

Ground was broken by the Central Pacific in January,
1863. Fifty miles had to be built before the government
subsidy began, and the cost of this Judah estimated at well
over $3,000,000. The company had not this kind of money.
Collis P. Huntington went east to see what he could do in
New York and Stanford, newly elected governor of California, attempted to arrange subsidies from the state and interested counties. Enough money was found to keep the work
going, though the first eighteen miles of track was not completed until January, 1864.

In the abstract everybody had been in favor of a Pacific
railroad. In the concrete there were a lot of people whom
the shining rails moved to tears. A Pacific railroad would
destroy overland stage and freight business, mail contracting,
and an overland telegraph monopoly; it would compete with
Sacramento River steamship lines, with Pacific mail steamers,
and with the Alaska ice monopoly; it also, locally, would
dominate the transportation picture. Everybody loved the

virgin, but on having to live in the same house many thought the lady a whore.

Moreover, the Big Four's policy was to make the lady pay her way. Stanford, Huntington, Hopkins, and Crocker had never been known as philanthropists; their reputation was that of merchants who tried to make a dollar grow where none had grown before. It was preposterous to think that the better angels of their nature had persuaded them to self-sacrificing public service.

The nigger in the woodpile seemed to be the Nevada mines. The Central Pacific was merely using federal, state, county, and municipal money to finance a monopolistic wagon road to Nevada. A correspondent of the *Daily Alta California* in May, 1864, thought it doubtful whether the railroad would go farther than the 20 miles to meet the wagon road. They called it "The Dutch Flat Swindle."

Judah himself may have had his doubts about the lady's virtue. The speculators associated with him were mainly interested in getting their railroad far enough into the mountains to enable them to underbid competition for the Nevada freight and passenger business; they wanted money out of the business at once. Judah could not get out of them any funds for extending surveys east of the California line, and to his angry expostulations they turned a deaf ear. He might be chief engineer, but it was their money and they proposed to spend it in their own way. One way they intended to spend it was to award themselves the construction contracts. Obviously, somebody had to go. Judah seems to have accepted $100,000 for his stock, and to have received options to buy out the other four for the same sum each. In the fall of 1863 he set out for New York. But, crossing Panama, he contracted yellow fever, and a week after reaching New York he died. The Big Four would henceforth stand or fall by their ideas of how the Central Pacific should be built.

However slowly or meanly the Central Pacific got on

toward the Sierras, progress in California was inspiring by contrast with what was being accomplished in the East. The Union Pacific's achievements were principally limited to spending $500,000 which could not readily be accounted for and which it was suspected had gone to line the pockets of its officers.

Even the amending of the Pacific Railroad Act in 1864 produced no action on the part of the Union Pacific. Lincoln had listened sympathetically to criticism of the first Act. The land grant was doubled, and other valuable concessions were made; also, and significantly, the Central Pacific was authorized to build 150 miles east of the California state line, to which it had been limited by the Act of 1862. In 1866 this provision was again amended, authorizing the Pacific railroads to build until they met.

Until the close of the Civil War the Central Pacific made no sensational progress. Financial conditions were difficult; the cost of shipping in supplies was ruinous; and litigation by hostile California interests tied up their energies. On top of all this, the labor situation was appalling. Men worked just long enough to get a stake to cross the Sierras to Washoe. During one period the C. P. shipped two thousand laborers over the mountains before they got a hundred willing to stay on the job.

By the summer of 1865, however, things were brightening. The courts were ruling in favor of the C.P.; the Confederacy had given up the long struggle; and the labor problem had been solved in gangs of Chinese graders. When the Union Pacific drove its first discouraged rails out of Omaha in July, the Central Pacific railhead was some fifty miles out from Sacramento. By the end of the year thousands of yellow men were toiling in the Sierras, and the Central Pacific really began to move. Charley Crocker stormed up and down the road "like," he remembered later, "a mad bull, stopping along wherever there was anything amiss, and raising Old Nick with the boys that were not up to time." Yet the road had not really got into the Sierras at the close of the year, and the builders had still to wonder whether Judah had been right in thinking the snows could be circumvented.

In 1866 the assault was launched on the Sierra Nevada. The coolies swarmed to the task of cutting and filling the formidable canyon grades and the engineers began their labor with the tunnels. In all, there were fifteen; the longest was the summit tunnel, 1,659 feet long. This tunnel was worked from four faces—from its eastern and western termini and two ways from a shaft sunk midway in its length. The job took a year. Working in 12-hour shifts, the drifters averaged no more than seven or eight inches a day. Dynamite, invented only this year, was not yet available. Nitroglycerine had been invented in 1846, but it was not commercially available either, though experimental use was made of it. Black powder sometimes had no effect save to blast back through the drill holes. The summit bore was not holed through until September, 1867—the world's last major tunnel driven by hand.

Most spectacular, though not most difficult, of the feats of 1866 was the circumvention of Cape Horn, a granite buttress rising a thousand feet above the American River. Chinese, lowered on slings, chipped out a shelf in the solid rock and this was widened to accommodate the roadbed. After May, 1866, the construction trains were able to puff cautiously around the Horn and on up toward the summit tunnels.

This yard-by-yard progress was disquieting, for after years of inaction, the Union Pacific had hired Major General Grenville M. Dodge as chief engineer, and Dodge's capacities for railroad building had been demonstrated under Grant and Sherman.

On arriving at Omaha, Dodge found that the Union Pacific amounted to nothing but "a rusty and uncertain line

that jutted out from the banks of the Missouri River on to
the prairies of Nebraska as far as the Elkhorn." Fresh from
campaigns against the Plains Indians, he was well aware that
construction to the Rockies would be hard and dangerous
work. He had one advantage over Crocker, however—the
Plains presented no such obstacle to the grading gangs as did
the Sierra Nevada. On the other hand, Crocker's coolie labor
was much less expensive than Dodge's Irishmen, and on the
whole quite as efficient; moreover, timber was readily available from the Sierran forests. Problems of supply were complicated for each.

Dodge got to work. His chief tracklayer, Jack Casement, assembled a choice lot of roughnecks—"Union and
Confederate veterans, Irish immigrants, Mexicans, bush-
whackers, muleskinners, and ex-convicts from eastern jails"
—moved them forty miles out of Omaha to the forlorn end
of the rusted track, and put them to work. Within a month
he was laying three miles of track a day. The shining rails
moved on over the horizon.

Hell on Wheels kept pace with the rails. The construction camps of the C.P. would have met with the approval
of the Women's Christian Temperance Union—sober and
decorous, whisky sellers kicked out of the camps within the
hour of their appearance. The U.P. camps, by contrast, were
loud, bawdy, drunken, and explosive; as the sun went down
each night, the construction gangs yielded themselves up to
the roaring delights of the flesh. Murder was the commonplace
of any evening; riots were a community recreation. The U.P.
rolled into the Indian country giving off bright, loud, vainglorious sparks.

In August, 1866, the Plains Indians began a long harass-
ment of the Union Pacific builders. Dodge swore at humani-
tarians in Congress who wouldn't clear up the mess consequent
upon government treaties impossible of fulfillment, and
while the railroad's finances tottered and swayed and mo-

mentarily threatened to collapse about him, drove his rails west beyond Cheyenne, where the increased mountain subsidy pumped new blood into the shaky corporation. By the end of 1867 he was deep into what was about to be created as the Territory of Wyoming. It had been a monumental twenty months' labor. And the Central Pacific was still embroiled with the Sierra Nevada. The Union Pacific began to envisage grading across Utah, into and through the Humboldt Valley, and on to the Sierra foothills before the C.P. could get out of the mountains.

To the Big Four that contretemps appeared all too probable. The snow had almost paralyzed them during the winters of 1865-66 and 1866-67. In March of 1867 fifteen feet of snow still blanketed Summit Valley, and all winter nothing was done there except in the tunnels. But the company could not let itself be balked by the snow or by the unfinished tunnels. A stage road was kept open and supplies were hauled over the summit by sled and wagon to construction camps in the Truckee Canyon. "The snow would fill up as fast as they could dig it out," Charley Crocker said, "so I moved them down on the Truckee River. We hauled locomotives over (when I say we, I mean myself) and we hauled iron and cars and all that sort of thing and built fifty miles. We hauled the locomotives on sleighs, but some of them on logs because we could not get sleighs big enough for some of the engines." In June, 1867, the construction gangs in the Truckee Canyon were brought back to the mountains, but a dozen feet of snow had to be shoveled off the survey before work could recommence.

The C.P. holed through the last tunnels and by midsummer the first locomotive reached the summit. By the end of the year the locomotive was across the state line into Nevada. The railroad in 1867 had come almost forty miles, more than in any previous year. Much had been done, as well, in the canyon of the Truckee, and work had begun on forty miles of snowsheds, a three-year job to render secure the passage of the Sierras. With every prospect of making good, Charley Crocker wrote in his journal a New Year's resolution of a mile a day as the construction program for 1868.

Down out of the Sierras came the Central Pacific construction gangs as the spring of 1868 wiped away the snows. The grading crews were across the Forty Mile Desert and far up the Humboldt Valley; surveyors were even farther ahead, their stakes marking a way clear into Utah, around the north shore of Great Salt Lake, and up Weber Canyon. It was the tracklaying crews and the construction engines, however, puffing down the Truckee and out upon the deserts, that brought to the land the names of stations and towns. Lake's Crossing of the Truckee, brusquely renamed Reno, was reached June 19th, and engine whistles and the chatter of wheels on steel was sufficient baptism for Wadsworth, on July 22nd. There was need for haste. The Union Pacific had surmounted the Continental Divide, finding a route through the Red Desert south of South Pass, and was smashing its way on to the Green and Bear rivers. The cost of getting through the Sierras had been almost double the government subsidy, but the construction cost east through the great valley of the Humboldt was far lower than the minimum subsidy, and here the C.P. stood to recoup something of its losses—if the U.P. did not get there first.

The grades were ready and waiting. The tracklayers marched out upon the Forty Mile Desert and up the lower valley of the Humboldt. Into the age-old silences moved the steel-and-iron clangor of the America which had found this pathway west and in this pathway was forging the irrevocable jointure. The bright glitter of sunlight on steel was the American will imposed upon the alien land. So was the outcast redeemed to tradition, the desolation mocked, the loneliness and the emptiness thwarted. Crocker fought his way north and east to the Big Bend of the Humboldt and the raw new railroad town named Winnemucca, and then east. By the end of the year engines were sounding in Palisade Canyon.

Far ahead of the tracklayers, the graders had moved into the upper valley of the Humboldt, observing the sharply clean new stakes announcing the ambitions of the Union Pacific. The U.P.'s Irishmen were grading in advance of their own rails to meet them. Soon the grading gangs of the two railroads were working parallel to each other, occasionally abandoning their work to crack skulls in pick-handle free-for-alls. The C.P.'s yellow men were slight of build, but they more than held their own with Casement's roaring Irishmen. The Irish discovered an innocent pleasure in blasting sky-high the C.P. grades and the Chinese; but their own grades began exploding under their feet. They assembled their dead, buried the fragments in style, and commended to the world that fine old workable philosophy of live and let live.

Ogden was the primary objective of each road; the one that first reached the valley of the Great Salt Lake might monopolize the Mormon trade. As for the Mormons themselves, they had tried to persuade both roads to build through Salt Lake City and south around Great Salt Lake. Failing in this, they hired out gladly enough to each company, taking subcontracts to build grades east and west from Ogden. The coming of the railroad must bring tremendous changes to the domain of the Saints, but to those optimistic souls who ventured to hope that the railroad might be the means of overthrowing the Mormons neck and crop, Brigham Young had sufficient retort: It was a poor religion that couldn't stand one railroad.

In March, 1869, the Union Pacific burst through the Wasatch into Great Salt Lake Valley, and celebrated entrance into Ogden. They had won that race; now they would build as far west as they could. The probable junction looked to be the summit on the Promontory Range, and after much argument and political maneuvering in Washington, it was agreed that the Pacific railroad should be joined there. Keeping up the terrific race to the end, with tracklaying competition in which the C.P. set a ten-miles-in-one-day record that still stands, the two companies on April 29, 1869, completed the gap save for two lengths of rail left for a final ceremony.

In special trains from Sacramento the C.P. officials arrived at Promontory on May 7th. The town was sodden with rain, its streets a black quagmire. Floods along the line, and incipient strikes by unpaid workers, held up the U.P. train. For three days the celebrants had to kill time awaiting their celebration.

May 10th was sunny but cold; an icy wind whistled through Promontory until early afternoon. As the crowd began to reach the ragged end of its patience, the U.P.'s *No. 119* pounded up to confront the C. P.'s *Jupiter*. Out of the U.P. cars piled officials of the road, newspapermen, prominent Mormons, officials of Utah counties and cities, and soldiers from Connor's Camp Douglas. In all, five or six hundred spectators were present—Irish and Chinese laborers, section hands, teamsters, freighters, train crews, strumpets, engineers, cooks, gamblers, and perhaps a stray Indian or two.

In the nation's cities the people listened to the news flashed over the telegraph lines. A laurel tie was embedded, and the final rail put in place by a smartly garbed squad of C.P. coolies. Presently the telegrapher tapped out encouragement to the nation: "We have got done praying; the spike is about to be presented."

Spikes were presented with flowery rhetoric; spikes of Comstock silver, other spikes from Arizona, Idaho, and Montana. California had provided a double spike of gold, with a silver sledge hammer for the driving. Another hour went by in preparation for the driving of the golden spike. At last Leland Stanford picked up the hammer and prepared for the final act. A telegraph wire was attached to the spike, and another to the hammer; the railroad would signal to the nation its own completion.

Out of the immortality of the moment emerges a fine, human touch, Americans stamping this hour with the fullness of their laughter. Listen to Alex Toponce, honest, shrewd, Gentile freighter standing down there in the crowd squinting into sun and splendor:

"When they came to drive the last spike, Governor Stanford, president of the Central Pacific, took the sledge, and the first time he struck he missed the spike and hit the rail.

"What a howl went up! Irish, Chinese, Mexicans, and everybody yelled with delight. Everybody slapped everybody else on the back and yelled, 'He missed it. Yee.' The engineers blew the whistles and rang their bells. Then Stanford tried it again and tapped the spike and the telegraph operators had fixed their instruments so that the tap was reported in all the offices east and west, and set bells to tapping in hundreds of towns and cities. . . . Then Vice President T. C. Durant of the Union Pacific took up the sledge and he missed the spike the first time. Then everybody slapped everybody else again and yelled, 'He missed it, too, yow!'

"It was a great occasion, everyone carried off souvenirs and there are enough splinters of the last tie in museums to make a good bonfire."

Forty-three years later, Alex had forgotten what was said on this momentous occasion, but he had not forgotten that the champagne was marvelous.

XX

Milk from the Cow Country

I N THE year of passage of the Pacific Railroad Bill, Orson Hyde had recited to Washoe the word of God in its fullness: "I will work a work in your day—a work which ye shall in no wise believe though a man declare it unto you." And the Apostle of the Lord had been so good as to declare this work unto them, and even to advise that God's dealings with a certain class of dwellers upon the earth should be "neither light nor on a limited scale." Washoe, which might have taken less as a fearful warning than as a generous promise the assurances of much rioting in debauchery, abominations, drunkenness and corruption, was of course quite incapable of seeing at once that the Apostle, droning his curse in the full authority of his priesthood, had put his finger squarely on the railroad.

The excitement of the Promontory celebration was still electric in the cars of the Central Pacific special train that rumbled west through the Humboldt Valley on May 11, 1869. Stanford had especial reason to be pleased with himself. Six years ago he had turned the first shovelful of earth; now he had driven the last spike (it would be said later, unkindly, that that was about all he did do to build the road). On this day the blood ran free in the veins.

The train banged and rattled on the rails. Beyond the car windows was desolation—the naked hills, the rolling valley bottom, the emptiness the West had accepted as a necessary condition of life. But it was desolation changed. Indians, thirst, alkali, dust, the saber stroke of the sun—these were vanquished by the rails, the long American pageantry of the Humboldt Valley severed from the Nevada earth. Civilization in twenty years had hardly made impress upon the river valley, yet raw new towns drawing sustenance from this feeding steel artery already were flexing their young muscles. Wells, Elko, Battle Mountain, Golconda, Winnemucca, Lovelock—treeless towns, smelling of new-cut lumber, sunbeaten, virile and young. Looking from the grimy windows of their special train, the C.P. officials could warm to a sense of their own power. They had wrought with the desert, and these beginnings were fruit thereof.

Back in Sacramento, the elation went quickly. Stanford, Huntington, Hopkins, and Crocker had never had time to realize the kind of bear they had by the tail. Just hanging on had been a way of life. Now all that was over.

All of them were tired, tired to the bone. Through six years the railroad had been their life. All of them wanted to have done with this thing that had fed so long upon their energies. They would have sold out for ten cents on the dollar. Crocker did sell out, his partners finally agreeing to buy the greater part of his interests for $1,800,000. This was twelve cents on the dollar, but his associates felt that Crocker had the best of the bargain. Through 1871 they labored to sell their own interests for a reported price of $20,000,000; the sale would have netted them twenty cents on the dollar, and they would have been delighted to take it. Stanford, his infant son enabling him to dream of dynasties, began to think he might want to stick to the railroad, but Huntington occupied the gloomy months wondering just what good money was. "If I had someone growing up to take my place, I would hardly name a price that I would take, but as I have not, what the Devil is the use of my wearing myself out?"

In September, 1873, however, a paralyzing panic struck the nation, ending all possibility of immediate sale of the Central Pacific, and calling in question whether the road would not go under. The Big Four rolled up their sleeves and went back to work. Crocker re-entered the partnership, and the men settled down to making their railroad pay. Quickly Washoe and the country of the Humboldt learned that making a railroad pay had much, very much, to do with them.

The expectation had been general, that the Pacific railroad would be an avenue to the Orient. However, in the year that Judah had gone to California a French engineer, Ferdinand de Lesseps, had become absorbed with an age-old dream, and through years of discouragement and disappointment he stuck to this endeavor. Only six months after the driving of the golden spike, the Suez Canal was formally opened, and it soon became clear that the Humboldt Valley would not be a latter-day Silk Road.

It had also been anticipated that passenger traffic would be great, but after the first few months the number of passengers sharply declined, and for days together the daily train carried no passengers at all. And the Mormon market proved a mirage, as Brigham Young established co-operative stores and local socialistic communities to further his ruling passion for Mormon self-sufficiency.

Making a railroad pay boiled down, finally, so far as the country east of the Sierras was concerned, to mine supply business and to building up towns in the desert—the development of "local traffic." Monopolistic control of California's transportation facilities gave the company the great proportion of its wealth and power, but no source of profits was passed by, and certainly not Washoe and the Humboldt.

By the terms of the Pacific Railroad Act, every alternate section of land not earlier alienated, for twenty miles back on each side of the tracks, belonged to the railroad. It was desert land, substantially worthless. But a railroad in the Humboldt Valley permitted a new perspective on the worth of the Humboldt land.

The towns began as a combination of supply bases for the mining camps and railroad sidings and division points. The railroad brought in many, the mines attracted others, freighters followed the line of least resistance, and there were those, even in the seventies, who came west in answer to the old fever still burning in American blood. "We drove as far as we could, went broke, and then, by God," an old-timer once told me, "we had to stop where we were." Many stopped in the Humboldt Valley. The West was filling up, and men who had gone to California or to Oregon were drifting back over the mountains in search of land. "Roll along, Mr. Immigrant," the *Humboldt Register* observed in 1864, "any fool can get to California, but it takes a smart man to get away from there." Smart men were now coming back in increasing numbers.

Elko and Winnemucca were most vigorous of the Humboldt towns. Elko was near the headwaters of the river, amid low, rolling hills green in spring but drying with summer

into dead tones of green, gray, and brown. Here the river
ran opaquely green through cottonwood brush, its waters
helpless to succor the hills. Winnemucca was in a spreading
wide valley at the Big Bend, 120 miles west. In 1850, a
French trader sold supplies to the Golden Army there. The
Frenchman departed, but the Humboldt mines lured others
than Mark Twain north, and in 1863, astonishingly, French
Ford boasted even a hotel. Two years later both a bridge and
a ferry spanned the river, with a wagon road north to Idaho
through Paradise Valley, so that Winnemucca in 1868 was
not, like Elko, the issue solely of the railroad's steel womb.

Southwest of Winnemucca, all the way to the Sink, the
Humboldt towns had hardly more dignity than was afforded
by yellow-painted station houses, lonely water tanks, and
piles of fuel for the wood-burning locomotives, with perhaps a straggling log cabin or two close by. Elko and Winnemucca, with Reno, the new town astride the Truckee, were
the railroad's nerve centers for the exploitation of this country east of the Sierras.

The towns were built to western specifications. One old-
timer remembered later that Elko, on his arrival in 1869,
consisted of two tents, but that it grew very fast as the
mining excitement mounted in the hills south. It was, he
remembered specifically, "rather a bad town, as many rough
men stayed there for a few days at a time on their way to
White Pine." In that respect Elko was blood brother to most
other Nevada towns. There is a saying in the West that a
man living alone means suicide, two means murder, but
three means dissipation. Call it "a hell of a good time." The
town that couldn't provide the good time has not existed
in Nevada since the Mormon exodus. A railroad might get
to a boom town late or never, but whores, whisky, and
gambling houses got there almost before groceries. Song, the
plunking of pianos, and a spattering of gunshots enlivened
any night of the week. Diversions were various. The Opera

House impartially alternated singers and dogfights with magicians and dramatic companies, but equally welcome were wearers of the cloth. Men "plumb out of Bible" found ministerial sound and fury as satisfying as a whirl at monte, though here as on Washoe fire fighting was supreme among the recreations of man. Raw, rough, unpainted, false-fronted, perpetually blanketed in dust, loud and young and sinful under the desert sun, the very sign and symbol of rugged individualism, the Humboldt towns nonetheless were instrumentalities of a monopoly. "Railroad trouble" soon became endlessly descriptive in the ailing economics of any of these towns.

They evolved a phrase for it—"all that the traffic will bear"—and for almost forty years the railroad maintained rate schedules on that basis. In California the lion's share of the profit of virtually every business was diverted into the hands of the railroad. Freight costs on goods brought in from the East were so high that merchants had to cut their profit almost to nothing. "The degree of prosperity of every business or industry," Oscar Lewis observes in *The Big Four,* "was directly dependent upon the officials at Fourth and Townsend streets who fixed the railroad's freight rates. . . . If merchants were found to be growing prosperous, rates were raised; if too many went bankrupt, rates were lowered. The manufacturer was allowed to earn enough to keep his plant in operation; freight rates on the farmer's products were nicely calculated to enable him to clear enough to plant and harvest his next year's crop and to support himself, not too extravagantly, in the meantime. . . . The producer was usually allowed to clear enough to continue to produce, but in good years the profit went, not to him, but to the railroad."

In the Humboldt country the milking went on both ways. Miners, stock raisers, and farmers paid a tariff to get

their products over the Sierras to California, and they paid
through the nose for supplies. The Central Pacific had killed
the wagon-freighting business over the mountains; railroad
rates now rose far above the old wagon rates. The railroad
also quickly discovered that useful institution, the long haul.
Merchants in any Nevada town who ordered goods from the
East had to pay for having them hauled first to San Francisco
and then back over the Sierras. The railroad justification
was that water competition had to be met, and with no water
competition Nevada should pay higher rates; moreover, han-
dling charges were less for bulk shipments, and it was to the
railroad's convenience to ship in bulk to its San Francisco
terminal and transship from there. Nevada might argue that
if the railroad could haul goods to the Pacific and then back
three or four hundred miles, and still meet water competition, there was no justification for the back haul, while if
water competition so far undercut rail profits on the transcontinental haul as to force operations at a loss, there was no
reason why the inland provinces should be taxed for the
benefit of coastal areas. Argument, however, availed Nevada
nothing until 1910, when the Interstate Commerce Commission intervened; shippers since have fared better, but the
long- and short-haul argument is one still normal to the
worries of the West.

The railroad talked tough. The C.P.—absorbed in 1887
into the Southern Pacific system—had built its road not as a
public service, not for the government, but for itself. The
business would be run to suit itself. The railroad entrenched
itself politically, and in California, for over thirty years, its
enemies struggled in vain to dislodge it. In Nevada also, railroad money was potent.

Nevertheless, resistance organized in Nevada against the
railroad. This resistance should not be construed as represented in that holdup of the C.P. train below Reno, on November 1, 1870. Engineered by Jack Davis, Washoe's courtly

stage robber, that was the Pacific Coast's first train robbery, and one of the first in the nation. Far from applauding, Nevada's officialdom quickly collared the miscreants. Cattlemen of the Humboldt Valley, whose coming was in large measure a fruit of the building of the railroad through the valley of the desert river, were a more orthodox spearhead of resistance.

From the time of Mormon Station, ranching had had a foothold in Nevada's valleys, and throughout the fifties men had trailed sheep, cattle and horses to California through the Humboldt Valley. The silver rush to Washoe opened nearer markets. Through the early sixties cattlemen herded stock along the bottoms of the Walker, the Carson, the Truckee, and the northern creeks. Nevada's cattle era, however, began with the Humboldt's cattle era—with the appearance of the longhorns which in 1866 began the famous trail drives north from Texas.

The longhorns came first to the ranges of Montana and Wyoming, but quickly the dust of their passing eddied westward. The Mormons remained indifferent to them, and Mormon range history is barren of their wild glamour, but the longhorns were welcomed in the Humboldt Valley. John Sparks, a Mississippi-born Texan who later became governor of Nevada, has been credited with driving in a herd in 1868. The longhorn was a good rustler and could take care of itself; it fattened well on the Nevada ranges, and brought a good price in California slaughterhouses. Ranches spread in the country which until then had belonged to the Indian.

These cattlemen were hard-handed, straight-thinking fighters, far more independent and belligerent than the miners. L. R. Bradley, Nevada's second governor, had come over the Sierras with stock in 1862. A. B. Maxon, a young man reared a strict Baptist in upstate New York, who came west in 1872, depicts his manner. "At Elko," he says, "a very pleasant old man passed through the car addressing every one as 'my son' and extending the greetings of the day. This was contrary to my teachings and I declined to answer him, but on our arrival at Humboldt House, where the passengers had supper, I observed that everybody spoke to him, and I asked the conductor who the old gentleman was, and he said, with a laugh, 'That is Old Broadhorns, the Governor of Nevada,' and then for the first time I realized that the customs of the West were certainly different from the teachings of the East and I said to him, 'Excuse me for not replying to you the first time you spoke to me, but my people at home had told me not to speak to any one unless I was introduced, and they had also told me that the trains of the West were filled with confidence men who parted the innocent eastern travelers from their money by innocent manners and by strap games, etc.,' whereupon the Governor told every friend on the train that he had been taken for a three-card monte sharp, and when he got to Reno he treated the house at the old Depot Hotel and told Chamberlain to give me the best in the house and send him the bill.''

The cattlemen had this ease of manner, this grace of informality. Railroad money could buy an efficient opposition in a state more corrupt than any in the Union, and mining was too chaotic in its ups and downs, its frenzies and its collapses, to present a stable front. But the range barons won friends; and they stayed with the land and drew strength from it.

The railroad's checkerboard landholdings down the Truckee, up the Humboldt, and through the desert valleys east into Utah gave them a powerful leverage. Holdings twenty miles back from each side of the tracks along the floor of the Humboldt gave the railroad a singular kind of control over the better-watered area. Legally the railroad owned only half of that 40-mile-broad strip of land, but the square miles of public domain between their own holdings were inaccessible except by trespass upon their land. On the

Great Plains cattlemen pre-empted the public domain, the watercourses especially, and ran their herds as upon a royal dominion, unchallenged until the coming of the homesteaders. In the Humboldt Valley a powerful corporation had land-holdings from the beginning. The railroad's thorough grasp upon the Humboldt Valley, even seventy years after, may be seen by a glance at a land-use map for the state of Nevada.

The panic of '73 overthrew cattle markets, but the price of beef rose through the seventies, during the same years that the Big Four buckled down to the job of making their railroad pay. The locking of horns was inevitable, complicated presently by the appearance of sheepmen and homesteaders. The cattle barons fought a four-cornered battle—with courage and not too many scruples.

Rate fixing gave the railroad a mobile artillery to pound enemy lines destructively. But the cattlemen, besides fighting the railroad in Carson City's legislative and judicial chambers, had a weapon in their home country—political control over the range counties. Taxation of railroad property by the counties was a means of reprisal.

War spread to the range itself.

In the Humboldt Valley, as upon the Great Plains, the big cattlemen came first to the land. Peter Haws had raised some garden stuff near the head of the river in 1854-55, and employees of the Overland Stage Company in 1862 planted garden truck and forage crops in Ruby Valley, but homesteaders had not come to the Humboldt when the longhorns began to be trailed west from Goose Creek Valley. Range was to be had for the taking, and the firstcomers took it. Water was scarce and valuable, and was first to be fought over.

As early as 1873 sheep were herded in considerable numbers on the Nevada ranges, and cattlemen who accepted the folk belief that the breath of sheep poisoned the range, who simply and wholeheartedly hated the guts of sheep outfits for no better reason than that sheep were sheep, or who knew that sheep in the long run, by closer cropping of the forage, could drive cattle from any range—these cattlemen bought Winchesters and hired men who could use them.

Today one may ride up into the O'Neil country north of Wells and find crumbled walls of forts built out of dire necessity in the years of the war for the range. The period of disuse is hardly a quarter of a century old. Old-timers in Elko and Wells who talk freely of the old days hesitate, and say nothing, when certain years of their life ripen in their talk. The statute of limitations has its limitations.

The migration of sheep from summer to winter range, or from an old range to a new, was marked by the crackle of rifle fire. A gentleman known as Diamondfield Jack Davis wrought especial havoc among sheepherders who had the temerity to wander into the Humboldt Valley.

The railroad, by invoking laws of trespass, made difficult or impossible of access the checkered public domain. But also the railroad could lease or threaten to lease its grazing land to sheep outfits, thus enabling sheep to get a foothold where they had not been before; and by sales of its land, the railroad could bring in another and dangerous antagonist of the cattleman, the homesteader who strung the bottom land with the new barbed wire.

The fight was unequal, but the big cattlemen held their own quite well through the eighties. The country of the Humboldt was not, when all is said and done, a homesteader's country—the land and the climate, here even more than on the Great Plains, fought for the cattlemen. Sheep could not be denied, but ranchers who bowed to the inevitable did so by putting their own sheep on their range—ungratefully, as witness the rancher who looked over a couple of his waddies on whom the years had begun to tell, and wondered out loud whether he could knock their brains out and make sheepherders of them.

The range was flowering and beautiful. Sam Furniss, who came to Elko in 1881, an English boy with an ambition to be a cowboy, remembers the waving grass on the ranges in all directions from the town; it sustained outfits running as many as 20,000 head. Others remember when in the valleys near by the antelope were so numerous that when they all moved at once, the earth itself seemed to be moving. Grass was so thick and high that the cattle first reaching it were lost to sight.

Through the seventies and eighties rain was abundant, and the range seemed inexhaustible. Nobody will ever know how many cattle roamed the range—there are estimates that around Elko alone there were 300,000 to 400,000 head.

But the very richness of this range in the end was a betrayal. Cattle prices collapsed in 1885. Instead of shipping to burst markets, the ranchmen kept their cattle on the home ranges and waited for prices to pick up. And in 1888-1890 came the blizzards.

The snows of those two winters are legendary in the West. Ranchers recite history before and since 1888 as other men reckon time from the birth of Christ. The cattle froze in the drifts or starved to death. It is said that not 5 per cent of the stock in the Humboldt country survived the two blizzard winters. When the spring of 1890 melted the snow from the range, nine stockmen in ten were ruined. Mining in Nevada was approaching what seemed its finish, and the agricultural development of the state was negligible. The wiping out of the cattlemen seemed the finishing stroke. The railroad still maintained itself (though events were shaping in California to strip it of power there, and the nation was moving in the direction of federal suzerainty over transportation; just twenty years later the long struggle with the monopoly would end with the defeat of the railroad and the beginning of the era of regulation), but the victory for the railroad in Nevada was hollow.

The cattlemen came back, and the towns of the Humboldt Valley, which essentially had become cow towns serving the ranchmen, revived also. But things were not as they had been before. The irresponsible years when grass was a loot like beaver and bonanzas were ended. The ranges filled again, but on a reduced scale, and the stockmen bought home ranches to grow winter feed. Fights for hay land continued, but land rights were maturing now along the bottom lands and meadows where water was to be had, and order replaced violence in the Humboldt range country. The type of stock on the range changed also; blooded stock was brought in, shorthorns and then Herefords. The blooded stock was too valuable for haphazard range practices, and exerted further influence toward the farm-ranch developments that were the result of the blizzards.

The warfare over sheep continued. Scots and Chinese had herded the first sheep in the Humboldt country, but they were replaced by Basques from California. The "Boscoes" loved sheep and fought for them like devils. Warfare was the more bitter because the rainy years ended at the turn of the century; "drought years" have been the rule since. The wild grasses grew more reluctantly, and the scanty feed was overgrazed. The waving meadows disappeared. Cattle outfits warred for what feed there was, one against another and all against the sheep. Feeling was the more bitter against the sheep because most of the herds had no home range. They were tramp outfits feeding on the public domain, paying no taxes, having no interest in the preservation of the range. They "et out" the feed and moved on; if the range was ruined, that was none of their affair. They were the last of the looters the Humboldt Valley has known from the time of Ogden; and their day ended with the passage of the Taylor Grazing Act in 1934, which had as one of its provisions for use of the public domain, the possession of home

range on which stock could be ranged during a part of the
year.

Except for the nervous irritability which must always
characterize the relations of railroad and shipper in sub-
marginal regions, the long, bitter, costly warfare in the
Humboldt country between railroad and stockmen is ended.
Since 1907 a second railroad through the Humboldt Valley,
the Western Pacific, has ensured the benefits of competition,
but today both Western Pacific and Southern Pacific are
held in check by the Interstate Commerce Commission, and
the railroads work in harmony; through parts of the Humboldt Valley one line carries the westbound trains of both
companies, while the other carries the eastbound traffic.

There has always been rustling and there always will
be, until God or glandular discoveries effect necessary changes
in human nature. Rustling today, however, is butchershop
business—by men in trucks who slaughter beef and dispose
of it to crooked butchers. But, more than by farms or by
mines, the Humboldt country today is sustained by its livestock. The ranges which once precariously sustained Diggers
are grazed by white-faced Herefords, by black-and-white
Polled Anguses, by Rambouillets and Suffolks. Cattle cars
roll east and west to stockyards, and wool and mutton are
shipped both ways from the sidings. In livestock the land
has come to terms with itself.

The towns became cattle towns and existed on that
basis. Sam Furniss remembered that when he arrived at Elko
in May, 1881, the town was a street on each side of the railroad track. "The rest was cow trails." Wind-worn and false-
fronted, faded with dust and sun, the towns sprawled on the
desert floor, strung along the westering river and the railroad. Travelers east and west upon the trains, inheritors to
the Golden Trail, looked out upon the desert towns, oppressed by the grayness and the loneliness. But the towns

always had a vitality outmatching their physical proportions. Their roots ran deep into the back country. A mining
camp beyond that range or the other freighted its supplies
from here; but also ranch houses over every horizon drew
sustenance from these gray clusters of buildings that out-
siders only reluctantly called by the name of towns.

It is somehow fitting that one of the Humboldt towns,
in this far province of the Cattle Kingdom, provided the
setting for almost the last exploit of the famous outlawry
of that kingdom.

Struthers Burt, in *Powder River*, teetered on the rungs
of his chair to gossip about "Butch" Cassidy and the "long
riders" who at the close of the century gave the country
some of its most cherished wild West traditions. I shall not
enlarge upon Mr. Burt's account of the Wild Bunch. But
the job at Winnemucca deserves this much commemoration.

With Harry Longabaugh and Harvey Logan, the ablest
and most dangerous of the Wild Bunch, Mormon-born Butch
Cassidy rode into Winnemucca at noon on September 19,
1900. From a saloon they trooped into the bank. One of
them leveled a carbine at the cashier and ordered him to open
the vault. When told that the vault could be opened only by
the bank president, that dignitary was ushered in. The three
long riders then passed out the back door, herding before
them the two bank officials, a bookkeeper, a stenographer, and
a horse buyer who happened to be in the bank. Mounting
their horses, the outlaws galloped out of town to their own
exuberant gunfire. The whole job had taken less than five
minutes, and the loot was $32,640.

The job had been carefully planned. A few miles east
of Winnemucca the outlaws abandoned their horses for three
blooded animals, one of which, ironically, had been stolen
from the bank president's ranch. Although the news had been
telephoned to Golconda, seventeen miles east, by the time
a posse was organized there, the long riders were half an

hour beyond the town. The combined posses followed the trail north, but beyond Soldier's Pass the outlaws had another four horses waiting. An Indian from Golconda got close enough to exchange a couple of shots with Harvey Logan, but the outlaws then ran away from the laboring horses behind. Four of the posse trailed the long riders clear into Star Valley, Wyoming, but the quarry had vanished.

Small boys of East and West re-enacted on willow nags that drama the papers reported out of Winnemucca. The organization for the job, the precision of its execution, and most of all the galloping through the waste places with sacks of gold coin, gilded life with a glamour that even today remains in many men a warmth out of their youth. The Winnemucca stickup however, was instrumental in the breakup of the Wild Bunch. Cassidy, Longabaugh, and Logan lit out for Fort Worth where, newly dolled up, they had their picture taken in company with a couple of friends. The photographer was pleased with his work and displayed a print in his gallery. A Wells, Fargo detective recognized Bill Carver, one of the group, and headquarters soon was able to identify the others. The gang skipped to San Antonio, where they hid out for a while in the red-light district, and then Cassidy, Longabaugh, and Logan moved back north to an old hideout in Montana. They held up a train at Wagner, Montana, on July 3, 1901, and then broke up forever. Cassidy and Longabaugh went to Bolivia, and history says they were killed there, though legend (and Mr. Burt into the bargain) thinks otherwise. Logan's end also is legend, and anyone is permitted his choice whether he died in Wyoming of a gunshot wound or in Colorado by his own hand.

XXI

Rain

THIS is a story that is minted of the West, and you're likely to hear it anywhere—as well on the High Plains of Kansas or Colorado, in Utah's desert outlands, in Texas or in Arizona, as in the country of the Humboldt.

So the story goes, one day a waddy out on the range incredulously squirted some tobacco juice at the nearest clump of sage. Sure enough, he saw a wagon, drawn by a couple of browbeaten horses. On the wagon box sat a gray-bearded stranger and in the wagon was a gleaming steel plow.

The waddy rode up and pointed to the plow. "Beggin' yore pardon, dad, what in hell is that?"

"Why, my boy," the old man said genially, "that's a plow."

"A plow. . . . What's it for? What do yuh do with it?"

The old man snorted. "Do with it? Why, you break up the earth with it. I'm agoin' to stop right here, pre-empt myself about eighty acres, fence it and plow it and raise corn, garden sass, mebbe a little wheat."

The waddy scratched his ear. "But look here, don't yuh hafta have a little moisture to raise that stuff—rain, for instance?"

The old man chuckled at this innocence. "Son, you've got behind times. Ain't you heard about this new dry farmin'? You can farm without rain." He filled his pipe and between puffs explained about the new way of using half the land and summer-fallowing the other half to store moisture.

"But yuh can't do that here," the cowboy objected. He thought up half a dozen reasons why. But the old man was stubborn; he cal'lated to have him a farm right here. At last the waddy sighed, pushing back his Stetson and mopping his brow with his sleeve. "Dad, I'll tell yuh a story.

"A while back an eastern dude inherited a lot of money. He'd heard about the West and he come out here, right out here, and he started to have him a farm. The first year he spent quite a lot of money, gettin' the land plowed, fenced, and planted. Well, dad, there wasn't no rain, and nothin' came up. He was a stubborn galoot, and he tried again the next year, and there wasn't no rain that year neither. He still had a lot of money left, though, and the third year he got a bright idee.

"He went into town and bought hisself a wagon, a big, strong wagon, yuh know, with four-inch tires. He put fourteen-inch sideboards on the wagon, and got a load of good soil—yuh gotta say that for him, dad, he got a load of good soil some'eres around. Nobody couldn't never figger out where he got that there good soil. Then he got a good team of horses, big, fast horses, and he hired a chore boy. Then he planted hisself another garden in that wagon, and he says to the boy, he says, 'Nick, I want yuh to keep yore eye skinned all the time, day and night. And if yuh see a cloud, no matter where it is, no matter anything, I want yuh to hitch up this-yere team and drive like hell till yuh get under the cloud. And if the cloud does percipitate, then the rain'll germinate the seed in the good earth on this-yere wagon, and damn if I won't have me a garden!'

"But the fack is, dad," the waddy said sorrowfully, "that rich dude, he went plumb, flat broke, buyin' oats for the horses and axle grease for the wagon."

Like many of the stories the West tells, this yarn has at its heart an unimpassioned disillusion. Elsewhere in the American wayfaring the land was always conquerable. Some land required a greater stubbornness of spirit, and its yield might be grudging. But soil always could be vanquished. It was not until Americans crossed the 98th degree, west longitude, that they realized how the condition of their triumph had been rain.

Rain! To the West the word is an invocation. Rain is the yardstick of the land's worth. It is the determinant of the level of life. Rain on the land itself, the rolling, illimitable earth, has, except for stockmen and the range grasses, the significance only of an unexpected beneficence; it is token of the interested, if weak-willed, benevolence of God. In the farther West rain means not rain upon the farmland so much as snow in the mountains, running water in the creeks, ground water from springs and wells. Man himself will bring the water to the farm land, and give thanks for the privilege. All that is expected of the Lord is that He shall precipitate the rain somewhere in the country, "that if not for us, He shall not be against us."

In the beginning none but the Mormons was willing to accept the West on those terms. The price of desert settlement was a lower level of subsistence, a greater measure of hardship and deprivation, a lesser return for the heart's blood. While other Americans went on to Oregon or California, the Mormons settled in the mountain-desert to work out their destiny. And from their center stake of Zion, planted in the valley of the Great Salt Lake, they carried the warfare to the desert.

Down the long valley of the Humboldt the Saints went to plant their western outpost under the Sierras; and in retreat they marched back up this valley to mountain-girt Zion. Save only outcast Peter Haws, in all these years there was none among these greatest of desert fighters who carried the war to the Humboldt earth. It was not only that the Humboldt Valley was America's thoroughfare, the highroad of empire, nor was it only that the Diggers of the West made perilous the whole land, for Mormon outposts dotted the Southern Route to California at oases even so poor and so isolated as Las Vegas, and there were no Indians for whom the Mormons could not feel fellowship. . . . In the Humboldt Valley the desert was enthroned. Mormon frontiersmen never here sought out the antagonist, the old enemy with which they warred even in the badlands of the Colorado Plateau. But in the end, when the pioneer years were finished, Mormons came to the Humboldt.

Bishop's Creek gathers itself from the west slopes of the Independence Mountains, a rapid mountain torrent eager to reach the Humboldt. This way the Golden Army came to the desert river, marching out of yellow-walled Emigration Canyon to that great, rolling plain from which the Ruby Mountains lift, gray-purple and gnarled, snow-mottled even in summer. The Golden Army could feel a lifting of the heart

at the renewed spaciousness of the world. Even a desert
plain, smelling of sun and dust and sage, was good to see.

Southwest across that rolling plain they went, that
valiant, ragged army. Through giant sage they marched, sage
that grew as tall as their heads, and there was none to think
that the trampled earth, the earth that clothed the day in
dust and soreness, contained its own dream.

With the years, other trails to California scarred the
earth in the valley south, shining rails and dusty wagon roads.
Over the flank of the hill a sun-dreary railroad town straggled
about the old Humboldt Wells. Here below the mouth of
Emigration Canyon, grazing cattle listened to the far, thin
screech of the Central Pacific engines sounding their arrival
at Wells. Down the river, west around the shoulder of the
Rubies, farms might begin to bulwark Elko, but here the
desert seemed secure.

The West has always had promoters. Sometimes they were
called empire builders, and the presumption then was that,
whatever they cost the country, the country got something
in return. Sometimes they were called speculators, and the
presumption then was that the country paid through the nose
for the privilege of knowing them and had no other joy
of their presence. The promoters who in 1911 came to this
spreading land where Bishop's Creek emerges from the mountains called themselves the Pacific Reclamation Company.

Reclamation! It was a flag for men's hopes. Capital
could build dams in canyons, and spread water upon the
long-barren land; by what God and Mormons had failed to
do with the desert earth, capital could measure its potency.
. . . Need it be added that the capital was eastern?

The agents of the Pacific Reclamation Company who
came into the Humboldt Valley to purchase some thirty or
forty thousand acres of land below the mouth of Emigration
Canyon were gratified by the co-operation they received from

everybody. Just beginning to get back on her feet after the destructive nineties, Nevada wished the enterprise well. The Southern Pacific agreed to build an 8-mile spur track and a $9,000 depot. The company laid out a townsite, plotted the streets of the business district, and built a $100,000 hotel, crown of glory for the town. Metropolis, they called it, this fated city of the desert.

The advertising literature glowed. By 1913 the company could print pages of pictures—oats as tall as a man's head, ripe and golden; fenced fields and houses ("This was nothing but sagebrush eighteen months ago"); spreading vegetable gardens, green and luscious, the dry mountains baffled in the distance. In nothing the land lacked. *Soil?* An alluvial deposit of rich loam, remarkable in its depth and in the entire absence of heavy gravel or boulders, hardly more than one-tenth of one per cent alkali. *Water supply?* Water in God's plenty from the streams that unite west of Metropolis to form the Humboldt River. The company possessed, in Bishop's Creek basin, one of the nation's finest and largest reservoir sites. "The Company's plans are conservative, and call for storage of more than one year's requirements, so as to guard against a possible dry year." *Climatic conditions?* All that could be desired in this latitude, though "we have no land suitable for orange-growing." *Products?* The finest varieties of beans, beets, sugar beets, celery, corn, cauliflower, cabbage, carrots, cucumbers, cantaloupes, spinach, parsley, parsnips, tomatoes, squash, turnips, rutabagas, asparagus, watermelons—anything and everything. Apples, pears, peaches, apricots, and berries all had been grown successfully in the immediate vicinity of the company's lands. "*At the Four State Fair oats grown on the demonstration farm of the Pacific Reclamation Company took first prize in competition with Utah, Idaho, and Wyoming.*" Barley, wheat, and other grains were grown with equal success. *Dry farming?* "The heavy sagebrush growth, the deep soil, with the added factors of an excellent clay sub-soil and proximity of water to the surface, with sufficient precipitation, make Dry Farming in this section an assured success." *Markets?* Nevada had always been dependent on imports for its food supplies; the products of the company's land had "practically no competition that has not at least a two hundred and fifty mile greater haul." And we would remind you again, gently, gently, that we are served by a transcontinental railroad only six hundred miles from San Francisco, "which in itself provides an excellent market, and upon the completion of the Panama Canal will enable farmers on our project to compete successfully in all the markets of the world."

The company was firm. "Our enthusiasm may entertain you, our confidence excite your interest, but it is facts that you are after if you mean business." It should be understood: "We have no cheap land, if by cheapness you mean low prices. We have a real live project, and this being the case we have no low priced land that we care to recommend to you. We think the most solemn warning of this decade was uttered by Mr. J. J. Hill when he said, 'There is only ONE crop of land.' The census of 1920 will show at least ten million more people in this country than we had in 1910, and come good times or bad they have GOT to be fed and the food has GOT to come from the soil. Ponder over this little problem in its relation to increasing land values."

This was the word scattered over the West, where land has always been a hunger in men's hearts. Farmers turned over the pages of the illustrated folder and felt their hearts lift to the thought that here was security, heritage for their sons. The pictured hotel, with its two stories of trim red brick and its new awnings, was an earnest of something strong and sure and stable. "Attention is called to the excellent investment offered in lots of the town of Metropolis. There has been for years a crying need for a first class town in this portion of Nevada, and the opening up of the lands of the Pacific Reclamation Company assured its existence. . . . Reference may be made here to the Hotel, modern in all its appointments; the city water system with its pure spring water under high pressure insuring ample fire protection; school building of the latest construction; cement sidewalks; electric lights, etc." A descriptive booklet might be had by addressing the Metropolis Commercial Club, Metropolis, Nevada.

So a new order of things had come to the West. Mormon pioneers of yesterday had come to the desert land by mid-winter pilgrimage, shivering in their wagons as the winter waned, building houses in the fashion of a fort, digging irrigation canals, fencing a Big Field and individual holdings, grubbing out sagebrush, working together and starving to-gether, and at last, with the passing of the years, achieving some measure of security and comfort. That had been the pattern of the past, the face of the war with the desert. But regard the superior technology of the modern age: Today there was benevolent eastern capital to build reinforced con-crete storage and diversion dams, railroad spurs, and $100,000 hotels. And to sell the land at a price.

Many journeyed to the new town at the head of the Humboldt to investigate for themselves. The hotel filled with them. Soon homesteaders' shacks could be seen in all direc-tions. The rolling sage plain was fenced off, teams of horses dragging lengths of steel rail to clear the land of sage. Other teams were raking the loose sage from the earth, sweeping clean a way for the plows. Here in the land was a dream to which the Golden Army had been blind, the reluctant earth subjected to man's will. Here amid green fields trees should rise, and houses of stone.

Warfare with the desert is a tradition bred into the Mor-mon blood and bone, and though this dream at the head of the Humboldt was alien to that tradition, Mormons came in numbers from the far places of the West to take up land below Emigration Canyon. Not all were Mormons who came to Metropolis. But it was the Mormons who stuck.

During the months before outbreak of the First World War, the population of Metropolis reached nearly a thousand. Some came hopefully to the dry farms beyond the silver network of irrigation canals. This dry farm land was to be bought for prices ranging from $10 to $15 an acre; between that asking price and the information that the land was to be had on the installment plan in ten annual payments with interest at 6 per cent on deferred payments, the company sandwiched the observation that "the average annual rainfall is 13.8 inches." Those who had more money and, out of an intuition of the desert's ways, were disinclined to gamble on dry farms, bought irrigated land at prices that ranged upward from $75 an acre.

Many of the settlers who came to Metropolis brought with them hardly more assets than their will to dream. There was even a philosophy about having too much capital: a farmer must get a large proportion of his living out of the soil, and if he had much capital, he might use it up or waste it, and neglect to raise a garden or to milk his cows. A man should live close to the earth.

But, during the first years, some capital was essential. No crop of proportions, under whatever favorable circumstances, could be expected before the second year. It took that long to subdue the land. Even as Metropolis prepared to boom, decay was working in its bones, men starved out before the struggle was well begun.

At first, however, there was rain. And wheat prices soared as war raged in Europe. Under the sun, round about Metropolis' tall red-brick hotel, wheatfields rippled their gold to the desert wind. But year by year the land seemed more reluctant, the wheat unrelieved by rain from the intolerable

sun. The dry farmers began to leave. And though the State
of Nevada, beginning in 1917, appropriated $5,000 a year
for an investigation of dry farming possibilities, five years'
work only turned the land back, at last, to the irrigation
canals and to the Herefords and the sheep which the farmers
had driven, for a time, north into the hills. In abandoned
shacks, buried under the litter the hot wind blew along the
floor, the folders of the Metropolis Reclamation Company
still held forth their promise of abundance: "The average
annual rainfall is 13.8 inches." By something like four inches,
that has been an optimism of the empire builders.

Retreat, then, to the irrigated farms and entrench in defiance behind the canals. The dream dies hard, and money is
strong. Money can build dams in the mountains, canals along
the shoulders of the hills; money can build hotels and schools
and paved sidewalks strung with electric lights. Money is a
force the desert farms of the West have never known. . . .

But the prospectus of the Reclamation Company had
not provided against the dryness. "The Company's plans are
conservative, and call for storage of more than one year's
requirements, so as to guard against a possible extra dry
year." Yes, but if the extra-dry years run two, three and
four in succession? That magnificent reservoir site, capacious
for all needs—of what use was it unless snow fell in the
mountains? And there was something else the company's
advertising men had failed to write into their hymns.

To those easterners rabbits were game to be hunted.
Here, in the fields around Metropolis, they were a ravenous
vermin. Without rabbit fences the farms were no more than
a benevolence of God to the rabbit cosmos. Rabbits were
fought with the means at hand, and the intervention of predators and plague thankfully accepted. In bad years the
farmers continued the stoic fight and could even see the
workings of a large determinism in this irruption of the land:

"We're going to have another depression in about two years. The rabbits are increasing to feed the poor."

Men gave up in despair, but there were others to take their places. As the sifting continued, Metropolis became a community of Mormons. The help and encouragement by state and federal governments and by the Southern Pacific Railroad had less to do with Metropolis' continued existence, during years that multiplied hardship and difficulty, than the social and religious organization that bound the people together and gave them hope.

"They were encouraged to struggle along and not give up; their leaders holding before them a promising and truthful picture of beautiful fields and a prosperous community," a Metropolis man has written. "The amusements fostered by the church were many and varied; they served to take the minds of the discouraged farmers off their troubles. There were dances and dramatics and concerts by home talent as well as religious gatherings." Up in the canyon above the diversion dam, where a warm spring bubbles from the south wall of the canyon, the settlers built a low pool, with a bathhouse at the upper end. This shallow swimming pool was also the baptismal font, where the community's children came at the age of eight to be baptized into the Church, the work of God served in the hard-handed desert. . . .

A boy who had been baptized in that pool came back with me in the summer of 1940. It was fifteen years since he had seen Metropolis. We drove north and west from Wells across sage uplands that opened out, eventually, upon farms green in the valley before us. This was the upper part of Metropolis. The nearer farm, gold and green in the hot afternoon, had been owned by a fellow best situated to avail himself of the precious water from the canyon above; something of a water hog, he had gone through periods of social ostracism. Water counted, however, for more than social grace. A group of trees, cottonwoods and Lombardy poplars, flanked his wooden shacks. Beyond were other houses; once this had been almost a community. A mile farther on, standing on the brow of the hill surrounded by Carolina poplars and other trees, was a tall stone house that had been built by the father of my friend. They had planted the trees, "and, Lord, how slow they grew!" There were no other trees in sight, except a scattered few toward the canyon mouth. We drove up a dusty road. A line that ran along the hillside south from the canyon was the canal which watered most of Metropolis. Only the farms in the foreground were watered from the creek bed. Now we saw that the fields and the road were crawling with repulsive life.

Imagine a loathsome grasshopper without wings, a grasshopper leaden black or bedbug red, a grasshopper as thick and long as a powerful man's thumb, a grasshopper that leaps and skitters along the ground or pauses to stare with an unutterable malignance. . . . Looking at a Mormon cricket, you suddenly disbelieve the stories the Mormons in Utah tell of sea gulls that came miraculously in 1848 to gorge upon them and save the crops. It is unimaginable that a sea gull could find courage to look a cricket in the eye, let alone actually pick a fight with one and eat it. A Mormon cricket looks strong and mean enough to jump on sea gulls and rend them limb from limb, feather from feather.

We watched the uneasy movement of the fields. There was no square yard that did not have a cricket or two. The crickets were capable of stripping a field as though it had been scorched with fire. The crickets had come to Metropolis since my friend's family departed. Like rabbits, they were the desert's gratuity to its conquerors. The irrigation canal was speckled with them; some of the crickets had just fallen in, and were still struggling, while others floated torpidly on the surface of the roily water. In Utah irrigation canals, bird predators, and hogs and poultry wiped out the crickets soon after the Mormon occupation of the land. But this cricket infestation, we presently learned, was in its sixth year.

We drove on up the canyon, a narrow defile down which a gray stream plunges tumultuously, water released in constant volume from the storage dam. Beyond the diversion dam which separates the water allowed to go down the channel from that diverted into the canal, we reached the warm spring. Although my friend remembered that it normally contained a few blow snakes, fallen into the water from the yellow canyon wall above, now it was empty of them. A few drowned crickets, however, floated in the water, amid yellow-green moss. We threw out the crickets, and gratefully shed our clothes to rid ourselves of two days' accumulation of dirt and salt dust. Down this narrow canyon, within yards of where we soaked in the pleasant warm water, the Golden Army had marched for California. . . . Ghosts stalked the afternoon, but we stirred to no imperative except that of being clean.

Feeling fine, we drove back down the canyon. The valley opened before us, the distant farmhouses and fields looking unutterably brave and little and lonely in the late afternoon sunlight, which lit the rye and alfalfa fields and cast tiny, dark shadows behind mounded gold hay. Passing again the stone house on the hill, we drove on down toward the heart of Metropolis. Jack rabbits sprang out every dozen yards, dashing frantically down the road ahead of us or into the sagebrush on either side. Now and then a tiny cottontail ran among the jacks. We flushed one jack who started straight down the road ahead of us, the sun gleaming strangely salmon-pink through his extraordinary ears. About every sixth leap he hopped into the air as though shifting gears, and Lord, how he traveled! Timed by the speedometer, he was going thirty miles an hour when finally, after some three or four hundred yards, he yielded the road to us.

So we came to Metropolis, to the hotel, the railroad station, the schoolhouses, the bustling, energetic town. Over the hill the grade school still stood. The high school, however, was gone. The meetinghouse was gone; some mean board shacks stood on the site. The depot was gone, and the railroad tracks. Both saloons were gone. The Consolidated Wagon Company building was an empty shell with high hollow windows. Next door south stood the storied hotel. Part of one wall extended to the top of the second story, but most of its red brick had fallen down to the level of the first. Nothing remained within but rusted steel girders. The floor was gone and the basement gaped empty.

We sat in the car, looking about us. Beyond the ruin of the hotel a length of concrete sidewalk ran irrationally under a farmer's barbed wire to end suddenly in the middle of a pasture. That was Main Street. The summer sun, sinking at an angle down the long Humboldt Valley, cast the blue shadows of fence posts and barbed wire across Main Street. The sidewalk once had bridged hotel and railroad station, and sputtering yellow arc lights along the concrete path had been evidence of the redemption of the desert land to the uses of civilization.

The land can have an eloquence outmatching the tongue. In another decade there would be nothing here but a red rubble of brick, nothing but the shacks, the corral fences, the sheds. That was the true level of life here. Metropolis had had the vitality only of a dream. No riches had come out of the earth in justification of this vision; here had reared no Aurora, no Virginia City, no Unionville, no bright flame of the desire and its fulfillment. Man had simply pitted himself against the desert—his energy and desire, his technological expedients, his driving will. The sun's rays threw upon the ground a ragged shadow, the hotel. A wind was beginning to rise; it blew in from the sageland, warm, spiced, sweet. The wind was a little sick with the smell of the sage, and it gathered up whorls of dust beyond the barbed-wire fence.

In nothing had the land been lacking. The soil was good, the slope of the land admirable for drainage, the climate equable. The men who had come to the land were desert-wise men, not easily discouraged or beaten.

Rain is the answer to so many things in the West. An inch or two of rain above the 10-inch mark means white-painted houses, trees tall and green (though perhaps yellowed by the dryness in late summer), the shocked gold of wheat, oats, and barley, the serried green of onions, potatoes, beets. Each half-inch loss from the year's precipitation takes something from the land and from the spirit. June grass grows where alfalfa once spread green. Sage marches in from the desert. Dust blows on the wind, a bitterness of the land ever present on the lips.

At length we left this dead city, driving up toward the benchland again, the rutted road frenzied at intervals with jack rabbits. We passed a lonely, dusty-looking building. My friend had lived here while his father was building the stone house on the hill. "I remember playing in the dusty yard in the hot sun. It looked then just as it looks now. My mother hated the place." The wooden walls of the house were warped by the sun. There was no greenery around, just arid sage and dust. We drove past fenced fields where, even at the time his family had departed from Metropolis, there had still been long plots of alfalfa and grain. June grass rippled there now, obscene in the wind.

A frame house, more pretentious than most we had seen, a few flowers growing around it, was our destination. A dozen sheds with open east face flanked the house. Farm machinery was lying around, and white Leghorns and sandy Rhode Island Reds were running about the place to the rear. On the east was the muddy irrigation ditch. Several horses, buckskin,

roan, and black, were in a corral with a couple of frail-legged
colts. As we stopped at the side of the house a young man
came out, a handsome young fellow whose skin was burned
red with much sun, his dark blond hair parted loosely on
one side, his blue eyes squinted against the glare of the sun.
The collar of his shirt was folded under so that his Mormon
undergarment was visible; he wore levis, work shoes and
heavy woolen socks.

My friend had gone to school with him, and they talked,
eying each other across this bridge of fifteen years. The
young man now was bishop of the Mormon ward here, which
had shrunk through the years to some fifteen families. Presently a younger brother came out, and then the father. The
old man had come to this country before the First World War
as a German immigrant; he had a wonderfully characterful
face, with gray, rather unkempt hair, straggling gray mus-
tache, and furrowed bronze forehead. A little bent, and
shorter than his sons, he stood in the dooryard with all the
blunt earthy strength of a German peasant. He and his sons
had dwelt here over twenty years.

We were invited inside. The mother, like her husband,
was of unmistakable German blood, with long nose, small
mouth, work-worn hands and hair, bent and heavy breasted in
a print house dress of violet and light green. The young
bishop's wife, dandling in her lap a three-months-old baby
boy, had the smooth-skinned, feverish fresh blondness, the
sun-bleached blue eyes, of so many girls who live in the desert.

For an hour or more we talked. It was a drought year;
the Metropolis farmers were hard up for water, though there
had been seventeen feet of carry-over in the reservoir. Things
had changed over the years. . . . Once there had been grain
fields, truck gardening, dry farming a few miles out from
the canal arteries. Then the dry farmers, beaten, quit the
unequal fight. On the irrigated farms, then, there had been
potato growing and dairy farming, with a co-operative mar-

keting association. The co-op had gone, too. But they were still here. They had a hundred head of cattle, part beef and part dairy, and they raised alfalfa, grain, and a sizable acreage of potatoes.

And they had, now, new hope in the community. The number of farmers had decreased until there should be enough water to go around, and the value placed upon the farms and water had been reduced. A committee, during recent years, had been pushing litigation to clear title to the water; only a few weeks ago the suit had ended, the farmers successful in ousting the land-promotion company interests. There had been help from the Mormon welfare organization; the Church had assumed in some way all the debts of the federal land bank, and the process had reduced valuation of the farms and water to about one-third. The refinancing process eliminated land and buildings, and all value of any holding depended on the amount of water right each farm possessed. Grasshoppers, squirrels, rabbits, and the crickets that had first appeared in 1934 were ever present, but these were the natural enemies of the land.

Listen to quiet voices talking of water and the land. ("I was in Salt Lake eight times last year working on the water suit.") Eastern capital thrown out. Rain could have supported a hotel, a two-story, red-brick, strictly modern hotel; with rain farmers could have paid not only for storage and diversion dams but even for such extravagances as $100,000 hotels. Subtract an inch of rain and the dry farms go; subtract another inch and the hotel sags in rust and rubble; subtract another and the railroad pulls up its steel rails and departs. ("A lot of our people, maybe twenty-five families, went to Gridley, California. I've been there and seen it. No good. Either too hot or too cold or something. Every time I went there I liked it less.") Unpainted inside and out, the house dwells sick within the fetor of sun-hot wood. Across this land had gone the Golden Army, another race of buccaneers. Down the desert river the hosts had marched. . . . In this land there had been a dream, a hard dream. When the old piracies were ended, men had come in pursuit of this dream—capitalists, men with money. ("Mostly, the company was eastern Jews.") Capital, the omnipotent instrument. But though money can be poured out upon the land like water, only by water is the earth made pregnant. Promotion has no margin for survival in the desert. For the desert is an honesty, a realism unchanged by persuasion or chicanery. Dreams, like opalescent soap bubbles, may drift above the sage, but the air is dry and the bubbles burst.

Think upon these things and see the white curtains at the window lift to the desert wind, and see them ranged across the room—grandfather, father, infant son—three generations to toil upon this desert earth and always know hope. And then go out again into the wind, saying the words of farewell, remembering smiles in sun-darkened faces, remembering brown-flowing water in the shallow irrigation canal. North in the sage uplands where a campfire leaps brightly in a circle of sage under a world of magnificent stars, you may wonder where fortitude is secure. The desert is patient and near.

XXII

Men and Desert

LIKE none other among the rivers of America, it
flows in the American story. The Humboldt challenged men,
not to live upon it but to live without it. There is a surly
integrity to its history. Men might travel its length or come
to dwell within its basin, but they came without invitation,
and the river conceded nothing to their presence. Necessary
river, unloved river, barren river—Desert River of the West.

There is no minstrelsy to celebrate it except the song
of hate. Yet light glints from it at all angles into American
history. Under a moon too large and white to be quite real,
men may sit around the fading embers of a campfire, their
buttocks hard against the white, baked resilience of the

alkali, and ghosts are summoned in a man's clear-throated
joyous bellow:

> Exciting times all round the town,
>   Glory, Glory to Washoe.
> Stocks are up and stocks are down,
>   Glory, Glory to Washoe.
>   Washoe! Washoe!
>   Bound for the land of Washoe.
> And I owned three feet
> In the "Old Dead Beat,"
>   And I'm bound for the land of Washoe!

The song echoes on the clear night air and all at once
America is young again. The hills that glow darkly on the
far horizons of this silvered world are again the Unknown
Land sought out by the great adventurers. Cibola no longer
lies over the rim of the world, nor the country of the Mun-
chies, but the land dreams with the nighttime and tomorrow
glows with yesterday. The voices of coyotes cry the primor-
dial, strange anguish of this earth, and the river lives perfectly, a flowing brightness in the night. So much is secure
in the American heritage, the poignance of all the past contained in beauty spacious and free.

But in the morning the world opens as a land set within
a circle of distant hills, low-lying mountains deep lavender
against the orange stain of the rising sun. Widely spaced
clumps of greasewood lift above the flat-caked white alkali
plain. As the sun rises, the alkali takes on color, the long
blue shadows of the greasewood brilliant in contrast to the
orange-silver where the light falls warm and free. A far
line of willows is the river meandering in this plain. The
night mystery is gone, and the timelessness; though the world
bears still the mark of strangeness, it is solid-set and bound-

lessly real in the clear light of morning. Suddenly the Humboldt has a dimension in today.

It is a world where people live on terms with the land, expecting not too much of it, even tempered, philosophical, friendly, with a healthy gusto for the business of living. It is an unspectacular, spacious world from which the frenzy is gone. On an alkali plain below Battle Mountain, as the sun renews its work with the desert world, you can begin to understand that the river has wrought with a people.

A son of the Humboldt Valley ponders upon those neighbors east, the Mormons, and suddenly the God-seeking and the social regimentation look self-righteous and strange: "My mother's father was a Methodist minister. I was married by a Baptist. My wife is an Episcopalian, but prefers the Roman Catholic religion. My little girl was baptized by a Methodist, but goes to a Congregational Sunday school. The last time I was in church, it was a Presbyterian." There is room for everybody and everything: I preach you no gospel of salvation, and will be responsible for my own soul.

The hills that roll north and south from the sundering westward thrust of the Humboldt Valley are a common denominator of life. Everybody is a prospector, by profession or by inclination. When out in the hills on any business, a man has an eye for the terrain around; and when vacations attend the normal course of the new urban life in the Humboldt Valley, a man is more likely to go prospecting·than to go fishing, though I offer assurance that better trout fishing is nowhere to be had than in some of the mountain creeks of the Humboldt country. In many Nevada homes hangs a placard or calendar picturing a twitching-eared burro standing by a hole in the ground from which the dirt is flying; its legend burlesques for their enjoyment that spirit of restless inquiry and hope that is the soul of prospecting: "Ten miles from wood, twenty miles from water, ten feet from pay dirt—*God Bless Our Happy Home!*"

They can laugh at their own earnestness, this race of prospectors. They tell you a story about a sheepherder who was making his camp as a prospector ambled up. The prospector made his own camp, and then strolled over to talk with the sheepherder. "I should think," said he, "that the bla-bla of the sheep would drive you crazy." "It does," the sheepherder admitted. "What do you do then?" the prospector wanted to know. The sheepherder grinned: "I go prospecting."

This land has, after all, the memory of the Comstock, that incandescence of bygone years. The Comstock symbolizes all the wealth ever found in Nevada's mountains, and the abundance of its life—its nervous energy, its overflowing vitality, its exciting gusto—is something more than a land's memory of its youth.

A Nevadan talks about the Comstock with warm affection and brightening eye. The Comstock brought Nevada statehood fifty years and more before its time; the Comstock enforced upon the land an appreciation of other values than mere scenery or the spreading wealth of farm land; the Comstock is the justification for all deserts everywhere. The Comstock was also a disease in the blood of this land; it telescoped or aborted social development, choked off agricultural development by flooding the state with men before the land, the reluctant desert land, was ready for such hosts. Between the miners and the stockmen, the scanty water was kept from farm lands, and the state has labored ever since under economic disability. The ruin of the Comstock was almost the ruin of the land; before the turn of the century, before the Tonopah discoveries that set off Nevada's second mining boom, and before the hamstringing of the railroad, Nevada seemed under sentence of death. The state has come back, now, with precarious irrigation projects on the lower Carson and at Rye Patch on the lower Humboldt, with federal control of the range lands, and with new mines, or old mines profitable with high prices for metals. In that resurgence the Comstock lives again, for the Comstock is a larger identity than mine shafts or towns. The Comstock is desire and belief, not ghost-ridden Sun Peak. Virginia City survives into the present, its buildings leaning drunkenly in this direction or that; the shafts that honeycomb the earth under Virginia City have caved in, in places, and the city has been wrenched by that obligation to its own past. The earth has been gutted, violated and torn, but the Comstock is betrayed, not in its own exhaustion and death but in the gray parasitism that would wring dimes and nickels from memory's splendor. The Bucket of Blood Saloon, the Museum of Memories—one who remembers the greatness of Washoe is saddened by the "joints" that clutter this monument to its own era. The Comstock lives most truly, not in Virginia City's battered houses and sunken shafts but in men's hearts, in him who walks off into the hills with an inquiring eye for "float."

The Humboldt was a man's trail. The Humboldt is a man's world today. The spreading ranches, the farms, and the mines are male, and the mark of the frontier is on them. The "clubs," the saloons, the stockades—all these answer to the old male need. Men who slept in shacks or dugouts, or who slept over some restaurant or saloon in beds, twenty and thirty to the room, gathered naturally to public places where there was laughter and good-fellowship to feed the hungers of the soul. The scented flesh of whore and hetaera answered to other hungers ancient as the flesh, and like the gambling hells gave outlet to the pent furious energies of men who might die before another nightfall with no other climax for their lives.

Survival of the frontier into today appears mere license to the latter-day traveler of the Humboldt trail; and Reno, that city risen in the Truckee Meadows at the far end of the

trail, seems either the fountainhead of evil or a garish absurdity—consciously wicked and therefore a contradiction in
terms, a lie . . . but in the absurdity a disturbing core of
realism. For money lost to the spinning wheel is gone; and
if you walk past the policeman and around the yellow-lit
stockade, although these hard mouthed young girls in pa-
jamas, nightgowns and play suits seem only the stage-dressing
of a drama for tourists, it is you, not the girls, who occupy
the stage. In Reno there is this air of the absurd and the
improbable, intermixed with the vicious, about this bequest
of the past; and in Las Vegas the amusements of the night
are glamorized. But in Nevada's other towns stockades,
"houses," and clubs serve functional needs in a male world—
and no catering to tourists. If "civilized" Nevada has not
always approved this realism about the bases of its life, the
townsfolk have been comforted to know that the land has a
safety valve, that their daughters are secure from women-
starved men in from the desert. It was with not altogether
unmixed feelings, perhaps, that Nevada early in 1942, at
Army behest, undertook to outlaw prostitution. The state
had done this before, and only driven it underground, re-
form made an agency of vice.

North of Wells you may camp upon a creek and pass
the time of day with a sheepherder who wanders over a ridge
in the midst of a blatting herd. He pauses to talk amiably,
and you can think of a land that is his world. He wants to
know the day of the week; he knows it's the 24th, because he
is supposed to have the sheep at Sun Creek on the 25th, but
he has lost track of the weekdays. He squints, and thinks
maybe he knows you. You think maybe he doesn't, because
you're from Salt Lake City. "Oh," he says, "I've been to
Salt Lake City." Salt Lake City sounds suddenly like Tim-
buktu or Singapore, a far corner of the earth. "Me and a
couple or three others in this outfit," he confides, "are goin'

to Salt Lake for the blow-in this fall. I've blown in in Denver, Boise, Portland, and other towns."

You suggest that a blow-in has potentialities for a good time. "Yeah, it all depends on the start you get. When three or four get together with four or five hundred bucks apiece, you can make things pretty hot for a while." You wonder out loud what he does after the money's all gone, and he is almost scornful: "Go back to work. You may not believe it, but herding sheep is skilled labor. Not anyone can do it."

You agree with all your heart. A herder must keep his flock in feed and water—a poor herder might bring the flock in weighing less than when it went out. And just try keeping 1,200 sheep together without losing 50 per cent, even though you can keep rough track with black sheep or bell sheep as markers. There is always some loss. The herder yawns. "The days are too long, now. I don't get a hell of a lot of shut-eye, have to get up at dawn with the sheep." A frolicsome pup, brown, and with docked tail, prances up to look us over; the herder calls the dog by an odd breed name. "The boss fell in with some dog breeder who gave him a song and dance about this breed dog being from Australia and so valuable they have to be smuggled out. The boss fell for it and bought one of them. The boss can believe that stuff if he wants to, but if you ask me, they pay you to haul the critters out of Australia. The boss and me don't see eye to eye on dogs, anyhow. He wants a slow dog, that'll meander out to the sheep and turn them slow. Trouble is, by the time one of them gets back you have to send him again. I like a fast dog that turns them so they stay turned. Of course, I can see the boss's viewpoint, you don't lose so much fat with a slow dog, and fat is what counts."

With thanks he refuses a cup of coffee: he stands there by the fire, likable, sun-browned, homely, with that curious expression about the eyes you sometimes see in men whose minds are too simple. "I got to be gittin' along. Expect the

boss today in the truck. About outa supplies. So long!" He
splashes through the creek in the wake of his sheep. . . .
For five minutes you have lived in one of the Humboldt's
worlds.

The Humboldt has so many worlds. The world of the
desert farmer, of the sheepherder, of the miner; of the gaunt
woman in green eyeshade who sits late at night under a yellow
light to deal cards on a green table; the world of air beacons,
great swinging arms of white light lashing the night world
up and down the river valley; the world of shining rails and
Challengers; the world of desert cities and of far-flung
ranches. They are worlds, mostly, of people who have come
to the land to stay, accepting it for what it is, and content
with it.

Those who came in the beginning looted the land in
passing, and did not return. Those who came later came to
make a stake and get out. But those came finally to whom
the land was good, an earth to be lived on. These are the
Nevadans who have made the Humboldt country their own.
Dilettantes have followed them. Stockbrokers of either coast
buy ranches to be run as a hobby; by no means incidentally,
to these men Nevada is convenient as a legal residence, for the
state prides itself on having no income tax, no inheritance,
gift, corporation or sales tax. The people of the Humboldt
Valley do not resent this influx of alien blood, though they
wonder whether the men of money will long be able to keep
their hands off state politics—millionaires of the past never
displayed this capacity for forbearance. Dude ranches have
come to serve the divorce trade around Reno and Las Vegas,
but dude ranches are few in all the long valley of the Humboldt, and the amused tolerance of most Nevadans for these
is announced in a sign, possibly apocryphal, said to have
adorned one dude ranch:

WE HAVE A SPEAKEASY IN THE WOODSHED,
A NIGHT CLUB IN THE BARN, AND THE HIRED
GIRL TAKES A BATH IN THE DINING ROOM TWICE
A WEEK. WE WANT OUR NEW YORK GUESTS TO
FEEL AT HOME.

The country's liberal good sense and easy tolerance has given it a name of looseness. Reno-vation, a Winchellism, is an expressive accession to the vocabulary of marriage. But Nevada's laws of residence, and the philosophy of her judges, answer rather to the political needs of a miner's world and to a moral realism that dispenses with evangelism and the sanctity of mere legal and social habit.

There is, of course, a sophistry to this. Nevada did not evolve its divorce laws as a catharsis for the marriage ills of the nation, but when the native genius of the legal profession discovered peculiar attractions in the scenery on the east slope of the Sierra Nevada, divorce was adopted into the family. Once, in 1913, the state consented in the nation's moral outrage, and sought to practice social virtue. The economic ruin that followed was visitation so prompt and pointed that the grim legislature which next sat made greatest haste to restore the old order of things. The occurrence reestablished the timeless creed: you tend to your soul and I'll tend to mine; if we go to hell, we'll not lack for good company.

A metropolitan glitter and sophistication wrestles with the frontier. The prospector down from the hills lounges in an ornate cocktail bar. The harness shop rubs elbows with the magazine racks and the coke signs of the glassy drugstore. The paradox does not endure, for the land itself has a paradox: the Comstock bequeathed an elegance and a bizarre attention to the mode. The contradictions resolve into a logic.

Possibly the glitter and the glisten derives in part from the divorce trail. But divorce is not a factor in the Humboldt Valley itself. The mark of modernity is that of the American highroad. For today, as a century ago, the Humboldt is the way of empire and the highroad for the restless American heart. A gas station in Lovelock with critical business acumen can plant its roadside signs as far east as Wyoming, and harangue its customers. Space and time have foreshortened, but the Humboldt is still the westward passage. The railroad runs hence, and the asphalt highway; and overhead the planes roar across the world's immensity.

It is still a big land, an empty land. You can hardly know its bigness or its emptiness unless you climb into a transcontinental bus and make the passage of the Humboldt Valley by night. Leave Reno as the sun is sinking behind the Sierras, the desert impassioned with the sunset, and see the darkness settle upon the earth. Night rushes beyond the windows, the river flowing in the darkness of the mind, and you stumble out of the bus in one of the Humboldt towns: lights burn yellow in the town and it is lonely and small in the great darkness. At a lunch counter coffee steams in fat white cups; a roof keeps out the stars. The bus terminal seems wind-littered and dusty, and the gloved bus driver appears and disappears about his business, rosy-cheeked and sleepless in a sleeping dingy world. The sailor who has been making hay with the girl who kissed her husband good-bye at the town east of Sacramento is hollow-eyed, blond and young and rumpled, as he steps out of the great bus and is fixed in the spurt of fire at the tip of his cigarette. Down the street a wan light shines from the dusty windows of the Ten Aces Club, and the men playing poker within seem wax-faced and empty with the night. . . . The bus rolls out of town again, the driver nervously sleepless and competent; heads roll on white pillows and the immense black night hurls itself past the windows, secure in its own great immensity, in

which the cities of the Humboldt are forlorn and small. . . .
When the sun whitens the sky, the bus is pounding its way
across the sterile salt desert, and the Humboldt has been
no more than this memory of the endless spaces of the night.

The Humboldt is still a bridge between the desire and
its fulfillment, an intervention of time and space in the exercise of the will. More than one wearied traveler on the Southern Pacific's trains has announced the discovery that Nevada
was created on the American continent only to enable the
railroad to sell more mileage on its passenger tickets; and more
friendly travelers have observed that no place in the country
is more in need of a good real estate agent. Science serves a
function in severing the traveler from the land, withdrawing
him from dust and sweat; the extent of the technology is the
extent of its success in the insulation from the land.

But the land remains. It is patient. It may yield to irrigation dams in the mountains; the desert river itself may be
dammed in the Lovelock Valley. Towns may force an existence from the land. Air line and highway and railroad may
have their triumphs. But the land remembers the ageless
levels of its being, and suddenly it is there, hard and old and
murderous with its reality.

The streamliner that plunged down into the Humboldt
on Sunday night, August 13, 1939, announced in blood and
agony that unrelenting endurance of the land. The ordered
grace of the civilized world exploded as the train smashed off
the rails and into the river. The worst train wreck in Nevada's history, they called it, as trainmen hacked, in the light
of blazing piles of railroad ties, at torn steel cars imprisoning
the living and the dead. A score of bodies were spread upon
the dark-swathed desert earth while doctors ministered to the
living. . . . The summer night was warm, and the stars
that had winked upon the passage of Fur Brigade and Golden
Army were the stars that winked upon this bloody violence.
The passengers of the streamliner walked dazedly about, re-

peating the details of what had happened as assurance that they still lived. "The lights went out suddenly. At once I knew we were in for a crash, and without a thought I jumped up and dived through the window." "The train hit the ties before we reached the bridge. Sparks began to fly and I thought there was another train bumping us. Ours was the last car to get across. I groped my way out and went back to the bridge where I heard Negroes groaning. One had both legs broken." If I had been there instead of here, if I had done this instead of that . . . I should now be dead. Walk upon this earth, smelling the stench of burnt June grass on the night wind, hearing the harsh clangor of metal upon metal as men with axes and crowbars, down in the river bottom, tear their way into steel cars where human flesh still can moan or scream. The desert is not distant, now, nor the ancestral knowledge of this passageway between civilizations. The river, westward flowing, tastes again of the salt of men's blood.

It is good, at last, that there should be deserts—and desert rivers. It is good that the past shall have an iron memory in the present, and that we shall know by the face of a land the stature of our race. The Humboldt has still an eloquence for America: this way went buckskinned Jedediah Smith with rifle and Bible; this way went Ogden on his starving horse, and Old Greenwood. This way went the sun-faded canvas of the undaunted emigrant wagons, the ragged legions of the Golden Army, and all the spectral multitudes. . . .

Stand in the sun and feel the power of its stroke. Look upon a world mountainous and dry and stern. Shoulder the sky, and see the dust rising in the plain. Here man must fight if he would live. Here the energy and the courage of the American wayfaring must be more than a memory. The physical frontier endures, and the desert is withstood only while the human spirit is valiant.

Acknowledgments

M ANY people by their aid and personal interest have enabled me to write this book, and I hope they will feel rewarded in the result.

Dwight L. Jones shared with me the experiences that were essential to the final writing, and I should like to think that this book will recall to him the black battlements of City of Rocks, the early morning sunlight on the aspens and white birches of Cottonwood Creek, the color of the Ruby Mountains, his evaluation of the Comstock, and many other things.

Maurice L. Howe was a source of greatest encouragement throughout the time I was building the book, and for innumerable suggestions and for contribution of important materials, especially from the National Archives, I extend warm thanks.

Charles Kelly permitted me to use his excellent library as though it were my own, and even more generously placed at my disposal his wide knowledge of the West and its source materials.

I might possibly have been able to write the book without the facilities afforded by the Salt Lake Free Public Library, but it would have been immeasurably a poorer work. Both circulation and reference departments have been of greatest service.

Miss Marguerite Sinclair and the Utah State Historical

Society are almost synonymous to anyone who knows either, and it is difficult to divide my thanks for many privileges granted me.

That this book is in many respects an original contribution to the history of the Mormons and Nevada rests primarily upon special courtesies extended by Alvin Smith, librarian in the Historian's Office of the Church of Jesus Christ of Latter-day Saints, and by the Writers' Project of the Utah Work Projects Administration. In the face of innumerable demands upon his time and knowledge, Mr. Smith remained helpful and genial, and he dug patiently into the archives of the church to enable me to substantiate, or try to substantiate, ideas I entertained about Mormon history. Supplementing the information from the church archives, the Writers' Project afforded me invaluable aid in permitting me to draw upon its important collection of pioneer manuscripts; the Conover and Huntington journals bulwark my narrative at vital points. I had the honor to supervise the Writers' Project during the period I was writing this book, so that I feel also a wider obligation to the Work Projects Administration in Utah, which is being terminated while this book is in press. I am glad to express my sense of the importance of the Work Projects Administration's accomplishments in Utah, and to say also that this book in all probability would never have been written except for the professional duties which gave shape and direction to my thinking about the West.

To Robert A. Allen, state highway engineer in the Nevada Department of Highways, I am indebted for a number of courtesies and especially for permission to draw upon the manuscript Reminiscences of Abner Blackburn, one of the most delightful historical documents I have seen. This narrative is to be published in the *Pony Express Courier*.

Miss Mary Ream, also of the Department of Highways, aided in shaping many of my ideas on the early Nevada trails, and we threshed out together the problems attendant on the moral derelictions of the Haws. I salute the resourceful integrity of her thinking. Miss Ream should not, however, be held accountable for conclusions reached in this book, which do not always square with her ideas.

Darel McConkey read the manuscript with constructive attention to detail, and his warm personal interest has been important to me in many other ways. I have a major obligation also to Mrs. Mina Hardy, who typed the manuscript with unfailing competence, invincible good humor, and stimulating good sense.

For valuable ideas and suggestions I express my appreciation to Miss Nellie B. Pipes and the Oregon Historical Society; the Writers' Project of the Nevada Work Projects Administration; Joseph E. Wilson and Sam Furniss of Elko; Nels Anderson of Washington, D.C.; F. N. Fletcher, now of Berkeley; and Miss Grace Winkleman and J. Roderick Korns of Salt Lake City. Quotation from Oscar Lewis' *The Big Four* is by permission of the author and the publisher, Alfred A. Knopf, Inc.

Although it is impracticable—and indeed impossible—to list all the sources upon which I have drawn, the bibliography gives the sources that have been my principal reliance. Since some of these materials are new to Nevada bibliography, and therefore important beyond the purposes of this volume, citation of individual sources in some instances has been pursued in detail.

Finally, and just before going to press, I desire to call attention to Richard G. Lillard's *Desert Challenge*, An Interpretation of Nevada. Published late in 1942 by Alfred A. Knopf, this book supplements my own, and I regard it as certainly the best book on the state yet written.

Bibliography

ABBEY, JAMES, *California: A Trip Across the Plains in the Spring of 1850.* New Albany, Ind., 1850.

ALTER, J. CECIL, *James Bridger.* Salt Lake City: Shepard Book Company, 1925.

ANGEL, MYRON (editor), *History of Nevada.* Oakland: Thompson & West, Inc., 1881.

APPLEGATE, LINDSAY, "The South Road Expedition," *Oregon Historical Quarterly,* March, 1931, Vol. 22, pp. 12-45.

BANCROFT, HUBERT HOWE, *History of California* (7 vols.). San Francisco: A. L. Bancroft & Company, 1884-1890.

—— *History of Nevada, Colorado, and Wyoming,* San Francisco: The History Company, 1890.

—— *History of the Northwest Coast* (2 vols.). San Francisco: A. L. Bancroft & Company, 1884.

—— *History of Oregon* (2 vols.). San Francisco: The History Company, 1886.

—— *History of Utah.* San Francisco: The History Company, 1890.

BARNARD, E. L., Letter, *Deseret News,* April 30, 1853.

BATCHELDER, AMOS, Journal of a Tour Across the Continent of North America from Boston, via Independence, Missouri, the Rocky Mountains, to San Francisco in 1849, Manuscript, quoted by courtesy of Charles Kelly, Fruita, Utah.

BEAN, GEORGE WASHINGTON, Autobiography and Journal (3 vols.), Manuscript, quoted by courtesy of Utah Writers' Project, WPA.

BEATIE, HAMPDEN S., "The First in Nevada," *Nevada Historical Society Papers,* Vol. 1, pp. 168-171.

BECKWITH, E. G., "Report upon the Route Near the Forty-First Parallel;" in *Reports of Explorations and Surveys to Ascertain the Most Practicable and Economical Route for a Railroad from the Mississippi River to the Pacific Ocean,* Vol. 2 Washington: Beverley Tucker, Printer, 1855.

BIDWELL, JOHN, *Echoes of the Past.* Chicago: The Lakeside Press, R. R. Donnelley & Sons Company, 1928. First edition, Chico, Calif., n.d.

———— *A Journey to California.* San Francisco: John Henry Nash, 1937. First edition, 1842, probably published at Weston or Liberty, Mo.

BIGLER, HENRY W., "Extracts from the Journal of Henry W. Bigler," *Utah Historical Quarterly,* Vol. 5, April, 1932, pp. 35-64; July, 1932, pp. 87-112; October, 1932, pp. 134-160.

BLACKBURN, ABNER, Reminiscences, Manuscript, quoted by courtesy of Robert A. Allen, Carson City, Nevada. To be published in *Pony Express Courier* (*q.v.*).

BLAIR, SETH M., Letter, *Deseret News,* April 30, 1853.

BLISS, ROBERT S., "The Journal of Robert S. Bliss with the Mormon Battalion," *Utah Historical Quarterly,* Vol. 4, July, 1931, pp. 67-96; October, 1931, pp. 110-128.

BONNER, T. D., *The Life and Adventures of James P. Beckwourth,* edited by Bernard DeVoto. New York: Alfred A. Knopf, Inc., 1931. First edition, New York, 1856.

BONNEY, EDWARD, *The Banditti of the Prairies.* Chicago: W. B. Conkey, n.d. (*ca.* 1850).

BRANNAN, SAMUEL, Proclamation "To the Saints in England and America," January 1, 1847, reprinted in *Millennial Star,* Vol. 9, October 15, 1847, pp. 306-307.

———— Letter to L. N. Scovil, June 18, 1847, *Millennial Star,* Vol. 9, October 15, 1847, pp. 305-306.

———— Letters to Brigham Young, October 3 and December 5, 1847; March 29, 1848, quoted in L.D.S. Journal History for these dates.

BROWN, JAMES S., *Life of a Pioneer.* Salt Lake City: George Q. Cannon & Sons Company, 1900.

BROWN, JOHN, *Autobiography of Pioneer John Brown,* edited by John Z. Brown. Salt Lake City: Privately printed, 1941.

BRYANT, EDWIN, *What I Saw in California.* New York: D. Appleton & Company, 1848. Reprinted, various editions, as *Rocky Mountain Adventures.*

BUCKLAND, SAMUEL S., "Indian Fighting in Nevada," *Nevada Historical Society Papers*, Vol. 1, pp. 171-174.

California Star, published weekly at Yerba Buena-San Francisco, 1847-1849.

CANNON, GEORGE Q., *Writings from the Western Standard*. Liverpool: Privately printed, 1864.

CARSON, CHRISTOPHER, *Kit Carson's Own Story*, edited by Blanche C. Grant. Taos, N. M.: Privately printed, 1926.

CHAPMAN, ARTHUR, *The Pony Express*. New York: G. P. Putnam's Sons, 1932.

CHITTENDEN, HIRAM MARTIN, *American Fur Trade of the Far West* (2 vols.), edited by Stallo Vinton. New York: Press of the Pioneers, Inc., 1936. First edition (3 vols.), New York, 1902.

CLARK, BENNETT, "Diary of a Journey from Missouri to California in 1849," edited by Ralph P. Bieber, *Missouri Historical Review*, Vol. 22, October, 1928, pp. 3-43.

CLAYTON, WILLIAM, *William Clayton's Journal*. Salt Lake City: Privately printed, 1921.

CLYMAN, JAMES, *James Clyman, American Frontiersman, 1792-1881*, edited by Charles L. Camp. Cleveland: The Arthur H. Clark Company, 1928.

CONOVER, PETER WILSON, Autobiography, Manuscript, quoted by courtesy of Utah Writers' Project, WPA.

CORBETT, ROGER, *Unionville, Pioneer Mining Camp*. Winnemucca: Privately printed, 1939, mimeographed.

CRAIG, COLUMBUS L., Letter, *Deseret News*, August 29, 1855.

CRAMER, THOMAS AMBROSE, "Journal," *Pocahontas Times* (weekly newspaper, Marlinton, W. Va.), February 7-May 16, 1940.

DALE, HARRISON C., *The Ashley-Smith Explorations and the Discovery of a Central Route to the Pacific, 1822-1829* (revised edition). Glendale, Calif.: The Arthur H. Clark Company, 1941. First edition, Cleveland, 1918.

DAVIS, SAM P. (editor), *History of Nevada* (2 vols.). Reno & Los Angeles: The Elms Publishing Company, 1913.

DELANO, ALONZO, *Across the Plains and Among the Diggings*. New York: Wilson-Erickson, Inc., 1936. First edition, Auburn, N. Y., 1854.

Deseret News, weekly newspaper published at Salt Lake City (later triweekly and now daily except Sunday). Issues more especially cited are those for June 20, 1855, June 5, 1856, February 4, May 13, and November 1, 1857.

DE SMET, PIERRE JEAN, *Life, Letters and Travels of Father Pierre-Jean de Smet,* edited by Hiram M. Chittenden and Alfred Talbot Richardson. New York: F. P. Harper, 1905.

DEVOTO, BERNARD, *Mark Twain's America.* Boston: Little, Brown & Company, 1932.

DODGE, GRENVILLE M., *How We Built the Union Pacific Railway.* Council Bluffs, Iowa: Monarch Printing Company, n.d.

DRURY, WELLS, *An Editor on the Comstock Lode.* New York: Farrar & Rinehart, Inc., 1936.

EGAN, HOWARD, *Pioneering the West,* edited by William M. Egan. Richmond, Utah: Privately printed, 1917.

ELLIOTT, T. C., "Peter Skene Ogden, Fur Trader," *Oregon Historical Quarterly,* Vol. 11, September, 1910, pp. 229-278.

ESCALANTE, SYLVESTRE VELEZ DE, "Diary and Travels," pp. 34-124 in W. R. Harris, *The Catholic Church in Utah.* Salt Lake City: The Intermountain Catholic Press, 1909.

EVANS, DAVID W., Letter, *Deseret News,* July 11, 1855.

FISHER, VARDIS, *City of Illusion.* New York: Harper & Brothers, 1941.

FLETCHER, F. N., *Early Nevada.* Reno: Privately printed, 1929. Substantially reprinted in James G. Scrugham (*q.v.*).

FREDERICK, J. V., *Ben Holladay, The Stagecoach King.* Glendale: The Arthur H. Clark Company, 1940.

FRÉMONT, JOHN CHARLES, *Memoirs of My Life.* Chicago: Belford Clark & Company, 1887.

———— *Report of the Exploring Expedition to the Rocky Mountains in the Year 1842 and Oregon and Northern California, 1843-44.* Washington: Gales and Seaton, 1845.

GOLDER, F. A. (editor), *The March of the Mormon Battalion.* New York: The Century Company, 1928.

GOODWIN, CHARLES C., *As I Remember Them.* Salt Lake City: Privately printed, 1913.

GREELEY, HORACE, *An Overland Journey.* New York: C. M. Saxton, Barker & Company, 1860.

HAFEN, LEROY R., *The Overland Mail 1849-1869.* Cleveland: The Arthur H. Clark Company, 1926.

HARLOW, ALVIN F., *Old Waybills.* New York: D. Appleton-Century Company, Inc., 1934.

—— *Old Wires and New Waves.* New York: D. Appleton-Century Company, Inc., 1936.

HARRINGTON, M. R., *Archeological Explorations in Southern Nevada,* Southwest Museum Papers #4. Los Angeles: The Southwest Museum, 1930.

—— *Gypsum Cave,* Southwest Museum Papers #8. Los Angeles: The Southwest Museum, 1933.

HASTINGS, LANSFORD W., *The Emigrants' Guide to Oregon and California,* edited by Charles Carey. Princeton: Princeton University Press, 1932. First edition, Cincinnati, 1845.

HEATH, EARL, "From Trail to Rail," *Pony Express Courier,* January-October, 1938.

HICKMAN, WILLIAM A., *Brigham's Destroying Angel,* edited by J. H. Beadle. New York: George A. Crofutt, 1872.

HILL, JOSEPH J., "Spanish and Mexican Exploration and Trade Northwest into the Great Basin," *Utah Historical Quarterly,* Vol. 3, January, 1930, pp. 3-23.

HODGE, FREDERICK W. (editor), *Handbook of American Indians* (2 vols.). Washington: Government Printing Office, Vol. 1, 1907; Vol. 2, 1910. (Bureau of American Ethnology Bulletin 82.)

HOLEMAN, JACOB H., Letters to Luke Lea, Commissioner of Indian Affairs, May 2, May 8, June 28, 1852. Quoted from originals in the National Archives, Washington, D. C.

HOUGHTON, ELIZA P. DONNER, *The Expedition of the Donner Party and Its Tragic Fate,* Chicago: A. C. McClurg & Company, 1911.

HULBERT, ARCHER BUTLER, *Forty-Niners.* Boston: Little, Brown & Company, 1931.

HUNTINGTON, OLIVER B., "Eighteen Days on the Desert," *Young Women's Magazine* (monthly, Salt Lake City), Vol. 2, November, 1890-March, 1891).

—— Journal, 3 vols., Manuscript, quoted by courtesy of Utah Writers' Project, WPA.

HUNTINGTON, OLIVER B., "A Trip to Carson Valley," pp. 77-98 in Robert Aveson, *Eventful Narratives*. Salt Lake City: Juvenile Instructor, 1887.

HUNTINGTON, OLIVER B. and C. A., Letter, *Deseret News*, December 7, 1854.

HURT, GARLAND, Letter to Brigham Young, September, 1856. Original in the National Archives, Washington, D. C.

HYDE, ORSON, Letters, *Deseret News*, June 27, August 1, October 10, 1855.

IRVING, WASHINGTON, *Adventures of Captain Bonneville in the Rocky Mountains and Far West*. New York: G. P. Putnam's Sons, 1849. First edition, New York, 1837.

JENNINGS, WILLIAM, "Carson Valley," *Nevada Historical Society Papers*, Vol. 1, pp. 178-183.

JENSON, ANDREW, History of Metropolis Ward, in History of Nevada Stake, Manuscript in possession of L. D. S. Church Historian's Office, Salt Lake City, Utah.

———— "The Pioneers of 1847," *Historical Record*, Vol. 9, 1890.

JONES, NATHANIEL V., "The Journal of Nathaniel V. Jones with the Mormon Battalion," *Utah Historical Quarterly*, Vol. 4, January, 1931, pp. 6-24.

KELLY, CHARLES, *Old Greenwood*. Salt Lake City: Western Printing Company, 1936.

———— *Outlaw Trail*. Salt Lake City: Western Printing Company, 1938.

———— "The Salt Desert Trail," *Utah Historical Quarterly*, Vol. 3, January, 1930, pp. 23-27; April, 1930, pp. 35-56; July, 1930, pp. 67-82.

———— *Salt Desert Trails*. Salt Lake City: Western Printing Company, 1930.

KELLY, WILLIAM, *An Excursion to California* (2 vols.). London: Chapman & Hall, 1851.

KERN, EDWARD M., "Journal of Mr. Edward M. Kern of an Exploration of the Mary's or Humboldt River, Carson Lake, and Owens River and Lake, in 1845," in James H. Simpson (*q.v.*), pp. 477-486.

KINKEAD, JAMES H., "The First Train Robbery on the Pacific Coast," *Nevada Historical Society Papers*, Vol. 3, pp 108-115.

LAMBERT, J. CARLOS, *The Metropolis Reclamation Project*. Carson City, Nev.: State Printing Office, 1925. (University of Nevada Agricultural Experiment Station, Bulletin 107.)

LANGWORTHY, FRANKLIN, *Scenery of the Plains, Mountains and Mines*, edited by Paul C. Phillips. Princeton: University Press, 1932. First edition, Ogdensburg, N. Y., 1855.

Latter-day Saints Journal History. Manuscript compilation of journal excerpts, letters, minutes of meetings, statistical data, and clippings, day by day from April 6, 1830, to December 31, 1900. In possession of L.D.S. Church Historian's Office, Salt Lake City, Utah, and consulted by courtesy of Alvin Smith, Librarian.

LEONARD, ZENAS, *Zenas Leonard's Narrative*, edited by W. F. Wagner. Cleveland: The Burrows Brothers Company, 1904. First edition, Clearfield, Pa., 1839.

LEWIS, OSCAR, *The Big Four*. New York: Alfred A. Knopf, Inc., 1938.

LOCKLEY, FRED., "Recollections of Benjamin Franklin Bonney," *Oregon Historical Quarterly*, Vol. 24, March, 1923, pp. 36-55.

LOOMIS, LEANDER V., *Journal of the Birmingham Emigrating Company*, edited by Edgar M. Ledyard. Salt Lake City: Privately printed, 1928.

LYMAN, GEORGE D., *John Marsh, Pioneer*. New York: Charles Scribner's Sons, 1930.
—— *Ralston's Ring*. New York: Charles Scribner's Sons, 1937. (For severe and detailed criticism of its Comstock chapters see Grant H. Smith, "Highlights of Comstock History," *Pony Express Courier*, May, 1938, pp. 7-14.)
—— *The Saga of the Comstock Lode*. New York: Charles Scribner's Sons, 1934.

MACK, EFFIE MONA, *Nevada*. Glendale: The Arthur H. Clark Company, 1936.

MACK, EFFIE MONA, and BYRD WALL SAWYER, *Our State: Nevada*. Caldwell, Idaho: The Caxton Printers, 1940.

MAXWELL, WILLIAM AUDLEY, *Crossing the Plains: Days of '57*. San Francisco: Sunset Publishing House, 1915.

MERKLEY, CHRISTOPHER, *Biography of Christopher Merkley*. Salt Lake City: J. H. Parry & Company, 1887.

MILLER, MAX, *Reno*. New York: Dodd, Mead & Company, 1941.
McGLASHAN, C. F., *History of the Donner Party*, edited by George H. and Bliss McGlashan Hinkle. Palo Alto, Calif.: Stanford University Press, 1940. First edition, Truckee, Calif., 1879.
Nevada Historical Society, *Biennial Reports*, 1908-1912 (3 vols.). Carson City: State Printing Office.
————— *Papers*, 1916-1926 (5 vols.). Carson City & Reno.
NEVINS, ALLEN, *Frémont, Pathmarker of the West*. New York: D. Appleton-Century Company, 1939.
New York Messenger, weekly newspaper published by Samuel Brannan, July 5-November 15, 1845; irregular or extra issues published until February, 1846.
NIDEVER, GEORGE, *The Life and Adventures of George Nidever*, edited by William Henry Ellison. Berkeley: University of California Press, 1937.
OGDEN, PETER SKENE, "Journal of the Snake Expedition, 1825-1826," edited by T. C. Elliott, *Oregon Historical Quarterly*, Vol. 10, December, 1909, pp. 331-365.
————— "Journal of the Snake Expedition, 1826-1827," edited by T. C. Elliott, *Oregon Historical Quarterly*, Vol. 11, June, 1910, pp. 201-222.
————— "Journals of the Snake Expeditions, 1827-1828, and 1828-1829," edited by T. C. Elliott, *Oregon Historical Quarterly*, Vol. 11, December, 1910, pp. 353-396.
————— "Letter to the Governor, Chief Factor and Chief Traders, July 10, 1825," in Frederick L. Merk, "Snake Country Expedition 1824-25," *Oregon Historical Quarterly*, Vol. 35, June, 1934, pp. 93-112. Also printed in *Mississippi Valley Historical Review*, Vol. 21, June, 1934, pp. 63-75.
PAINE, SWIFT, *Eilley Orrum, Queen of the Comstock*. Indianapolis: The Bobbs-Merrill Company, 1929.
PERKINS, J. R., *Trails, Rails and War: The Life of General G. M. Dodge*. Indianapolis: The Bobbs-Merrill Company, 1929.
Pony Express Courier, monthly newspaper published at Placerville, Calif., 1934—.
PRATT, ORSON, "Extracts from Journal," *Millennial Star*, Vols. 11, 12, 1849-1850, *passim*.

REDDING [REDDEN], JACKSON, Letter, *Deseret News*, December 1, 1853.

REED, JAMES FRAZIER, "Narrative of the Sufferings of a Company of Emigrants in the Mountains of California, in the winter of '46 and '7," *Illinois State Journal*, Springfield, Ill., December 9, 1847.

—— "The Snow-Bound, Starved Emigrants of 1846," *Pacific Rural Press*, March 25 and April 1, 1871.

REESE, JOHN, "Mormon Station," *Nevada Historical Society Papers*, Vol. 1, pp. 186-190.

REMY, JULES, and JULIUS F. BRENCHLEY, *A Journey to Great Salt Lake City* (2 vols.). London: W. Jeffs, 1861.

ROGERS, FRED B., *Soldiers of the Overland*. San Francisco: The Grabhorn Press, 1938.

ROOT, FRANK A., and WILLIAM ELSEY CONNELLEY, *The Overland Stage to California*, Topeka, Kans.: Privately printed, 1901.

ROSS, ALEXANDER, "Journal of Snake Country Expedition, 1824," *Oregon Historical Quarterly*, Vol. 14, December, 1913, pp. 366-388.

RUXTON, GEORGE FREDERICK, *Life in the Far West*. Edinburgh & London: William Blackwood & Sons, second edition, 1851.

SABIN, EDWIN L., *Building the Pacific Railway*. Philadelphia & London: J. B. Lippincott & Company, 1919.

—— *Kit Carson Days* (2 vols., revised edition). New York: Press of the Pioneers, Inc., 1935. First edition, New York, 1914.

Salt Lake Tribune, daily newspaper, Salt Lake City. Issues of August 14, 1939, *et seq.* for accounts of train wreck near Carlin.

SAWYER, LORENZO, *Way Sketches*, edited by Edward Eberstadt. New York: Edward Eberstadt, 1926.

"Scalping a Woman on the Plains, Her Extraordinary Fortitude," *San Francisco Daily Evening Bulletin*, September 19, 1857. (Compare with account in Maxwell, *q.v.*)

SCHERER, JAMES A. B., *The First-Forty-Niner*. New York: Minton, Balch & Company, 1925.

SCRUGHAM, JAMES G., *Nevada, A Narrative of the Conquest of a Frontier Land* (3 vols.). Chicago & New York: American Historical Society, Inc., 1935.

SIMPSON, JAMES H., *Report of Explorations across the Great Basin of the Territory of Utah for a Direct Wagon-Route from Camp Floyd to Genoa, in Carson Valley, in 1859*. Washington: Government Printing Office, 1876.

SMITH, JEDEDIAH S., *The Travels of Jedediah Smith*, edited by Maurice S. Sullivan. Santa Ana, Calif.: The Fine Arts Press, 1934.

SMITH, JOSEPH, *History of the Church*, edited by Brigham H. Roberts (7 vols.). Salt Lake City, 1902-1932.

STANSBURY, HOWARD, *Exploration and Survey of the Valley of the Great Salt Lake of Utah*. Philadelphia: Lippincott, Grambo & Company, 1852.

STEWARD, JULIAN H., *Basin-Plateau Aboriginal Sociopolitical Groups*. Washington: Government Printing Office, 1938. (Bureau of American Ethnology Bulletin 120.)

—— "Native Cultures of the Intermontane (Great Basin) Area," Smithsonian Miscellaneous Collection, *Essays in Historical Anthropology of North America*. Washington: Smithsonian Institution, 1940, pp. 445-502.

STEWART, GEORGE R., JR., *Ordeal by Hunger*. New York: Henry Holt & Company, 1936.

SULLIVAN, MAURICE S., *Jedediah Smith, Trader and Trailbreaker*. New York: Press of the Pioneers, Inc., 1936.

TALBOT, THEODORE F., *The Journals of Theodore Talbot*, edited by Charles Carey. Portland, Ore.: Metropolitan Press, 1931.

Times and Seasons, biweekly newspaper published at Nauvoo, Illinois, 1840-1846.

TOPONCE, ALEXANDER, *Reminiscences of Alexander Toponce*. Ogden: Privately printed, 1923.

United States Geological Survey, *Guidebook of the Western United States, Part B. The Overland Route*. Washington: Government Printing Office, 1916. (U. S. Geological Survey Bulletin 612.)

VAN SICKLES, HENRY, "Utah Desperadoes," *Nevada Historical Society Papers*, Vol. 1, pp. 190-193.

VICTOR, FRANCES FULLER, *River of the West*. Hartford: Columbia Book Company, 1870.

WARE, JOSEPH E., *The Emigrants' Guide to California*, edited by

John Caughey. Princeton: Princeton University Press, 1932. First Edition, St. Louis, 1849.

WEBB, WALTER PRESCOTT, *The Great Plains*. Boston: Ginn & Company, 1931.

WIER, JEANNE ELIZABETH, "The Mystery of Nevada," in Thomas C. Donnelly (editor), *Rocky Mountain Politics*. Albuquerque: University of New Mexico Press, 1940.

WILLIAMS, E. G., Letter to Heber C. Kimball, June 11, 1855, quoted in L. D. S. Journal History for this date.

WILLIAMS, THOMAS S., Letters to Brigham Young, June 24 and July 30, 1852, quoted in L. D. S. Journal History for these dates.

WILLIAMSON, DAVID E. W., "When Major Ormsbee Was Killed," *Nevada Historical Society Papers*, Vol. 4, pp. 1-28. Reprinted in *Pony Express Courier*, May and June, 1942.

WOODRUFF, WILFORD, Letter, *The Mormon* (weekly newspaper, New York City) October 11, 1856.

WOOLLEY, EDWIN D., Letter, *Deseret News*, July 30, 1853.

WORK, JOHN, "Journal of the Snake River Expedition, 1830-31," edited by T. C. Elliott, *Oregon Historical Quarterly*, Vol. 13, December, 1912, pp. 363-371; *ibid.*, Vol. 14, September, 1913, pp. 280-314.

Work Projects Administration, Nevada Writers' Project, *Nevada: A Guide to the Silver State*. Portland, Ore.: Binfords & Mort, 1941.

——— *Nevada Notes: Lost Mines*. Reno: Nevada Writers' Project, *ca.* 1940, mimeographed.

——— *Nevada Notes: Nevada Towns*. Reno: Nevada Writers' Project, *ca.*, 1940, mimeographed.

WYETH, NATHANIEL, Journals and Letters, in Franklin G. Young (editor), *Sources of the History of Oregon*, Vol. 1. Eugene, Ore.: Oregon University Press, 1899.

YOUNG, BRIGHAM, Letter to Samuel Brannan, April 5, 1849. Quoted in L. D. S. Journal History for this date.

——— Letter to James C. Snow, August 15, 1857. Original in Archives of L. D. S. Church Historian's Office.

Index

Lahontan, Lake 7
Land Rights 313, 316-317
Larkin, Thomas O. 115-116
Las Vegas 323, 343, 345
Lassen's Meadows 223
Lent, Uncle Billy 255
Leonard, Zenas 52, 54, 56
Lewis and Clark 13, 17-18
Lewis, Oscar 309
Lincoln, Abraham 99, 258, 265, 278, 294
Linn, Lewis F. 80, 82-83, 93
Little Humboldt River 6, 28-29, 43, 108
Little (Bear) Lake 20, 24
Logan, Harvey 318-319
Long Haul 310
Longabaugh, Harry 318-319
Longhorns 311-313
Loveland, Chester 239-240, 243
Lovelock Valley 7, 305, 347-348
Lyman, Amasa M. 178
Lynch Law 210-212

Mackay, John 255
Mackenzie, Donald 33, 39
Mail 232-233, 268-279, 281-282
Malaria 63, 99
Malheur River 27, 85, 91
Maps, Early 13, 63, 87
Mark Twain's America 263
Marsh, John 63-64, 77
Marshall, James W. 175-176, 178
Mary's Lake 64, 86-88
Mary's River (modern) 6
Mary's River, Name of 5, 46
Maxon, A. B. 311-312
Maxwell, Lucien B. 81, 167
McCutchen, William 132-133, 139-140, 153, 156-158
McCutchen, Mrs. William 145-148
McKay 37
McKinstry, George 163
McLaughlin, Pat 252
McLoughlin, John 33-34, 37
Meek, Joe 46
Metropolis 323-337
"Miss Ella" 183
Mississippi Saints 121
Monk, Hank 283
Montgomery, Allen 101
Moore, Steve 237-238

Morals 167-169, 206-220, 246, 249, 254-255, 264-265, 308-309, 340, 342-343, 345-346
Mormon Battalion 168, 170, 173-176, 179, 198, 203
Mormon Station 199-202, 207, 216, 226, 311
Mormons
  Migration West 82, 103, 114, 116-117, 121, 132, 166-179
  In California 166-168, 171, 173-179
  In Utah 169-171, 173, 185-186, 197-200, 273, 277, 286-287, 301-302, 306-307, 311, 327-328
  In Nevada 199-207, 239-247, 249-251, 257, 323, 330, 335-338, 340
  Morals 209, 213-221
  Explorations 222-232
  Express to Carson 234-245
  At Metropolis 330, 335-338
Mott, Gordon N. 285
Moultry, Sept 149-150, 154-155
Mount Diablo 64, 77, 91
Mountain Meadows 94-95
Mountain Men 44-47, 61, 83-84, 98, 106, 144
Murphy, Bill 142
Murphy, Landrum 153
Murphy, Mrs. Lavinia 156-157, 161, 164
Murphy, Lem 142, 145
Murphy, Martin, Sr. 99
Murphy, Simon 157
Murray, Carlos 217, 219-220
Muddy River 14, 94
Munchies 45, 339
Murdock, John 243

Name, of River 5-6, 108, 111
New Helvetia 103, 105, 116, 129, 148
Nickerson 243
Nidever, George 56
North Fork of Humboldt 6
Nye, James W. 258

Ogden, Peter Skene 5, 18, 27-43, 45-46, 48, 108, 117
Ogden, Utah 301
Ogden's Lake 117
Ogden's River 5-6, 45-46, 48
Old Pancake (see Comstock, H. T. P.)
Old Virginny 249, 251-252, 255